HARVARD HISTORICAL STUDIES
VOLUME LXXIII

*Published under the direction
of the Department of History*

From the income of
THE HENRY WARREN TORREY FUND

Patriots and Partisans

THE MERCHANTS OF NEWBURYPORT

1764–1815

Benjamin W. Labaree

HARVARD UNIVERSITY PRESS

Cambridge, Massachusetts

1962

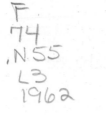

© Copyright 1962
By the President and Fellows of Harvard College

Distributed in Great Britain by
Oxford University Press, London

Library of Congress Catalog Card Number 62-19217

Printed in the United States of America

FOR MY PARENTS

PREFACE

This study of the merchants of Newburyport, Massachusetts, has been undertaken in the belief that historians can better understand the revolutionary changes that took place in America during the half-century 1764–1815 by examining what happened on the local level. Because of its maritime interests Newburyport was not a typical American community of the period, but in most ways it was representative of a dozen or more New England seaports. The problems that faced the merchants of Newburyport concerned most of their contemporaries as well. How they responded to these problems and how the events of the period affected their lives is the subject of the present volume.

During the critical half-century under study two distinct generations of merchants dominated Newburyport. The colonial generation had carried on a profitable trade within the British Empire and seemed to have little quarrel with the imperial system. When the revolutionary crisis developed, however, these merchants joined the radical cause. In the chaos that followed the war they sought stronger state and national governments, but even before the adoption of the federal constitution, the fortunes of most of the older merchant families were lost in the lingering depression. By the 1790's an entirely new group of merchants, unrelated to the earlier generation, came to profit from the neutral trade made possible by the Napoleonic Wars. Although not originally interested in politics, these men soon became fanatical in their devotion to the Federalist party. By 1815, their prosperity ruined by Embargo, the War of 1812, and finally European peace, the merchants of Newburyport stood on the brink of secession.

Why did the colonial merchants support a revolutionary cause which threatened their means of livelihood, and why did they endorse a centralized national government? This book attempts to answer these questions and to explain why the colonial merchants were succeeded by a group so different from themselves, a group which forsook the nationalism of its predecessors for an increasingly narrow sectionalism.

In carrying out this study I have had the invaluable assistance of many friends and colleagues. Oscar Handlin guided the project in its earlier stages as a doctoral dissertation, while Bernard Bailyn, Donald H. Fleming, and Walter M. Whitehill have contributed many constructive suggestions. I would like to express my appreciation to Mrs. Carl Pitha for her many helpful editorial comments. I am also grateful to Sheila Stannard and to Dorothy Dawson, who typed the final drafts of the manuscript.

B. W. L.
1962

CONTENTS

List of Maps and Illustrations

Patriots and Partisans

The following abbreviations are used in the notes and in the Bibliographical Note.

Boston Public Library	BPL	Library of Congress	LC
Essex Institute	EI	Massachusetts Historical Society	MHS
Harvard University Library	HUL	Newburyport Public Library	NPL
Historical Society of Old		New York Public Library	NYPL
Newbury	HSON	Yale University Library	YUL

Chapter I

COLONIAL NEWBURYPORT
AND ITS MERCHANTS

At the time of the American Revolution most of the small seaports scattered along the New England coast were dominated by a merchant aristocracy. In Newburyport, Massachusetts, these men enjoyed their greatest power in the years between 1764 and 1782. Only the economic chaos which followed the war could dislodge them from their positions of authority, and in many cases these merchants continued to run the political affairs of their community long after they had lost their fortunes. How this minority group of less than 200 men managed to control a town of over 3500 persons can best be understood by a study of the economic, social, and political institutions of colonial Newburyport.

Forty miles north of Boston the Merrimack River opens into a long narrow bay as it reaches the Atlantic Ocean. On this site, well endowed with natural advantages for maritime activity, rose the port of Newbury in Massachusetts Bay. The sandy arm of Plum Island provided adequate protection against the pounding action of the open sea, virtually landlocking the harbor. The river itself abounded with fish, especially sturgeon, and small craft could easily reach the cod banks lying offshore. While the swift flow of the river created ever-shifting bars at its mouth, this current served to keep the harbor free from winter freeze-ups. Oakstands of excellent quality flanked the river for most of its 120 mile course, providing the timber which made shipbuilding the basis of local industry. As settlements pushed upstream—first Amesbury, then Haverhill, Methuen, Nashua—Newbury became the entrepôt for the entire Merrimack Valley. These factors molded the principal economic course of the

town during the period of its greatest prosperity, the late eighteenth
and early nineteenth centuries.

Newbury was settled in 1635 by a group recently arrived at Boston
that was persuaded to assist in establishing the northern boundary of
Massachusetts Bay Colony against rival claims. The colonists at first
concentrated their settlement on the northern edge of the Parker
River, although by 1707 lots had been laid out along the southern
bank of the Merrimack River, termed "the waterside." The early
inhabitants engaged solely in agriculture, but within fifteen years
some began to seek their livelihood in the rich resources of the
river itself.[1]

By the turn of the century the business of utilizing the Merrimack's
resources was the leading activity of the settlement at the river's
mouth. River and ocean fish, cured by salting and drying, became
a valuable commodity principally to the West Indian plantations,
where lumber was also increasingly in demand. At first many of
these products were carted overland for shipment from Boston, but
the second important maritime activity of Newbury—shipbuilding—
soon permitted the town to develop its own carrying trade. Shipbuilding and the West Indian trade, well established by the early
1700's, became the foundation for a prosperous expansion of the
waterside settlement throughout the rest of the century.[2]

The growing number of Newbury inhabitants who looked to the
sea for a living constituted the town's new mercantile class. Although
increasing its domination of the Merrimack settlement, this group
repeatedly failed in its attempts to wrest control of the entire community from the incumbent farming interests. As the decades of the
eighteenth century passed, the ambitions of those dwelling along
the "waterside" became steadily less compatible with the older, agricultural community. The incident which precipitated the final break,
of little importance in itself, involved the prospective location of a
new town house. So much accumulated rancor had burst forth
during the debate that although the new section of town won the
battle, 208 of its inhabitants shortly petitioned the General Court

[1] John J. Currier, *The History of Newbury, Mass., 1635–1902* (Boston, 1902),
p. 31; Records of the Town of Newburyport, Mass., I, 35–36, on deposit in the Office
of the City Clerk, Newburyport, Mass. Hereinafter referred to as Town Records.
[2] E. V. Smith, *History of Newburyport* (Newburyport, 1854), pp. 25–27.

for their part of Newbury to be set off and incorporated as a separate town. The petitioners cited as the basis for their request the
irreconcilable breach that had split the two segments of the population and went on to enumerate some of the difficulties which had
arisen as a result. A bill providing for the incorporation of the
"waterside" as the town of Newbury Port was soon enacted into
law, and on February 4, 1764, the maritime interests won their
independence from the farmers. Four days later the inhabitants held
their first town meeting to elect officers and to settle various problems arising from the division of property with Newbury.[3]

The area separated from Newbury and established as the town of
Newburyport resembled a long rectangle except for the irregularities
of the river's shoreline, which formed the northeastern boundary.
The town seemed to stretch even farther than its two-mile length
because its southwestern edge was but a half-mile inland from the
river. Only a long triangular wedge into the great pasture behind
the town tied it to an agricultural past. Into these 647 acres crowded
2882 inhabitants, most of whom looked down the river and out to
sea for their fortune.[4]

The main stage for Newburyport's economic life was the waterfront. If the river itself was the backbone of the town, then Merrimack and Water Streets were its main arteries, paralleling the bank
and leading into the heart at Market Square. Side streets, parallel to
each other and sloping back from the river up to High Street, linked
together the residential and commercial areas of the town at a dozen
junctures. At the time of incorporation some 350 houses lined this
network, homes for the town's more than 500 families. Most commercial activities took place on the several wharves that reached
into the river, two of which were "long wharves," maintained by
the town. Between these two were others owned by leading merchants. Several important shipyards lined the river upstream, while
mastyards, sail lofts, and other maritime enterprises crowded into
the remaining spaces. Interspersed among the wharves and yards

[3] Petition for separate incorporation, Town Records, I, 2–9; Province Laws, 1763–
1764, vol. IV, ch. 20.
[4] John J. Currier, *History of Newburyport, Mass., 1764–1905* (Newburyport, 1906),
I, 27.

were a number of public landings maintained for the convenience of the less-affluent inhabitants.[5]

Not all of the townsmen directly contributed to maritime activities, of course. A variety of artisans provided the skills needed to erect houses, make shoes, and operate forges. Painters and chair-

TABLE 1

Occupation of Adult Males—1773

I. MERCHANTS AND PROFESSIONAL MEN			
Distiller	14	Butcher	1
Esquire	8	Cabinetmaker	11
Gentleman	6	Carver	1
Lawyer	2	Chairmaker	6
Merchant	36	Chaisemaker	2
Minister	4	Clockmaker	2
Physician	7	Combmaker	1
Shipbuilder	7	Coppersmith	2
Shipmaster	83	Cordwainer	28
Teacher	6	Currier	1
Total	173	Dyer	1
Percent of adult males 24.8		Glazier	3
		Goldsmith	3
		Gunsmith	2
II. SHOPKEEPERS AND INNHOLDERS		Hatter	4
		Housewright	9
Apothecary	1	Joiner	39
Bookseller	1	Leatherdresser	1
Innkeeper	3	Painter	5
Shopkeeper	21	Perukemaker	2
Tobacconist	1	Potter	3
Total	27	Saddler	5
Percent of adult males 3.9		Sawyer	1
		Silversmith	2
III. DOMESTIC ARTISANS		Stonecutter	1
		Tailor	8
Baker	9	Tallowchandler	1
Barber	1	Tanner	3
Blacksmith	14	Tinplater	2
Bricklayer	3	Total	177
		Percent of adult males 25.3	

[5] Town Records, I, 36–39; Currier, *History of Newburyport*, I, 333–360; John J. Currier, *"Ould Newbury": Historical and Biographical Sketches* (Boston, 1896), pp. 153–156, 279–285.

IV. MARITIME ARTISANS		V. LABORERS AND OTHERS	
Blockmaker	6	Laborer	18
Boatbuilder	10	Mariner	30
Caulker	15	Porter	2
Cooper	18	Teamster	1
Mastmaker	7	Truckman	2
Rigger	7	Yeoman	27
Ropemaker	3	Total	79
Sailmaker	9	Percent of adult males 11.3	
Shipsmith	1	VI. UNKNOWNS	
Shipwright	60	Total	107
Total	136	Percent of adult males 15.3	
Percent of adult males 19.4		Total adult males	699

A note on the procedure followed in formulating this table is in order. First the author compiled a list of all adult males living in the town in 1773, obtaining his data from birth and marriage records, deeds, tax lists, biographical sketches, militia records, shipping records, and newspaper references. Where there was reasonable doubt that an individual was actually resident in Newburyport that year or was at least twenty-one years old, his name was dropped from the list. A total of 699 adult males was thus reached. From the same sources, particularly the deeds and wills on file at the Essex County Probate Court in Salem, the author then discovered the occupations of 594, or 84.7 percent, of these men.

Little explanation for the grouping is necessary. Shipmasters are included with merchants not only because of their great authority in a maritime community ("Captain" was a title of considerable distinction) but also because many of them retired from the sea at an early age to open their own mercantile houses. It is often impossible to tell precisely when such a captain left the quarterdeck for the countinghouse. Shopkeepers have been placed in a separate category because they were neither importers on the one hand nor were they, strictly speaking, artisans. Many of the latter, of course, kept their own shops to sell products of their labor. Finally, the 107 men of unknown occupation have been placed in a separate category, although many of them were undoubtedly laborers of little property.

makers joined clockmakers, tanners, and stonecutters in offering their craftsmanship to the community. Though Newburyport was a town nearly bereft of agricultural lands within its boundaries, a number of yeomen raised and sold their produce to the town's three thousand inhabitants. Many of the artisans maintained their own shops or sold their products right at the anvil or cobbler's bench, while some twenty retailers offered the public a wide variety of wares from their shops in Market Square. Foodstuffs were readily available, as were rum, wines, and of course tea. For clothing a customer needed only to enter one of several shops for the necessary woolens, linens, or the vast quantity of English cloth goods available. Tailors and dyers were on hand to provide those services for people unable to make their own clothes. Nor were the goods available in Market Square simply confined to the essentials of life. A cosmopolitan variety of specialties was offered, ranging from tobacco and snuff to an assortment of drugs and including such unrelated objects as mooseskin breeches, rhubarb, hair powder, and garden seeds.[6]

At the same time that Newburyport's economic life demonstrated the basic interdependence of its inhabitants upon each other, the prosperity of all depended on the relation of the town to the world around it. Its back yard, running far up the river into New Hampshire, played a doubly important role. Not only did this area serve as a market for the many goods imported or produced by Newburyporters, but also its timber provided the foundation for Newburyport's major industry, shipbuilding. At the time of the town's incorporation, shipyards along the Merrimack River produced enough vessels to make it New England's greatest shipbuilding center. In the decade 1756–1765 no less than 427 Newbury-built vessels had cleared or entered the custom districts of Boston and Salem. How many more were sold in England or were sailing other routes cannot be ascertained. Tradition states that in the summer of 1766 there were in all seventy-two vessels in the process of construction in the various yards along the Merrimack River, some of which of course were not actually located within the boundaries of Newburyport. And another observer stated that Newburyport yards launched ninety vessels in 1772 alone.[7]

Many of the ships built in Newburyport sailed for England, where they were sold to merchants eager to purchase American vessels whose cost was far below English-built ships. The protective arm of the British colonial system, requiring that all vessels engaged in empire trade be of English or colonial construction, made this practice possible. One authority has estimated that by 1775 colonial shipyards supplied Britain with almost one third of the vessels

---

[6] "Inholders and Retailers Licenses," Ichabod Tucker Papers (EI); *Essex Journal and Merrimack Packet,* 1773–1776 *passim.*

[7] Samuel E. Morison, *The Maritime History of Massachusetts, 1783–1860* (Boston, 1921), p. 101; *English Shipping Records* (EI); Sarah A. Emery, *Reminiscences of a Nonagenarian* (Newburyport, 1879), p. 225; John J. Currier, *Shipbuilding along the Merrimack* (Newburyport, 1889).

registered as English. A good share of these must have come from yards along the Merrimack.[8]

The forests lining the upper Merrimack River also provided timber necessary as a salable commodity in Newburyport's foreign commerce. Shipped to the West Indies, usually in the form of shingles, boards, and staves, these lumber products were exchanged for molasses, which when distilled into heavy New England rum found its way back into the Merrimack Valley in payment for the timber, completing an economic cycle. Commerce with the British Isles depended partly on profits from the West Indies trade, and partly on such native American products as tobacco and flaxseed. Newburyport merchants imported from England a wide range of goods, particularly cloths, hardware and household items, and of course tea and spices. In addition, vessels called at Quebec for wheat, at Malaga for fruit and wine, at Charleston for rice, among many other ventures. Colonial Newburyport looked out to sea; the world upon which the town depended lay beyond the river's treacherous bar. It was the world of the Carolinas and the West Indies, of Bristol, Cork, and Cadiz.[9]

The business of Newburyport may well have been centered along the town's extensive waterfront, but activities other than economic claimed their share of the inhabitants' attention and energy. Perhaps symbolic of the close relation between church and commerce in eighteenth-century New England was the fact that Newburyport's First Religious Society was prominently situated in Market Square. Its minister, John Lowell, looked after the spiritual needs of his mercantile flock, and in turn the merchants took more than a casual interest in religious affairs, many of them serving as deacons

[8] Lawrence A. Harper, *The English Navigation Laws* (New York, 1939), pp. 358–361.

[9] Compiled from the following business papers: Jackson & Bromfield's Ledger, 1 March 1766 to 1 March 1772; Patrick Tracy Jackson, Jr., Collection (Boothbay Harbor, Maine); "Letterbook 1765," Jackson & Bromfield, Henry Lee Shattuck Collection (MHS); Jackson & Bromfield invoice book, 4 August 1764–December 1771, Henry Lee Shattuck Collection (MHS); Jackson, Tracy & Tracy's Ledger, 11 April 1774 to 9 August 1787, Patrick Tracy Jackson, Jr., Collection (Boothbay Harbor, Maine); "Letterbook 1774," Henry Lee Shattuck Collection (MHS). See also Kenneth W. Porter, *The Jacksons and the Lees* (Cambridge, 1937), I, 262–263, 265, 275–277.

and providing lay leadership in the Congregational tradition. When the occasion directed, they took the initiative in forming a new church. At the senior Lowell's death in 1767, for instance, disagreement over the appointment of his successor led to a division of church, plate, and stock, and the establishment of a new society, soon known as the North Congregational Church. Earlier deviations from the straight Puritan brand of Protestantism had led to the construction of Queen Anne's Chapel in 1711, replaced by St. Paul's Church in 1739, and the formation of the First Presbyterian Society in 1746.[10]

Secular education, on the other hand, was provided by a somewhat more haphazard system. At the time of incorporation, Newburyport apparently had two schools within its jurisdiction. In the next few months, however, the education system underwent complete reorganization, with the establishment of a grammar school near the First Religious Society meeting-house and two writing schools, one at each end of town. Private instructors also offered a variety of special curricula to supplement public education. John Vinal, who during this period was master of the North School, took the opportunity to augment his eighty-pound annual salary by teaching navigation evenings. Several private schools catered to the educational needs of the town's young ladies, and dancing classes enjoyed modest popularity. For more advanced learning a number of young Newburyport residents studied with Master Moody at Dummer Academy, recently opened in South Byfield. Somewhat surprising is the impressive number of inhabitants whose education was completed at Harvard College, many of the local merchants', lawyers', and ministers' sons receiving the benefits of four years in Cambridge. Social prestige and cohesiveness were as much the result as erudition.[11]

Other professions had representation in Newburyport at this time as well. Although the ubiquity of the lawyer had not yet reached full flower, two or three had established practices before the Revolution. Seven doctors seemed more than adequate to care for the medical needs of the town's inhabitants. The professional men, most of whom qualified for recognition by birth, education, or marriage,

[10] Currier, *History of Newburyport*, I, 252–280; Emery, *Reminiscences*, pp. 206–207.

[11] Town Records, I, 15, 19, and 20; Currier, *History of Newburyport*, I, 309–311; *Essex Journal*, 10 March 1774, 22 March 1775.

were fully accepted by members of the mercantile class and were in fact as much a part of that group as the merchants themselves.

Newburyport was by no means an isolated community, despite the forty miles separating it from Boston. The town's maritime activities brought many of its inhabitants into contact with the world beyond the mouth of the river Merrimack. Those who wished relatively fast and dependable transportation to such distant points as New York, Philadelphia, or points south, had merely to make suitable arrangements with the master of any one of several vessels that cleared for these ports each week. But water travel was not Newburyport's only link with other towns. "The Portsmouth Flying Stage Coach" provided one overland connection, stopping at Wolfe Tavern on its weekly trip between New Hampshire and Boston. Ezra Lunt, versatile printer, militia captain, and innholder, operated the first four-horse stage in the colonies, which ran between Newburyport and Boston three times a week.[12]

There was no need to leave Newburyport in order to establish contact with the outside world. Postal service, although dependent on stagecoach schedules, provided communication to and from both Boston and Portsmouth on a twice-weekly basis. With the mails came Salem, Portsmouth, and Boston newspapers and periodicals from England. These items were available mainly by subscription, though Bulkeley Emerson, the principal stationer in town, distributed various newspapers and magazines in addition to the books he offered for sale.[13]

In early 1773 an attempt was made to publish a weekly newspaper in Newburyport, to be called the *Essex Mercury and the Weekly Intelligencer*, but the intended editors failed to attract a sufficient number of subscribers to make the undertaking feasible. In December of that year Isaiah Thomas and Henry Tinges established the *Essex Journal and Merrimack Packet*, providing an important link with other towns and printing the latest advices from abroad. One department of particular interest was the Marine List, announcing the arrivals and departures of all vessels.[14]

Some inhabitants found the existing opportunities for informal

---

[12] Currier, *History of Newburyport*, I, 29, 379–381, 395–396.
[13] *Essex Journal* advertisements; Bulkeley Emerson to Henry Knox, 16 February 1773, 11 March 1774, Henry Knox Papers (MHS).
[14] Issues of the *Essex Journal* for the years 1773–1776.

social gathering inadequate and therefore organized more definite groups. One was St. John's Lodge of Free and Accepted Masons, founded in 1766. Many of those citizens prominent in commercial or professional life participated in the activities of this lodge, and its popularity grew to such an extent that by 1772 another lodge— St. Peter's—was organized to provide for the overflow.[15]

The most prominent social club in this port town was the Newburyport Marine Society, established in 1772. Its membership was restricted to active and retired masters of sea-going vessels. Like several associations of its period, the Marine Society was more than a social organization, frequently calling for the improvement of navigational aids along the coast, for instance. As a mutual benefit association the society's funds were made available to needy members, their dependents, and descendants. The Marine Society also formed in late 1775 its own fire society whose primary purpose was to look after its members' property in case of fire.

Other fire companies were organized around the various engines purchased by private subscription. In addition to the camaraderie offered, membership in one of these societies provided real protection and, by vote of town meeting, exemption from service in any other town office.[16]

The position of the merchant group in the social affairs of Newburyport went virtually unchallenged from any other class. With a firm grip on the religious and educational activities of the port, the merchants and their associates were also the people who had the best opportunities for contact with the outside world. Their awareness of developments in Boston, Philadelphia, and London naturally gave them a distinct advantage in providing intelligent leadership at home.

The merchants who controlled the social institutions of Newburyport came for the most part from distinguished backgrounds and had strong connections with each other through college friendships and by marriage. The most prominent local family was headed by Patrick Tracy, who had immigrated to Newbury before the middle

[15] Currier, *History of Newburyport*, II, 119–120.
[16] William H. Bayley and Oliver O. Jones, *History of the Marine Society of Newburyport, Mass.* ([Newburyport], 1906), pp. 482–486; Town Records, I, 17; Currier, *History of Newburyport*, II, 22–25.

of the century from County Wexford, Ireland, and who had soon become a prosperous merchant. His elder son Nathaniel was educated at Harvard before returning to carry on the family interests with his brother John. In 1774 the Tracys took into partnership Jonathan Jackson, the son of a wealthy Boston merchant and a graduate of Harvard, who had married Patrick's only daughter Hannah two years before. Jackson built a house on High Street next door to his college-mate, the young lawyer John Lowell, son of the First Church minister, and the two remained lifelong friends. John's son, Francis Cabot Lowell, married Jonathan's daughter Hannah and was associated in business for many years with his brother-in-law, Patrick Tracy Jackson. The close relationship of these three families illustrates the concentration of economic and social power in colonial Newburyport.[17]

Another intermarriage of merchant families involved the Daltons and the Hoopers. Michael Dalton had established a prosperous mercantile house in Newburyport during the middle decades of the century. His son Tristram continued the business after finishing college and married the daughter of Marblehead's most prominent merchant, Robert "King" Hooper. Tristram's brother-in-law, Stephen Hooper, settled in Newburyport as a merchant upon graduating from Harvard in the same class as Jonathan Jackson. Although not permanent partners, Tristram and Stephen often associated together in business enterprises during the colonial period. When Tristram's father died, his mother married the widower Patrick Tracy, connecting the Daltons with still another prominent family.[18]

Allied with the Newburyport merchants were several lawyers. Benjamin Greenleaf was perhaps the most prominent in the colonial period, along with John Lowell, already mentioned. Theophilus Parsons, son of a Newbury minister, who had been a Harvard classmate of Nathaniel Tracy, opened a practice during the Revolution and married Greenleaf's daughter Elizabeth. Together these three lawyers provided business and political advice to the mercantile leaders of Newburyport.[19]

[17] Currier, *History of Newburyport,* II, 216, 220–221, 244–245, 261; Porter, *Jacksons and Lees,* I, 259–260.
[18] Currier, *History of Newburyport,* II, 191–193, 213–214, 216.
[19] Currier, *History of Newburyport,* II, 262, 284–285.

Not all of the merchant leaders enjoyed second-generation wealth and position. Jonathan Greenleaf, Benjamin's poor cousin, started as a shipwright, married his employer's daughter, and established a profitable shipbuilding and mercantile business on his own. Nathaniel Carter was another merchant of obscure beginnings, but on the eve of the Revolution he was one of the wealthiest residents of Newburyport. Joseph Marquand was the son of a successful ship-captain who later became a merchant, but the Marquands' social standing did not match that of the Tracys, Daltons, and Jacksons until after the Revolution. Still less prominent in the colonial period were other captains and shipyard owners whose economic interests bound them to the merchants.[20]

Domination by the merchants of Newburyport's economic and social activities in turn gave them the power to govern the town politically. By their control of the town meeting, the merchants assured themselves of election to the board of selectmen, to *ad hoc* committees of special importance, and as representatives to the General Court. Only in this way could the merchant leaders maintain their authority over the affairs of Newburyport.

The statutes of the colony provided several means of qualifying to vote in town affairs. Possession of an estate ratable at £20 was perhaps the most common. Unlike the better-known forty-shilling freehold qualification for voting in provincial elections, the £20 requirement meant that the would-be voter needed to possess an estate assessed at £20—that is, one which if rented would bring a return of £3/6/8 annually, since the assessed value was that sum which an estate brought if rented for six years. The law provided an alternative means for enfranchisement. Any resident who paid in estate taxes an amount equal to two thirds of a poll tax for that year gained the right to participate in town meetings and elections. This method in fact was used by Newburyport's tax collector in 1771.[21]

Fortunately "A List of Voters Agreeable to the Tax of 1773" has

[20] Currier, *History of Newburyport*, II, 207–209, 239–240.

[21] *Acts and Resolves of the Province of Massachusetts Bay*, II, 761–762; Robert E. Brown, *Middle-Class Democracy and the Revolution in Massachusetts, 1691–1780* (Ithaca, 1955), pp. 80–81. Brown has contributed the most comprehensive study of voting in colonial Massachusetts. Daniel Balch's Tax Collector's Book, 1771 (NPL).

survived, which when combined with the material in Table 1 gives
us a clear picture of the electorate in colonial Newburyport as seen
in Table 2. Two important facts revealed in this table should be
emphasized. First, the merchants and shipmasters, with their professional allies, the lawyers, doctors, and other gentlemen, constituted only about one third of the electorate, placing nominal political
control in the hands of the shopkeepers, artisans, and laborers. In
the second place, only three out of five adult males were qualified
to vote in town affairs in 1773.[22]

TABLE 2

Voters and Nonvoters by Occupation—1773

Group	No. of voters	No. of nonvoters	Total no.	% of group qualified to vote	Voters in group as percent of total electorate
Merchants and professional men	137	36	173	79.1	32.8
Shopkeepers and innholders	21	6	27	77.8	5.1
Domestic artisans	113	64	177	63.8	27.1
Maritime artisans	70	66	136	51.5	16.5
Unknowns	48	59	107	44.8	11.5
Laborers and others	29	50	79	36.7	7.0
Total adult male population	418	281	699	59.8	100.0

Some of the nonvoters were young men just getting started in
their various trades and in a few years would attain sufficient prosperity to become voters. Others were older men who had retired
from active life to live with a son or daughter. But a good many
adults never did acquire enough property to meet the qualification.
Most of them rented a dwelling place, lived in a boardinghouse, or
at best owned part of a house. For many it was a life balanced on the

[22] In fact, there seems to have been an abnormally high number of voters in this
year. The list of legal voters for 1769 includes only 229 names, for an adult male
population which could hardly have been less than 500, making 45.8 percent voters.
The list for 1774 shows 335 names. If one assumes no change in population from the
previous year, the percentage of men qualified to vote had dropped to 47.9. Perhaps
the pattern can be explained in the fact that 1770–1773, with the removal of nonimportation agreements, was a most prosperous period. Unfortunately, no other
voters' lists have been preserved to give us more evidence for understanding these
fluctuations.

line of subsistence, finding employment as it came along, on the docks as wharfingers or at sea as fo'c's'le hands. For these men, perhaps a quarter of the town's adult male population, there was little hope, and perhaps little ambition, for a role in town meeting.

Between 1764 and 1773 thirty-three times out of forty-six the town meeting turned to a merchant or professional man to serve as select-man. Two thirds of the twenty-six different men chosen for this office were of the uppermost class. The town's representative in the General Court during this period was consistently a merchant or lawyer, and other important political posts—the assessors, wardens, and members of special committees—were invariably controlled by the merchant group.[23]

To some extent this political domination can be explained by the mercantile class's greater interest in public affairs. Its members probably attended town meeting more regularly than other voters and may well have constituted a majority of some meetings. For the merchants, often neighbors with one another on the better streets in town, interrelated by marriage, and members of exclusive social groups, public responsibility was difficult to abdicate. Certainly a "stake-in-society" attitude played some role in sustaining their interest in town affairs.

The artisans and laborers, on the other hand, constituted a more unwieldy political action group. Comparative ignorance of the important issues of the day, and the difficulty of identifying with their significance, probably led to considerable apathy at the polls. With little time off from the workbench, and without the independence which wealth brings, only a few artisans and other workers could have filled political office even if offered.

Most significant, however, in explaining why merchants and professional men dominated the political affairs of Newburyport was that these men were long used to command. Not only the active shipmasters, but also many of the merchants who had but recently retired to more sedentary careers, spoke with a quarterdeck authority which by the traditions and laws of the sea few citizens dared to challenge in this maritime community. Since many of the artisans and laborers had shipped before the mast in their youth,

[23] Town Records, I, 1–167 *passim*.

and others continued to do so, it is little wonder that they obediently listened when the same voices commanded their attention in town meeting. This habit of deference, to borrow a phrase from Walter Bagehot, must have been strong indeed in the maritime context of an eighteenth-century New England seaport.

True political democracy had not yet come to Newburyport. Four of every ten adult males were by law prohibited from taking an active role in politics. And town meeting itself only reflected the economic and social stratifications of the community. Artisans and laborers who did qualify to vote were not well organized and rarely held important political office. At best they wielded only negative power in town meeting. The domination which the merchants enjoyed in economic and social affairs of the town enforced their claim to unchallenged political leadership.[24]

[24] From the present study I have a rather different view of democracy in pre-revolutionary Massachusetts than that presented by Robert E. Brown in his *Middle-Class Democracy and the Revolution in Massachusetts*. After showing that the franchise was held by 60 to 90 percent of adult males in various towns, Brown concludes that Massachusetts was "very close to a complete democracy with the exception of British restraints." I maintain that wherever social and economic democracy does not exist, political democracy is impossible.

Chapter II

THE ROAD TO INDEPENDENCE

Aᴌᴍᴏsᴛ from the beginning of the crisis with England the merchants of Newburyport supported the revolutionary cause. As the dominant group in town meeting, they drew up resolutions denouncing each step of the British Parliament which seemed to abridge their liberties. As merchants, they joined nonimportation movements and limited their commercial activities accordingly. As Americans, they pledged their lives and fortunes for the independence of their new nation.

Newburyport was virtually without Tories. One lawyer, who died in 1776, a shipmaster, a shopkeeper, and a potter were suspected of Loyalist leanings, but among the merchants themselves and throughout the town as a whole the march toward independence met only approval. Why the mercantile class unanimously endorsed the radical movement, unlike the merchants of Salem, Marblehead, and of course Boston, can be partly explained by the distance separating Newburyport from the colonial capital. Government privilege rarely reached as far as the Merrimack, for none of the local merchants was among the tightly knit group surrounding the governor. He and his establishment were paid little allegiance, and the Newburyporters had few business connections with Boston merchants. When the revolutionary crisis developed, therefore, the Newburyport merchants saw Great Britain not as a defender of their economic privileges but rather as a threat to their political freedom. And it was in political terms that they argued their cause.

In 1765 the most serious problem confronting the people of Newburyport was economic depression. The late war with France had created an unusual demand for foodstuffs and military supplies, bringing unaccustomed prosperity to farmers and artisans as well as to exporters. But the restoration of peace and the withdrawal of British troops plunged the colonies into an uncomfortable period of adjustment. None of the Newburyporters had reason to suspect that he and his fellow colonists stood on the threshold of a decade of political struggle. By the end of this period their vessels would be carrying cannon in place of cargo—outward-bound on familiar routes but with an intent far different from peaceful trading voyages.

Logically one would expect the merchants of Newburyport to support the protest against the Sugar Act in 1764 because of the importance of rum manufacture to the town. There is no evidence, however, of any particular concern over the new duty and its strict enforcement, perhaps because the inhabitants were preoccupied with establishing their new town government. But in the fall of 1765 Newburyport did join the increasing opposition to the Stamp Act that stirred Americans all along the Atlantic seaboard. Suddenly in late September a tumultuous riot shattered the town's normal decorum. John Boardman had accepted the post of stamp distributor for Newburyport and was promptly hanged in effigy from what subsequently became known as "Liberty Tree." [1]

A few days after the riot a town meeting convened to condemn the Stamp Act, labeling any inhabitant who accepted the office of stamp distributor "an enemy to his country." At the same meeting, however, violence was denounced as a means of protest. On October 21 another session adopted a lengthy resolution of instructions to

---

[1] Cf. Arthur M. Schlesinger, *The Colonial Merchants and the Coming of the American Revolution, 1763–1776* (New York, 1918), pp. 50–54; Oliver M. Dickerson, *The Navigation Acts and the American Revolution* (Philadelphia, 1951), pp. 82–87; Joshua Coffin, *A History of Newbury, Newburyport, and West Newbury* (Boston, 1845), p. 231. The only documentary evidence of this particular riot is the bill presented by tavern-keeper William Davenport to "Messrs Joseph Stanwood & others . . . for Sundry Expenses at My House on Thursday Septr 26th A.D. 1765, at the Greate Uneasiness and Tumult on Occasion of the Stamp Act." Currier, *"Ould Newbury,"* p. 499. The "Sundry Expenses" amounted to nearly eight pounds lawful money as the assembled company consumed three triple, twenty-seven double, and six single bowls of punch before supper, followed by eight more double bowls and a single afterwards. Apparently the party lasted through the night, as the final item of the bill included "Breakfast of Coffee for Sd Company. . . ." Three years later Davenport was still trying to collect the bill, finally resorting to an appeal to the town meeting, which voted him six pounds six shillings compensation. Town Records, I, 125.

its representative in the General Court, Dudley Atkins. Political theory, not economic distress, was the primary concern of the authors.

The Liberty of the Subject [of the British Constitution] is so interwoven in every Part of it, that the least infringement of that Liberty is a Blow aimed at the Vital of the Constitution. To this happy Constitution in all its Branches, and in its fullest Extent, we apprehend the Inhabitants of this Province are entitled, as free born British Subjects.

After professions of loyalty to the king and respect for Parliament, the writers vehemently protested the jurisdiction of Admiralty Courts in recovery proceedings.

Are we not treated as Slaves indeed, when our Brethren and Equals, who in all Matters, where Life, Liberty, and Property are concerned, are to be the Judges by the British Constitution, are here excluded and we are obliged to Submit to a Jurisdiction naturally foreign to it.[2]

The interdependence of political freedom and property rights played as important a role to these colonial merchants as to the eighteenth-century political economists from whose writings they borrowed so much. Yet the argument remained essentially political, for it was liberties with which they were primarily concerned. On this basic principle the resolution closed.

That a People should be taxed at the Will of another, whether of one man or many, without their own Consent is Rank Slavery. For if their Superior sees fit, they may be deprived of their whole Property, upon any frivolous Pretext, or without any Pretext at all. . . . for Liberty, or even Life itself, without the Enjoyment of them flowing from Property, are of no Value.[3]

But while the merchant leaders were occupied with writing instructions to their representative, the local Sons of Liberty continued to prevent compliance with the offensive Stamp Act. Some transgressors apparently required several lessons at the hands of the mob before they acquiesced. John Boardman came in for further harrassment in February 1766, when the Sons of Liberty learned

[2] Town Records, I, 52, 54–55; cf. Edmund S. and Helen M. Morgan, *The Stamp Act Crisis* (Chapel Hill, 1953), pp. 99–113; Schlesinger, *Colonial Merchants*, pp. 71–82; Edmund S. Morgan, "Colonial Ideas of Parliamentary Power," *William and Mary Quarterly*, 3d ser., V (July 1948), 320–325.

[3] Town Records, I, 54–55

that he possessed a stamped clearance for his aptly named schooner *Defiance*. After being required to deliver up the paper, Boardman was brought before a local justice where he swore never again to make use of such a document until allowed by the province. Although dismissed with three cheers by the crowd, the next day Boardman was once again hanged in effigy, and "the detestable clearance was fixed on a Pole with a Chain, carried thro' the Town with Drums beating, & Flag flying, and other Music."[4]

When word of the Stamp Act's repeal arrived in May 1766, it called for spirited celebration. On the 20th a town meeting laid out careful plans for the occasion, providing at public expense for the firing of guns and illumination of the Town House. The constables were given strict instruction to brook no disturbance of the peace. These precautions apparently succeeded, for no riots such as were witnessed in Boston marred the celebration. Newburyport in fact went on record against such doings once more when in July a town meeting recommended that "the Losses sustained by the Sufferers in the late Tumults in Boston" should be compensated for by funds from the public treasury of the Province.[5]

In the year that had passed since Newburyporters first learned of the Stamp Act, they found it necessary to examine their thoughts concerning the rights and privileges they enjoyed as Britons. To many this process must have been a novel exercise. The lengthy resolution of instruction to Dudley Atkins was a practical application of the political theories with which the more literate Newburyporters, especially those who were graduates of Dummer Academy and Harvard College, had long been acquainted. Not only did the Stamp Act crisis teach a valuable lesson to many of the townsmen, but this crisis also brought the more sober citizens of Newburyport face to face with the specter of mob disorder. Although caught unprepared when word of the act first arrived, those in charge of town affairs quickly learned the need for a firm hand. After these initial disturbances in the fall and winter of 1765–1766, Newburyport was unusually free of similar activities in the decade to follow.

[4] *Boston Gazette*, 10 March 1766.

[5] Town Records, I, 81, 85; Arthur M. Schlesinger, "Political Mobs and the American Revolution," American Philosophical Society *Proceedings*, XCI (August 1955), 245; Ronald S. Longley, "Mob Activities in Revolutionary Massachusetts," *New England Quarterly*, VI (March 1933), 108–109; Morgan, *Stamp Act Crisis*, pp. 123–128.

Perhaps most important, the Stamp Act crisis brought the inhabitants closer to their fellow colonists. Participation in a common cause was a small but significant first step toward independence.

Repeal of the Stamp Act, though assuaging the ruffled feelings of the colonists, did little to restore prosperity to the prewar level, as many had hoped. The pace of business in Newburyport slowly picked up, however. The merchant Jonathan Jackson and his partner, John Bromfield, expanded stock somewhat, and net profits increased by 25 percent over the previous year. But caution was still the rule, especially in the acceptance of credit so eagerly extended by British merchants.[6]

The year 1767 was already one of general uneasiness when news of the Townshend Acts arrived to precipitate another round of protest and countermeasures by American colonists. Reaction in Boston at first took the form of a nonconsumption agreement, to which other towns in the province were invited to subscribe. On December 17 a special town meeting called in Newburyport to consider the Boston proposals appointed a committee of seven to draft a reply.[7]

The committee worked hard in the early months of 1768 to determine what action their town should take in response to the Boston proposals. The question was no longer simply whether Newburyport should agree with other Massachusetts towns not to consume imported articles. Nonconsumption ultimately meant nonimportation, and at this the Newburyporters hesitated. A special town meeting in March adopted the committee's report rejecting a nonimportation agreement. The reason was clear:

[6] Schlesinger, *Colonial Merchants,* pp. 86–87; Jackson & Bromfield (Newburyport) to Messrs. Barnard Harrison & Co. (London), 30 May 1767, "Letterbook 1765," Henry Lee Shattuck Collection (MHS).

[7] For this whole movement see Charles M. Andrews, "Boston Merchants and the Non-Importation Movement," in Colonial Society of Massachusetts *Publications,* XIX (1918), 159–259; John C. Miller, *Origins of the American Revolution* (Boston, 1943), pp. 255–311; Schlesinger, *Colonial Merchants,* p. 107; Town Records, I, 117. For an erroneous report that Newburyport had immediately agreed to the Boston regulations, see *Boston Gazette,* 28 December 1767. Members of the committee were the merchants Patrick Tracy, Tristram Dalton, Nathaniel Carter, and Jonathan Jackson, shipyard owner Ralph Cross, Judge Benjamin Greenleaf, and the signer of the report, lawyer John Lowell, Jr.

This Town has been in a great Measure Supported for many Years past by the Building of Ships which have been purchased mostly by the Inhabitants of and for the use of Great Britain: the manner in which we have been paid for the Ships has been mainly by British Manufactures So that the Importation and Purchase of these and our Staple Business (if we may so express it) have been almost inseperably [*sic*] united.

The town meeting did give its moral support to Boston for its patriotic endeavors and supported the proposition that frugality ought to be strictly observed. And so it would appear that Newburyport's mercantile class firmly balked at nonimportation as an appropriate protest to the Townshend duties.[8]

In April 1768, however, a group of Newburyport merchants in response to a letter from their Boston colleagues came into a private nonimportation agreement. The Newburyporters were headed by Tristram Dalton, Jonathan Jackson, and William Morland, the first two of whom had been on the committee drafting the outright rejection of nonimportation scarcely a month before. Among the twenty-four firms endorsing the proposals, moreover, were the other two merchants who had been on the earlier committee, Patrick Tracy and Nathaniel Carter. But the merchants refused to ban English goods imported in exchange for ships sold abroad. Adding to their list of exceptions carpenters' tools, steel, and dying stuffs, the cautious Newburyport committee also excepted all other articles which Boston, Salem, or Marblehead merchants might refuse to ban. There seems to have been no complaint that the merchants were playing the game unfairly. Other towns probably recognized that Newburyport stood to be doubly penalized by a general nonimportation agreement because of its shipbuilding industry.[9]

The merchants had a convincing economic reason for wanting to adopt nonimportation at this time: they had imported too many goods the previous year, and these stocks were moving slowly. Times were uncertain; retrenchment would give them opportunity to collect their debts, reduce their wares, and consider their next policy. But in Newburyport a number of voters would be put out of work if the shipyards closed, and the proposal from Boston town meeting made no suggestion for excepted articles. The merchants

---

[8] Town Records, I, 121–122.
[9] Savage Papers, II, 1751–1829 (MHS).

therefore probably decided that a private agreement was their best course.[10]

But the merchants' reaction also had political overtones. Jonathan Jackson in his private and business correspondence during the spring of 1768 indicated how strongly he felt about the current state of affairs between England and the colonies. Writing to his London merchant friend Stephen Sayre, Jackson pointed out that the colonists would willingly give their lives in defense against "the Encroachments of an usurping Minister [Hillsborough]." Jackson then heartily endorsed the arguments advanced by the Pennsylvania Farmer, John Dickinson, although mistakenly identifying the author as "Mr. Delaney of Virginia."[11]

To Henry & Thomas Bromfield, like Sayre's a partly "American" firm in London, Jackson & Bromfield catalogued a rather lengthy list of grievances: "the Great Scarcity of Cash among us . . . the Hardship of Infringement on our Libertys by the late Duty on Paper Glass &c confessedly laid for the purpose of raising a Revenue —the Embarrassments of our W. India Trade . . . occasioned by the Sugar Act . . . & the late more rigorous Execution of it—the increase of Crown Officers by the late Board of Commissioners & their power of Substitution. . . ." Jackson & Bromfield felt that the present crisis was stirring up every bit as spirited a commotion as did the Stamp Act, except that "the better sort of People are [now] more generally rouzed & firmly bent on an Assertion of their Rights." The Newburyport partners then indicated one of the reasons why they and their colleagues favored nonimportation. Pointing out that the common people in Great Britain were not thoroughly acquainted with the recent ill treatment of the colonies by the mother country, the writers concluded that "no one thing will give them so convincing a proof of what importance America is to them, as ceasing to import their Manufactures will."[12]

[10] Jackson & Bromfield to Messrs. Henry & Thomas Bromfield (London), April 1768; also printed in Porter, *Jacksons and Lees*, I, 197–199; Jackson & Bromfield to Messrs. Tappenden Hanbey & Co. (London), 27 June 1768; Andrews, "Boston Merchants and Non-Importation," pp. 181–198.

[11] Jonathan Jackson (Newburyport) to Stephen Sayre (London), 24 February 1768, "Letterbook 1765." Sayre was the American-born partner of Dennys DeBerdt, agent for Massachusetts during the Stamp Act crisis.

[12] Jackson & Bromfield to Henry & Thomas Bromfield (London), April 1768, "Letterbook 1765"; also printed in Porter, *Jackson and Lees*, I, 197–199. Henry Bromfield was a brother of Jackson's partner John; Thomas was their cousin.

Still another London firm received gloomy news from the colonies when Jackson & Bromfield addressed a lengthy letter to Messrs. Tappenden Hanbey & Co. in June. It was clear to the Newburyport partnership that if Hillsborough were to go through with his threat to enforce the collection of duties by military power, "it would throw this Country into such Convulsions, as it never before knew, & perhaps give a greater Shock to Britain than his Lordship may be apprehensive of. . . . He may be assured that his Rigors will be opposed with a firmness that is only discovered in those whose All is at Stake." Jackson & Bromfield concluded by announcing that the uncertainty of political conditions had determined them not to import further goods till more encouraging prospects developed.[13]

Through the letters of this period from Jackson & Bromfield to their fellow merchants in London ran two threads. First was that the colonists considered themselves "Englishmen born in America," a relation in which England was repeatedly referred to as "home." On the other hand, a new interpretation of the relation between mother country and colonies began to appear, one which implied a balance between two parts within the Empire. Jackson & Bromfield even passed along the opinion of some that England had grown so luxurious and depraved that the power of Great Britain was on the wane and that "in time America may be the Seat of Universal Empire." But just how distinct they thought the two parts were the Newburyporters did not seem to know, as is apparent in the following confused passage: "What *our* Fate or the *common* Fate of the *Nation* will be is much to be feared, if more true Patriotism does not preside in *our* public measures & if the Earl of Chatham is that true Friend to *our united* Interests which we *Americans* supposed him to be may God continue his health & stengthen [*sic*] him in his Abilitys to serve us." [14]

In the late summer of 1768 the merchants and traders of Boston held a series of meetings to decide what action to take in response to Philadelphia's rejection of the nonimportation proposal. It was agreed to go ahead without the assurance that any of the other large ports would cooperate. The Boston merchants therefore

[13] Jackson & Bromfield to Messrs. Tappenden Hanbey & Co. (London), 27 June 1768, "Letterbook 1765."
[14] To Stephen Sayre, 24 February 1768; to Messrs. Barnard Harrison & Co. (London), 30 May 1767; to Stephen Sayre, 24 February, 9 May 1768, "Letterbook 1765." Italics mine.

unanimously voted not to order any further goods for fall shipment and not to import any goods from England with the exception of coal, salt, and other articles necessary to the fishing industry. Dutied goods such as tea, glass, and paper were particularly singled out for blacklisting until such time as the duties be repealed. Newburyport merchants quickly followed suit, agreeing to a resolution similar to Boston's in early September 1768, and a year later they sought and received approval from town meeting to continue the nonimportation agreement until January 1770. Those who bought any goods imported contrary to the agreement were to be branded enemies to their country, and a committee of six was appointed to aid enforcement. With these actions Newburyport town meeting now at last firmly supported its merchants in protesting the Revenue Acts of Great Britain.[15]

Newburyport's attitude toward duted goods during this period is best seen in the popular reaction against tea-drinking. Writing in the spring of 1767 to their London correspondents De Berdt, Burkitt & Sayre, Jackson & Bromfield noted that "Tea is an Article which affords us scarce any Profit & yet is as necessary in our Business as almost any one thing." Less than two years later, in November 1768, the Newburyporters wrote to Peter Contencin, the London merchant who had been supplying most of their tea: "as for Tea it is growing daily out of Use in this Country—the Generality begin to be convinced how unnecessary an Article it is & are roused to the disuse of that and every Thing of the kind, from the great Indignity put upon us by sending military Troops, to enforce, they don't know what, now they have come—"[16]

In the eighteen months between these two letters the drinking of tea had become a symbol of acquiescence to the British policy of taxation for revenue. In addition, abstinence was in keeping with the principles of frugality that had been urged upon the populace since late in 1767. The protest movement also encouraged the cultivation of native American tea. In Newburyport at a spinning bee held at the Presbyterian parsonage in the spring of 1768 the

---

[15] Schlesinger, *Colonial Merchants*, p. 120; Andrews, "Boston Merchants and Non-Importation," pp. 204–206; *Boston Gazette*, 15 August 1768; Town Records, I, 131, 132.

[16] 30 May 1767, 21 November 1768, "Letterbook 1765."

young women drank "Labradore Tea" with such gusto that they finished their work long before nightfall. Not to be outdone, the Congregationalists had the opportunity to display their patriotism at the ordination of the Reverend Mr. Marsh by sampling imitation Bohea tea which had been cultivated in Maine.[17]

After the colonists learned early in 1770 that Parliament had withdrawn revenue duties on all articles but tea, attention focused on prohibiting consumption of that product, though there was continued effort to enforce the nonimportation agreement as a whole. In fact a new cycle of belt-tightening came in March 1770, partly perhaps as a reaction to the Boston Massacre early that month. In Newburyport a town meeting convening on the 28th resolved not to use or buy foreign tea and to discourage its use by others. Less than a week later another special meeting considered the charge that a number of merchants had brought into town goods imported contrary to the agreement. A sense of urgency was introduced by the suspicion that "in a few days past a Waggon Load of Tea thus imported [against the agreement] had been brought into this Town and received by some of our Traders &c." The meeting forthwith appointed a Committee of Inspection to discourage further violations. Particular care was to be exercised while examining the actions of those shipbuilders who were permitted to receive English goods in payment for vessels sold abroad. Public opinion was the principal means of enforcement by the threat of publishing the names of unrepentant offenders as "pests of Society & Enemies of ye Country."[18]

The Committee of Inspection also circulated a pledge to be signed by all inhabitants determined not to buy, sell, or use India tea. Those refusing to sign were to be reported to the next town meeting. The resulting list of nonsigners totaled forty-four men, plus the wives of four men who apparently did sign, and three widows. These men, about 6 percent of the town's adult males, were in fact

---

[17] *Boston Gazette,* 9 May, 21 November 1768. "Labradore tea" was probably made from the swamp weed of that name.

[18] Schlesinger, *Colonial Merchants,* pp. 181–182. Town Records, I, 141–143. The Committee of Inspection membership consisted of merchants James Hudson, Daniel Balch, Robert Roberts, Moses Little, Jacob Boardman, Samuel Tufts, and Nicholas Tracy; gentlemen Benaiah Young and Jonathan Bradbury; and cordwainer Edmund Bartlet.

a remarkable cross-section. Each social group was represented approximately in proportion to its share of the population, although there were fewer merchants and shopkeepers and more maritime artisans than one would expect. Of the thirty-seven still alive in 1773, twenty-one were members of town meeting and therefore must have known of the seriousness of their nonconformity. The only clue to understanding why some of these men refused to sign the pledge lies in their age: at least eighteen were over forty years old. In their cases, therefore, habit probably played an important part in their decision not to abandon tea drinking. Although the people of Newburyport were quick to single out those guilty of deviation in the matter of tea consumption, it is apparent that they were just as quick to forgive. Fully one fourth of those proscribed in 1770 subsequently held elective office at the bidding of the town, and there is no evidence of persecution of any sort.[19]

Despite apparent popular interest in anti-tea pledges, protest over the principle of taxation for revenue waned rapidly after word reached the colonies in the spring of 1770 that Parliament had voted to withdraw the duties on all articles except tea. Technically, of course, the nonimportation agreements were to remain in force until revenue duties were repealed on *all* imports. But the line began to crumble in most of the commercial towns before the end of the summer, and when the Boston merchants decided on October 12, 1770, to resume importation of all British goods, the great protest movement was at an end.[20]

Enforcement in Newburyport had been an intermittent problem since early in the year. In July reports reached Boston that Newburyport, among other Essex County towns, had been remiss in main-

[19] "A List of Persons that refuse to sign against . . . Tea . . . ," Eben F. Stone Papers (EI). The list included seven from the merchant group, four shopkeepers, ten domestic and twelve maritime artisans, five laborers, and six men of unknown occupation. Town Records, I, 167. One of the widows, Sarah Atkins, had ordered a chest of tea from Messrs. Hutchinson in Boston, but the coaster by whom it was to be sent to Newburyport, Captain David Stickney, refused to take it aboard his vessel, and the chest remained in Boston untouched. *Boston Gazette*, 11 September 1769.

[20] Schlesinger, *Colonial Merchants*, pp. 214ff., 233; Andrews, "Boston Merchants and Non-Importation," pp. 236–259.

taining the agreement, and a visiting committee was therefore appointed to look into the situation. The suspect communities apparently passed the examination satisfactorily and were accorded the congratulations of the committee for their determination. But by the end of the year life had returned to normal. In November 1770 Jackson & Bromfield once again sent out orders for goods to their English correspondents, for the first time in almost three years. During the period of nonimportation the Newburyport firm had been able to balance most of its English accounts. Now it was free to rebuild its stocks of popular English goods, and orders for cloth of all sorts, hardware, and household goods went out to England.[21]

Calm though the years 1771 and 1772 may have been, they were not so prosperous as the merchants had hoped. In July of 1772, scarcely eighteen months after the reopening of trade, Jackson & Bromfield were writing their London correspondents that "we are determin'd to import no more good till the present dull prospect brightens and Some Chance arives [sic] of their leaving us a living Profit." This and other letters written in the summer of 1772 merely announced a policy of nonimportation which the Newburyport firm had been following for purely business reasons since the beginning of the year.[22]

On the political front all remained quiet until late in the fall of 1772 when Samuel Adams, who had been struggling in vain behind the scenes to preserve anti-British sentiments, proposed to Boston town meeting the appointment of a standing committee of correspondence. Adams urged that this committee be directed to publicize particulars of British maltreatment of the colonies with the obvious purpose of stirring up old feelings on issues nearly forgotten in most towns of the province. The unanimous approval of his list of grievances on November 20, 1772, indicated that the Boston merchants had lost control of town meeting. The Adams report, accompanied by a letter from the Boston Committee of Correspond-

---

[21] Schlesinger, *Colonial Merchants,* p. 185; Jackson & Bromfield Invoice Book, Patrick Tracy Jackson Collection (Boothbay Harbor, Maine); Jackson & Bromfield to Henry & Thomas Bromfield, 11 November 1770, "Letterbook 1765"; order sent to Henry Cruger, Jr., of Bristol, November 1770, Jackson & Bromfield Invoice Book.
[22] Jackson & Bromfield to Hayley & Hopkins (London), 2 July 1772, "Letterbook 1765"; Jackson & Bromfield Invoice Book.

ence, was sent round to the various towns in the province with hopes that a general response would follow.[23]

Newburyport immediately rose to the bait. A special town meeting on December 23 appointed a twelve-man committee "to report to the Town as soon as may be what they think proper for the Town to do in order to procure a redress of our publick Grievances." On January 1, 1773, the committee submitted to town meeting a letter for the Boston Committee of Correspondence. The town pledged its support of the Boston committee and instructed its representative in the General Court, Jonathan Greenleaf, to join in a petition to Lord Dartmouth "in Behalf of an injured and oppressed People."[24]

It is curious that Newburyport merchants should be so willing to play the Boston radicals' game of trying to keep the spark of protest alive. Obviously their quarrel with Great Britain was primarily political in nature, not to be turned aside by the promise of economic prosperity. Such was not the case in the other Essex County ports. Twenty-nine merchants in Marblehead repudiated their town's resolution supporting the Boston letter, and Salem did not reply until early June, pleading "the uncommon Hurry of Business" as the reason for delay.[25]

The efforts of Sam Adams notwithstanding, the political scene remained calm through most of 1773. But in September when word reached the colonies that Parliament had given the East India Company the right to export tea directly to the colonial retailer, merchants and others were once more convinced that they were being sorely oppressed. One fear, it seemed, was the possibility that the East India Company would make even further inroads into other mercantile activities of the colonies in the future.[26]

Throughout the fall of 1773 tension mounted in Newburyport as elsewhere in anticipation of the first shipments of tea sent under

[23] Schlesinger, *Colonial Merchants,* pp. 256–260; Miller, *Origins of the Revolution,* pp. 329–330.

[24] Town Records, I, 161–162.

[25] Schlesinger, *Colonial Merchants,* p. 260; Salem Town Records, June 7, 1773, quoted in J. Duncan Phillips, *Salem in the Eighteenth Century* (Boston, 1937), p. 314; Boston Committee of Correspondence to Newburyport Committee of Correspondence, 9 January 1773, Bancroft Collection (NYPL).

[26] Schlesinger, *Colonial Merchants,* pp. 262–268; Miller, *Origins of the Revolution,* pp. 337–352.

the new arrangement. On December 9 town meeting selected a committee of prominent citizens "to draft something suitable for this People to do on this occasion." This group quickly drew up a short resolution stating that Newburyport acquiesced in the proceedings taken by Boston to protest the importation of tea and that "[we] are Determined to give them all the Assistance in our power even at the Risque of our Lives & Fortunes." [27]

When word of the Boston Tea Party reached Newburyport, some citizens thought the town should reaffirm its vote of the previous week. On December 20 a meeting of the town voted unanimously to address the Boston committee in its strongest language yet:

Gentlemen It is with Astonishment that we reflect on the unremitted Efforts of the British Ministry & Parliament to fasten Infamy and ruin upon these Colonies. . . . we loose all patience when we Consider, that the Industerous [sic] Americans are to be stript of their honest earnings to gratify the Humours of Lawless and ambitious Men & to Support in idleness & Luxury a parcell of worthless Parasites, their creatures & Tools, who are swarming thick upon us and are already become A notorious Burden to the Community.[28]

Anticipating complaints that the meeting was not sufficiently publicized in advance, James Hudson, chairman of the Newburyport Committee of Correspondence, took especial pains to point out in his covering letter to Boston that notices had been posted in public places throughout the town. "After a Serious consideration of ye matters before them," Hudson averred, "they passed a Vote (none dissenting) expressing their Acquiescence in the Proceedings of ye People at Boston." Hudson concluded with the hope that no one would regard this action "a piece of Parade & meer show." The Town Clerk, Stephen Sewall, apparently was showing similar concern when he carefully noted in the Town Records that the draft letter had been "distinctly read" at the meeting.[29]

Agitation concerning the landing of East India tea was as much the reopening of an old and familiar argument as it was opposition to the new measure of Parliament. For at a meeting on December

[27] Town Records, I, 178–180.
[28] Town Records, I, 178–180.
[29] Newburyport Committee of Correspondence to Boston Committee of Correspondence, 21 December 1773, Bancroft Collection (NYPL); Town Records, I, 180.

16 the town had voted to exert all affort to prevent the landing of East India Company tea *"whilst the Same is Subject to a Duty Impos'd by the British Parliament."* A letter written sometime in 1774 by a Newburyport man to a correspondent in the West Indies gives further evidence of the Newburyporters' attitude. The author apparently had recently returned from a voyage to one of the West Indian colonies, where many of the residents opposed the destruction of East India Company's tea.

Suffering the tea to be landed would have been construed as an implicit assent to the act, and consequently, the right of the British Parliament to tax the Colonies. . . . Thus we are bound to prevent the landing of the tea, or submit to the act, there was no alternative.[30]

In Newburyport as elsewhere direct action soon supplanted words as the language of protest, according to a newspaper communication in January 1774, signed by "Philo Patriae & Oppide." After pointing out that several other towns had published their patriotic doings relative to tea, the author informed the public "that a large quantity of the aforementioned pernicious stuff was consumed . . . [as in Boston and Charlestown] by fire and water . . . and to the further honour of the town it was done not in the manner of some others, on the wharves and in the public streets, but by each one under his own roof, and, as if by general agreement, about the same time." Although this last assertion strains the imagination somewhat, such a general purge of tea on hand appears a plausible occurrence.[31]

While waiting through the early months of 1774 for word of Parliament's reaction to the Boston Tea Party, Newburyport inhabitants showed signs of their tension by engaging in petty newspaper debates. Some citizens were uncertain what sort of behavior was expected of them, while others shed more heat than light on the matter by labeling the timid as outright Tories. No doubt a few Newburyporters privately felt that the destruction of tea was wrong and that the East India Company ought to be compensated for its property losses. But when the town learned of the Coercive Acts, the first response was decidedly radical. On the evening of May 12

[30] Town Records, I, p. 178, italics mine; *Essex Journal,* 28 September 1774.
[31] *Essex Journal,* 26 January 1774.

several merchants gathered to read the acts. "I shou'd not have conceived People here so generally & so soon wou'd have caught the flame of Resentment," Jonathan Jackson wrote to his brother-in-law Oliver Wendell the next day. The merchants immediately pledged to break off all trade with the West Indies and Great Britain if the other Massachusetts ports would agree to it, until Boston port was reopened or the disputes between the colonies and Great Britain were satisfactorily settled. To Wendell, Jackson was optimistic about the plan:

... with due moderation & firmness we may bring this Province into so general a Sentiment of Enthusiasm or rather manly Virtue I will call it, as to *break off every Connection with G. Britain* & live within ourselves— not with a scanty Pittance like Savages, but like Men wishing for no more than reasonable Nature requires, in a Land that improved as it may be, will flow with Milk & Honey– . . .[32]

In Boston Sam Adams had quickly learned of the proposal, for he wrote James Warren about it on the 14th, praising the Newburyport merchants for their "noble example of publick Spirit." Adams concluded his letter with the wish that "Plymouth which has hitherto stood foremost would now condescend to second Newbury Port." Adams' own town meeting had met the previous day and adopted a resolution suggesting similar action.[33]

Jonathan Jackson's letter to Oliver Wendell clearly indicates the

[32] *Essex Journal*, 16, 23, 30 March 1774; *Essex Gazette*, 17 May 1774; Jonathan Jackson to [Oliver Wendell], 13 May 1774, Massachusetts Historical Society *Miscellany*, No. 2, 15 July 1955. Italics mine.

[33] Samuel Adams to James Warren, 14 May 1774, Adams-Warren Papers (MHS); Schlesinger, *Colonial Merchants*, p. 313; Miller, *Origins of the American Revolution*, pp. 355-376. Other evidence that Newburyport's action preceded that of Boston is found in a letter from Newburyport's Committee of Correspondence to its counterpart in Boston. "We have to acknowledge the receipt of your esteemed favour of the 12th ult. wherein you acquaint us of that unrighteous Act of the British Parliament called the Boston Port Bill. . . . Previous to our receipt of yours we had sent you the minds of most [of] the principle Merchants and Traders in this Town, we are anxiously waiting to know if the plan we then propos'd will be accepted." Newburyport Committee of Correspondence to Boston Committee of Correspondence, 4 June 1774, Bancroft Collection (NYPL). It is possible that the letter from Boston which the Newburyport Committee described as being "of the 12th ult." was in reality the circular letter sent out on the 13th along with Boston town meeting's resolution of that day. By mid-July the editor of the *Essex Journal* assumed as common knowledge that his town had been the first in the province to protest the port bill by proposing a cessation of trade. *Essex Journal*, 20 July 1774.

profound effect of the Boston Port Act on the deteriorating situation between colonies and mother country. His evidence that the people were greatly stirred up shows how deeply concerned the town was for Boston's future. Although the Newburyporters stood to gain from the summary closing of Boston harbor, no one suggested that its plight be exploited; quite to the contrary, all forms of aid and assistance were to be offered throughout the summer and fall.

The fact that Jackson rejected conciliation was not surprising in the light of his strong resolves throughout the previous six years. Perhaps he did not mean to imply political independence in advocating that "[we] break off every Connection with Great Britain & live within ourselves," but his phraseology seems to suggest that he was prepared to support it if necessary. Jackson's idealization of America as the land of milk and honey was a sentiment common enough perhaps among colonists in general, but rather unusual for a merchant who only six short years before habitually referred to England as "home." Whether Jackson himself believed at this time that American independence was the only solution to current troubles with Great Britain is impossible to determine. The more practical, modified plan proposed by the Newburyport merchant group, of which he was a part, was based on the principle that redress of grievances could ultimately be gained. The leverage counted upon was the familiar one of putting pressure on Parliament from West Indian planters and English merchants who suffered when the continental colonies halted commercial intercourse.

But a proposal by the town's merchants in an informal gathering was a different matter from a resolution adopted by a legally constituted town meeting held after sober second thought took command. When the town received a letter from the Boston Committee of Correspondence on June 8 calling for a "Solemn League and Covenant" against commercial intercourse with Great Britain, Newburyport town meeting moved cautiously. In the end, four more men—all merchants—were added to the Committee of Correspondence, making it a group of six merchants, two shipyard owners, and a shipmaster. Four days earlier, the committee in its letter to Boston had freely talked in terms of the advisability of calling "a speedy Congress of Merchants from all parts of the Continent." After more statements about their God-given rights being violated, the authors had closed with a dark hint of the future: "if by the wicked Machinations of our, and the Nation's, Virulent Enemies we should be drove to the last Extremity I think you may Chearfully expect all that Assistance that reasonable Men may desire in this case." Despite the strong language used by its committee, town meeting failed to take any immediate action on the suggestion of a Solemn League. In this regard the town agreed with the position taken by both Salem and Marblehead as well as many of the other towns in the province.[34]

But the decision to resist, while not made at once, was inexorably determined by small steps taken almost daily, while the road to conciliation fell further behind. In June a subscription was raised through the authority and offices of the town to aid the poor of Boston. Contribution was in fact less than voluntary, for the assessors were empowered to collect £200 by levies in proportion to each inhabitant's last province tax, though they were carefully instructed not to make demands on those well-disposed but needy persons "who would willingly contribute if in their Power and who would feel a Pain in Refusing." Others who were unable or unwilling to contribute were legally quite free to refuse, though it is safe to assume such lack of patriotism did not pass unnoticed by their fellow citizens.[35]

During the summer numerous amateur political analysts attempted to explain why their world seemed to be in such a turmoil and what could best be done about it. In addition to the many tracts blaming "ministerial tyranny" some correspondents offered more original theories. One writer advanced the idea "not doubted by many sensible men, that it has been a plan long concerted by the execrable Thane to set one of the detested Stuart race upon the British throne." "B——— C———," on the other hand, argued that God was using the British ministry as a rod to punish the colonists for "the oppression, bondage and slavery exercised upon our poor

[34] Town Records, I, 191; Newburyport Committee of Correspondence to Boston Committee of Correspondence, 4 June 1774, Bancroft Collection (NYPL); Schlesinger, *Colonial Merchants*, pp. 323-325.
[35] *Essex Journal*, 22 June, 20 July, 17 August 1774; Town Records, I, 195.

brethren the Africans." A Negro resident signing himself "Caesar Sarter," agreed, pointing out the absurdity of the colonists' "exertions for liberty while you have slaves in your houses." Though perhaps somewhat irrelevant, these arguments nonetheless struck home to those slave-holding patriots such as Jonathan Jackson, who less than two years later freed his man-servant Pomp.[36]

The summer also brought a rumor of the imminent landing of tea. On July 20 the *Essex Journal* reported that a ship with several chests of "that political plague tea" was shortly expected to arrive in port, and the editor fervently hoped that his townsmen would block its landing. Pleas for unity continued to give evidence of the educational process affecting the colonists. Longstanding jealousies between townsman and farmer, New Englander and southerner, and other divisions of colonial society had to be put aside before effective action could take place. Common citizens joined the printers of patriot newspapers to enlighten the populace.[37]

With rumors and accusations indiscriminately filling the air some citizens, self-appointed or otherwise, regarded it their duty to label suspected fellow residents as "Tories" if their words or deeds did not measure up to some vague standard of patriotism. First in Newburyport to show signs of the strain was not a merchant but rather the versatile potter, Daniel Bayley. Writing an open letter to the *Essex Journal* on August 3, he thanked those in the town who had recently helped extinguish a fire in his shop. Bayley went on to say that he "Also takes this opportunity of exculpating himself from sundry reports, which have been spread to his prejudice, that he has been inimical to the town & has propagated many stories against their liberties," reports which he insisted were entirely groundless. "Notwithstanding," Bayley continued, "he readily acknowledges he has (considering the spirit of the times) been too free in speaking his political sentiments which have (perhaps unfortunately for him) been somewhat different from the major part of the people; but this consolation he has, that (if he has been in an error) he has ever spoken his honest sincere and unbiased sentiments—but is determined in future, not to converse on politics which seem so generally to disgust." [38]

[36] *Essex Journal*, 20 July, 27 July, 17 August 1774.
[37] *Essex Journal*, 20 July 1774.
[38] *Essex Journal*, 3 August 1774.

More important topics than a relatively harmless potter's lack of patriotism demanded the consideration of Newburyporters. Since shortly after the announcement of the Port Bill the major towns had been discussing the feasibility of a congress of all the American colonies. Massachusetts, when accorded the privilege of designating place and time, quickly decided upon Philadelphia and September 1. At the same meeting the General Court selected delegates to what was described as "a politico-mercantile congress." Merchants in Newburyport showed great interest in the eventual decisions of the impending session. On July 29 twenty-one merchants and traders headed by the venerable Patrick Tracy petitioned the selectmen to call a special town meeting. Their idea seemed to be that the congress would include delegates from the towns, for the petitioners hoped Newburyport would send "some Gentlemen well Acquainted with the Nature & present State of our Commerce." The plan to send a separate delegation was subsequently dropped, but the town chose a committee of five merchants to draw up a letter of information for the Massachusetts delegation respecting Newburyport's trade, and it was voted unanimously that "this Town will stand by the result of the Congress even if it be to the Cessation of all Trade." As adopted one week later, the report reiterated the town's determination to comply with the final decision of the Congress, expressing only the hope that if any exceptions were to be made to a complete cessation of trade, "our Trade and Commerce may be preserved in the same State and with the same Indulgences as that of the other provinces." [39]

While the Congress met in Philadelphia in early September, the towns of Essex convened in Ipswich to consider the current state of public affairs, particularly the effects of the "Act for the better Regulating of the Government of Massachusetts Bay." The convention report, which Newburyport town meeting endorsed shortly thereafter, closed with the warning that the people of Essex County were ready "to appeal to the last resort of states" in support of their rights. In its instructions to the General Court representative, Jonathan Greenleaf, the meeting made its determination clear: "We design not madly to brave our own destruction and we do not thirst for the Blood of others, but reason and Religion demand

[39] Town Records, I, 192–193, 195–198.

of us that we guard our invaluable Rights at the risque of both." [40]

Strong words were not expected to stand unsupported, and on October 24 Newburyport town meeting voted that all the inhabitants of the town should arm themselves as soon as possible. The Committee of Safety reported somewhat to its surprise that the inhabitants were "tolerably well furnished with fire Arms and Ammunition." Newburyport had already been divided into four companies, and every male over sixteen years of age (with some exceptions for occupational or physical reasons) was obliged to join one of them for military training. The Independent Military Society, ostensibly a company of artillery but in these prewar days apparently more social than military in nature, also went into training during the fall. Musters were usually followed by supper and drink at the General Wolfe Tavern, where on one occasion the proceedings closed with a series of forty-five toasts.[41]

Meanwhile the decisions of the Continental Congress demanded the attention of all patriots. Newburyport wasted no time setting up machinery for enforcing provisions of the Continental Association, especially the ban on importations from the British Empire, effective December 1. The Committee of Safety and Correspondence joined the selectmen in preparing to take charge of illegally imported goods and to encourage frugality within the community. Among the committee's expanded membership of thirty-five were eleven merchants and seventeen other gentlemen who were lawyers, doctors, shipmasters, or shipbuilders. While as a group the merchants in other colonial towns had lost control of local affairs by the end of 1774, in Newburyport they wielded more power than ever.[42]

The committee went about its business with great efficiency, using newspaper advertisements and announcements in town meeting to publicize the correct procedures which the merchants and retailers should follow during the period of transition to a restricted economy. All goods brought into Newburyport after December 1 had

[40] Town Records, I, 198–201, 203, 206–208; Jonathan Jackson, Jonathan Greenleaf, Tristram Dalton, Stephen Cross, and John Bromfield were the delegates to the Essex convention.

[41] Town Records, I, 211, 213–214; Essex Journal, 21 September, 19 October 1774.

[42] Schlesinger, Colonial Merchants, pp. 423–428; Miller, Origins of the Revolution, p. 231; Town Records, I, 204, 215.

Essex County, Massachusetts

The Center of
Newburyport
Massachusetts
At the beginning of the
Nineteenth Century

0   125   250   375   500
SCALE IN FEET

Merrimack — River

KEY

1. Moses Titcomb
2. Frothingham
3. Bassett
4. Joseph Williams, distiller
5. John Lowell, lawyer
   John Tracy, merchant
6. Jonathan Jackson, merchant
   Timothy Dexter, merchant
7. Titcomb [?]
8. Somerby
9. Capt. Benjamin Lunt [?]

10. Rev. James Morse
11. Capt. Tristram Coffin
12. William Faris, merchant
13. Abner Wood, merchant
14. John Pettingell, merchant
15. Widow Bass
16. Capt. Benjamin Wyatt
17. Samuel A. Otis, gentleman
18. Carey
19. Philip Bagley, auctioneer
20. Jacob Pierce, cordwainer

21. Jonathan Marsh, mercha
22. Daniel Bayley, potter
23. St. Paul's Church
24. Enoch Toppan, blockma
25. Deacon Parker
26. Cooper
27. Packard
28. Horton [?]
29. Horton [?]
30. Daniel Farnham, lawye
    William Farnham, lawy

68. Old Wolfe Tavern
69. Dr. Micajah Sawyer
70. Ebenezer Stedman, bookseller
71. Mrs. Burt
72. Nathaniel Tracy, merchant
    James Prince, merchant
73. Widow Wood
74. Nicholas Pike, schoolmaster
75. John Peabody, merchant
    New Wolfe Tavern
76. Joshua Carter, merchant
77. Capt. Nicholas Tracy
78. Clement
79. Stephen Greeley, cordwainer
80. Town house
81. Newburyport Bank
82. David Wood, watchmaker
    [?]
83. Joseph Moulton [?]
84. Col. Stephen Bartlet [?]
85. Benjamin Balch, merchant
86. Jonathan Marsh, merchant
87. Daniel Balch, watchmaker
88. Rev. John Andrews [?]
89. Tristram Dalton, merchant
    Moses Brown, merchant

90. John B. Titcomb, merchant
    [?]
91. John B. Titcomb, merchant
    [?]
92. Samuel Tenney, merchant
93. Richard Pike, merchant
    Capt. Jonathan Moulton
94. Ebenezer Greenleaf,
    merchant
95. Academy Building
96. Daniel Marquand, merchant
    Joseph Marquand, merchant
97. Moody
98. First Baptist Church
99. John Woodman
100. Fourth Religious Society
101. Woodbridge Noyes
102. Jacob Perkins, whitesmith
103. Capt. Peter LeBreton
104. Benjamin Perkins
105. Toppan [?]
106. Col. Edward Wigglesworth
107. Capt. Stephen Holland
108. Enoch Thurston, joiner
     Edward St.L. Livermore,
     lawyer
109. Stephen Cross, shipbuilder

110. Jonathan Greenleaf, ship
     builder
111. Nathaniel Knapp, caulker
112. Joshua Toppan, shopkeeper
113. Anthony Davenport,
     merchant
114. Abraham Wheelwright,
     merchant
115. Ebenezer Stocker, merchant
116. Capt. Ebenezer Wheelwright
117. Andrew Hills
118. Old Jail
119. William Bartlet, merchant
120. First Presbyterian Society
121. Capt. Nicholas Johnson
122. Old Almshouse
123. Mark Haskell
125. Capt. Samuel Swett
126. Richard Pike, merchant
127. Capt. John O'Brien
128. William Coombs, merchant
129. Rev. Jonathan Parsons
130. Zachariah Atwood,
     merchant
131. John Coombs, merchant

to be accompanied by a certificate from a committee of inspection asserting that the goods had been imported into the colonies before the cut-off date, or that the method of their disposition had been approved. The committee carried out other aspects of the association too, exhorting the merchants to hold to their usual prices and recommending the boycott of all funerals which did not conform to the requirements for simplicity in mourning.[43]

Enforcement of the association's provisions occasionally fell into hands other than those authorized by town meeting. Dutied tea having been put on the nonconsumption list by the association, the Committee of Safety and Inspection apparently apprehended a small shipment and deposited it in the town powderhouse pending final disposition. Although conclusive verification is missing, the tale of what next occurred is perfectly plausible. Shipbuilder Eleazer Johnson led a band of his workers to the town house where entrance was gained by axe. After carrying off the chests to Market Square, the group dumped the contents into a pile which was forthwith put to the torch. The Committee of Safety naturally regarded such goings-on as an infringement of its authority and feared that a similar fate would overtake any other goods which it sought to dispose of by orderly means. The members therefore appealed to the town to support their administration of the regulations peacefully. At the annual March meeting for 1775, the town voted its unanimous approval of the committee's past conduct and services and pledged its cooperation for the future. The meeting then protested such unlawful behavior as that committed by Johnson's band, declaring that "the manner in which the Tea was taken out of their [the committee's] hands by no means Justifiable." [44]

The strength of public opinion as a means of demanding adherence to the resolves of the Continental Association or conformity to a particular pattern of behavior was demonstrated almost daily. In early November, for example, a merchant about to send a cargo of sheep to the West Indies changed his plans and returned the animals to the country when informed of the ban on such ship-

[43] *Essex Journal,* 28 December 1774.
[44] Emery, *Reminiscences,* pp. 213–214; D. Hamilton Hurd, ed., *The History of Essex County* (Philadelphia, 1888), II, 1742; Currier, *History of Newburyport,* I, 538–539; Town Records, I, 226.

ments. Even the most prominent inhabitants of the town did not escape the scrutiny of their neighbors. The young lawyer John Lowell, who had been called upon to serve his town in several responsible positions during the developing crisis, found in December 1774 that his past was costing him the respect of his fellow townsmen. In the previous May Lowell had signed one of the addresses drawn up by some merchants and gentlemen of Boston, Salem, and elsewhere, bidding farewell and Godspeed to the departing Governor Thomas Hutchinson. This particular address contained several expressions of obeisance to king, country, and even to the incoming governor, General Gage. Scarcely six months later, Lowell, who incidentally was the only Newburyport resident to sign one of the documents, hastily atoned for his sin by writing an open letter to the "Inhabitants of Newburyport." Noting the fact that his action had distressed some of his fellow citizens, Lowell pointed out that he had been motivated only by a desire to serve his country. He had no idea that such a step could have done any harm, he said, and concluded that "if I had I never should have taken it, and am heartily sorry I ever did." Lowell's complete restoration in the affections of the town is evidenced by his re-election as selectman in the annual March meeting.[45]

The venerable Nathaniel Carter similarly found the persistent stare of the public eye uncomfortable. Carter stood accused of raising prices and shipping goods to Boston contrary to various articles of the association. In April the Committee of Safety publicly announced that Carter had realized his errors, which it said had stemmed from a misunderstanding of the articles, and had assured the committee of his strict conformity to the regulations in the future. The committee then expressed its hope that "he will be considered a good citizen." When mourners at a local funeral violated the association's restrictions on the dress appropriate for such occasions, they came in for a severe tongue-lashing from a correspondent in the *Essex Journal.*[46]

For the individual merchant adherence to the Continental Association required innumerable adjustments in the established pattern

[45] *Essex Journal,* 16 November 1774, 4 January 1775; *Essex Gazette,* 31 May 1774; Town Records, I, 225.

[46] *Essex Journal,* 15 February, 12 April 1775.

of his particular business. Jonathan Jackson and his partners, Nathaniel and John Tracy, found the new regulations demanded a swift succession of changes. Having warned one of their English correspondents in an earlier letter that they would comply with whatever the Continental Congress decided, the Newburyporters pointed out that "where there was one Man raised to a determined Opposition to unconstitutional Acts of Parliament in the year 1765 there are three now—." When they learned of the final decision of the Continental Congress in respect to trade restrictions, Jackson, Tracy & Tracy wrote to the English firms with whom they had been doing business to inform them of the resolves and to cancel all unexecuted orders for goods as soon as possible.[47]

In less tangible fashion the rapidly changing scene during the fall of 1774 and the winter following made planning ahead almost impossible. The uncertainties of the times required the widest of latitudes in orders to captains engaged in buying and selling abroad. Thus after withdrawing an order for the purchase of fruit in Lisbon (which would have been contrary to the association), Jackson, Tracy & Tracy gave Captain Edmund Freeman of their brigantine *Success* instructions permitting him a range of action. He could attempt to find employment in the freighting business, or he could purchase salt and carry it to Newfoundland. In the event his vessel were to prove "weak & crazy," Freeman had authorization to sell it, the proceeds in any case to be forwarded to Lane Son & Fraser for credit to the Newburyport firm's account there. To Cruger & Mallard, Jackson sent even more explicit orders for the sale of one of its vessels, bound to London or Bristol with a cargo of rice from Charlestown. In all procedures Lane Son & Fraser was solemnly cautioned "not to conduct contrary to the late Resolves of the Continental Congress."[48]

---

[47] Jackson, Tracy & Tracy to Lane Son and Fraser (London), 26 September 1774, "Letterbook 1774"; to Messrs. Lane Son & Fraser, 19 December 1774, and to Cruger & Mallard (Bristol), 19 December 1774, *ibid.* Also printed in Porter, *Jacksons and Lees*, I, 285; to Messrs. Thomas & Isaac Wharton (Philadelphia), 16 November 1774, "Letterbook 1774"; also printed in Porter, *Jacksons and Lees*, I, 282-283.

[48] Jackson, Tracy & Tracy to Capt. Edmund Freeman (Falmouth, England, or Bilboa, Spain), 9 December 1774, "Letterbook 1774," pp. 39-70; also printed in Porter, *Jacksons and Lees*, I, 284-285; to Messrs. Cruger & Mallard (Bristol), 25 January 1775, "Letterbook 1774," pp. 53-54; to Lane Son & Fraser, 12 January 1775, *ibid.*, pp. 50-51; also printed in Porter, *Jacksons and Lees*, I, 287-289.

To the partnership of Jackson, Tracy & Tracy, general uncertainty and restrictions of the Continental Association in particular dictated a policy of contraction. The Newburyport firm's business activity in fact slackened off for several nonpolitical reasons in the spring of 1775, and at the same time the partners continued the policy of gradually transferring vessels into the coastal trade (mainly with Philadelphia) or encouraging their sale.[49]

Nearly a decade had passed since Newburyport town meeting had asserted in October 1765 that "the British Inhabitants of America" were entitled to the "Privileges of Britons." For the next ten years the Newburyporters joined in resolutions and economic sanctions designed to bring about a restoration of these British rights by what they considered constitutional means. But even by 1774 a militant nationalism had begun to replace the earlier language of protest. In January of that year, for instance, a distinction between the two countries was abundantly clear to at least one inhabitant. "The *people* of the *Amer. world* are millions strong—countless legions compose their united *army* of free-men," he wrote in the *Essex Journal*. "Let the Britons fear to do any more so wickedly as they have done for the *Herculean arm* of this *new world* is lifted up—and woe be to them on whom it falls." On April 19, 1775, Newburyport dispatched its first company of 115 men to join in the fighting around Boston. As Jonathan Jackson explained it to the Spanish merchant Jose Gardoqui that summer, "We are now at War with the Troops of G. Britain—& if she will not give up Taxation over us, this War will continue as long as we are able to hold it—God grant 'till we are established as Freemen." [50]

---

[49] Jackson, Tracy & Tracy to Thomas and Isaac Wharton (Philadelphia), 25 January 1775, "Letterbook 1774," pp. 56–57; also printed in Porter, *Jacksons and Lees*, I, 294–295. This shift in trade patterns was not peculiar to the Jackson, Tracy & Tracy partnership. During a ten-week period in early 1774 out of a total of thirty-eight outward-bound voyages from Newburyport, twenty-eight vessels had cleared for various West Indies and other Caribbean ports of call, while six had listed coastal ports as their destination. In a comparable period in early 1775, however, only sixteen of thirty-one outward-bound vessels were headed for the Caribbean, at the same time that eleven cleared for coastal ports. Thus while the number of West Indies voyages dropped nearly in half, the coastal trade about doubled. Compiled from Marine Lists, *Essex Journal*, January–April 1774 and January–April 1775.

[50] Town Records, I, 55; *Essex Journal*, 5 January 1774; Jackson Tracy & Tracy to

Word of the Declaration of Independence reached Newburyport in mid-July. In a letter immediately dispatched to his friend Elbridge Gerry, still in Congress at Philadelphia, Tristram Dalton spoke for his townsmen.

I wish you joy on the late full Declaration,—an event so ardently desired by your good self and the people you particularly represent. We are no longer to be amused with delusive prospects. The die is cast. All is at stake. The way is made plain. No one can now doubt on which side it is his duty to act. We have everything to hope from the goodness of our cause. The God of justice is omnipotent. We are not to fear what man or a multitude can do. We have put on the harness and I trust it will not be put off until we see our land of security and freedom,—the wonder of the other hemisphere,—the asylum of all who pant for deliverance from bondage.

Here in a simple paragraph from one Essex County merchant to another is revealed the aspirations of a continent of men. Dalton was one of Newburyport's wealthiest merchants, a communicant of the Episcopal Church, and a son-in-law of Marblehead's most prominent Loyalist. But with this vision of his native land Tristram Dalton abandoned his British ties and declared himself an American.[51]

Jose Gardoqui & Sons (Bilboa), 10 July 1775, "Letterbook 1774," p. 76; also printed in Porter, *Jacksons and Lees,* I, 308–309.

[51] Tristram Dalton to Elbridge Gerry, 19 July 1776, Peter Force, ed., *American Archives* (5th ser., Washington, D.C., 1848), I, 461.

Chapter III

THE CONSEQUENCES OF INDEPENDENCE

To the merchants of Newburyport the immediate consequence of independence was the assumption of new responsibilities. With the outbreak of war in 1775 some of the younger men had joined militia units to participate in the fighting around Boston. But for the most part the merchant class fought its war on the sea, outfitting its vessels as privateers and importing powder and other material to support the military effort. At the same time, the mercantile group continued to administer local government through domination of town meetings as well as through control of the board of selectmen, the Committee of Safety, and the town's delegation to the General Court.

On the provincial level of government even greater responsibilities were thrust upon the Newburyport merchants. The departure of the royal governor and his Loyalist supporters in March 1776 created a void temporarily met by the General Court, governing under the provincial charter of 1692, with the Governor's Council trying to fulfill the functions of an executive. As the scene of warfare moved farther south, men in Massachusetts turned to the problem of drawing up a permanent state government. Newburyporters made a significant contribution to the framing of a constitution for the Commonwealth, and after its adoption in 1780 some of the more experienced among them assumed places of responsibility in the new government.

But at the same time independence brought economic ruin to the merchants of Newburyport. Privateering was not a profitable business for most shipowners, and when peace came in 1783, the few vessels they had left were mostly unfit for trading voyages. Worse, however, was that the terms of peace with England understandably excluded the Americans from the trading privileges they had enjoyed as members of the British Empire. Finally, a general depression among the farmers of Massachusetts and the financial instability of state and national governments made marketing conditions at home uncertain. This was the price Newburyport merchants paid for political independence, and it was a high price indeed, for with their capital tied up in unredeemed government notes and in unsold stock, few of them were able to weather the economic chaos of the 1780's. By 1786 most of the prominent colonial merchant families were on the way to losing their fortunes.

Dissatisfaction with the makeshift form of government that Massachusetts Bay adopted at the beginning of the war seemed general throughout the province. Newburyport joined other towns in Essex County in the spring of 1776 to protest the underrepresentation of eastern towns in the General Court, and shortly thereafter a new plan increased Newburyport's delegation to five members. But the western communities still controlled the lower house, and when some of them proposed in the summer of 1776 that a new constitution be drawn up by the two houses sitting together, Newburyporters resisted. In October town meeting proposed instead that House and Council meet separately for the purpose, obviously expressing the desire of the eastern commercial centers to take full advantage of their control of the upper body. Underlying the issue was a deep resentment toward the farmer harbored by rich and poor alike in the seacoast towns. Agricultural prices had risen sharply in recent months, and farmers were suspected of reaping unreasonable profits at the expense of urban-dwellers.[1]

To Jonathan Jackson in Newburyport the troubles besetting the Commonwealth seemed to mount in number and seriousness almost daily: "threatened with an powerfull Invasion . . . having internal Difficulties & Disensions not a few—Jealousies between Country & City—ville Practices among a few on both side—a Medium tottering & will fall to the Ground if not supported in every part." The

---

[1] Currier, *History of Newburyport,* I, 68–70; Town Records, I, 253, 263, 270; Samuel E. Morison, *History of the Constitution of Massachusetts* (Boston, 1917), p. 14; *Journals of Each Provincial Congress of Massachusetts in 1774 and 1775* (Boston, 1838); Oscar and Mary Handlin, *Commonwealth: A Study of the Role of Government in the American Economy: Massachusetts, 1774–1861* (New York, 1947), pp. 8–9.

most critical problem, it appeared to Jackson, was the desperate
need for a new state constitution.

[There are] but a few Manufacturers [of constitutions] who are thorough Workmen—to be received & go down with most People it must have
a good Outside Shew, to pass with the Judicious it must be thoroughly
finished, Part answering to Part, & together forming one harmonious
Whole, in which every thing will bear strict Scrutiny & Examination &
when thus framed, if not cordially adopted & every part carefully kept
to perform its Function immediately . . . arises Disorder.[2]

The House and Council, meeting in joint session after all, finally
submitted a constitution to the towns in January 1778 for approval
by two thirds of the freemen voting. But the document met with
almost immediate opposition from all quarters. In the first place,
the procedures for drawing up and adopting the constitution alien-
ated many persons from the start. Some of the towns had preferred
that a special convention be given the authority for this task. Others,
like Newburyport, had wished the two branches to meet as separate
bodies. The greatest weakness of the plan, however, was the provision that the towns accept or reject the proposed constitution as
submitted, without provision for conditional approval or suggested
amendment. Furthermore, a bill of rights was entirely absent. No
attempt had been made to create a balance either between the
branches of government itself, or between the elements of population
which were to be represented. As Jackson summed it: "I hope [the]
Constitution will not be ratified—I meet nobody that likes it—I
think it will never go down, if it does, it will never give Quiet." [3]

The most effective campaign against the proposed constitution
was waged by the merchants and lawyers of Essex County. Their
manifesto, *The Essex Result,* exposed all the shortcomings of the
document and then advanced the principles upon which they

[2] Jonathan Jackson (Newburyport) to Oliver Wendell (Boston), 8 May 1777,
Austin H. Clark Collection (Washington, D.C.).

[3] Morison, *History of the Constitution,* pp. 15, 16; Handlin, *Commonwealth,* p. 22;
"Rejected Constitution of 1778," in Appendix to *Journal of the Convention for
Framing A Constitution of Government. . . . 1779 . . . 1780* (Boston, 1832), pp.
255–264; Jonathan Jackson (Newburyport) to Oliver Wendell (Boston), 28 August
1778, Austin H. Clark Collection.

thought government ought to be based. In this attack Newburyport led the way. In a meeting held on March 26, 1778, the town resolved that the method of representation under the proposed constitution was inequitable and that some parts of it were fundamentally unsound. The selectmen of the town were then ordered to write circular letters to the other towns in Essex County proposing a convention for the purpose of reforming the document "agreeable to the Natural rights of mankind and the true principles of government." To this convention, which met at Ipswich on April 28, Newburyport sent five of its ablest citizens, Theophilus Parsons, Tristram Dalton, Jonathan Greenleaf, Jonathan Jackson, and Stephen Cross.[4]

Little is known of the actual day-to-day proceedings of the convention, but publication of *The Essex Result* has preserved its conclusions. The first session adopted numerous resolutions criticizing the proposed constitution of 1778, and then the convention turned to the task of making constructive suggestions. Most of the work was done by a special committee selected to devise a scheme of government more closely adhering to the "true principles" first vaguely referred to in the Newburyport resolution. And the man who wrote the actual document was the young Newburyport lawyer, Theophilus Parsons, at that time but twenty-seven years old. It is the second part of *The Essex Result* which reveals clearly the kind of state government most desired by the merchants and professional men of Newburyport and other Essex County towns.[5]

The first of the true principles upon which Parsons constructed his proposed constitution came directly from a familiar source—John Locke. "All men are born equally free. The rights they possess at birth are equal and of the same kind . . ." wrote Parsons. "Each individual surrenders the power of controlling his alienable rights only when the good of the whole requires it. . . . Over the class of unalienable rights the supreme power hath no control." Before the

<hr>

[4] Full title of the manifesto: *Result of the Convention of Delegates Holden at Ipswich in the County of Essex who were Deputed to Take into Consideration the Constitution and Form of Government proposed by the Convention of the State of Massachusetts-Bay* (Newburyport, 1778); Town Records, I, 299; Currier, *History of Newburyport*, I, 61, 678.

[5] Morison, *History of the Constitution*, p. 16.

ratification of any constitution the people's rights should be specifically guaranteed, he argued. The absence of a bill of rights, as in the 1778 constitution, could therefore not be tolerated.[6]

Parsons' second fundamental principle came from Montesquieu, somewhat less directly, as well as from Locke. Government should represent the various elements of society in balance: ". . . among gentlemen of education, fortune, and leisure, we shall find the largest number of men, possessed of wisdom, learning, and a firmness and consistency of character. That among the bulk of the people we shall find the greatest share of political honesty and a regard to the interest of the whole, of which they comprise a majority. . . ." The legislative body should be bicameral to embrace these diverse interests, the upper house representing the property of the state, and the lower branch the people. Thus a law affecting property would have to be approved by the representatives of those holding a majority of the property. This principle of balance is carried to its logical end by the suggestion that the three branches of government, legislative, judicial, and executive, be kept separate and independent of each other.[7]

Parsons and his colleagues frequently made specific suggestions. Determined to avoid weaknesses of the existing lower house, they firmly believed that a body composed of too many members was totally unable to conduct business efficiently. Another problem they felt was that the method then in practice of apportioning representatives to the General Court was inequitable for the larger eastern seaboard towns.[8]

In order to assure that the lower house numerically reflected the population, Parsons developed a rather elaborate and politically impractical system. The membership of this body, fixed at 100 delegates, was to be apportioned among the counties according to population. Essex, for example, with about 15 percent of the state's population, was entitled to fifteen representatives, chosen by an annual county convention in the following manner. The freemen in each town would choose delegates to the county convention in proportion to the town's population. All freemen would be entitled

[6] *The Essex Result,* in Theophilus Parsons, *Memoir of Theophilus Parsons* (Boston, 1859), pp. 365–367, 374. All subsequent references are made to this copy.

[7] *The Essex Result,* pp. 370, 372, 374, 376.

[8] *The Essex Result,* pp. 376, 389–390.

to vote without qualification because, Parsons reasoned, the lower house was to represent all the people. This convention would divide the county into as many districts as it rated representatives in the house, and the delegates (or electors) for each district then would elect its representative. In this manner a majority of the 100 members of the legislature would always represent a majority of the state's population. But Parsons' solution to the problem of disproportionate representation would certainly have met with bitter opposition. No longer were towns to be directly represented in the legislature, although the larger towns in each district of a county could probably control the election of that particular district's representative.[9]

In his plans for reorganizing the Senate Parsons revealed his purpose even more clearly, for his scheme gave the eastern counties full control of that chamber. Following the principle that this branch should represent the property of the Commonwealth, the young lawyer recommended that its forty members (which included seven extra men to be chosen for a privy council) be apportioned according to the amount of state tax paid by the citizens of each county, assuring control of the Senate by the wealthier eastern counties. The proposal suggested that each town elect delegates to a county convention in proportion to its share of the state tax. These delegates, in turn, meeting just before the regular county convention, would select the requisite number of senators to represent their county. The kind of property qualification required for those choosing senatorial electors was an innovation, for Parsons did not want such an important matter to depend on the individual's own estimate of his worth, especially during an era of wildly fluctuating currency. He suggested that only those citizens who paid a state tax of £3 for every £100,000 levied that year be qualified to vote for senatorial electors. In practice, of course, many eastern as well as western property-holders would be excluded from senatorial representation. In 1772, for instance, when the average state tax paid by all Newburyport property-holders was in the ratio of about £2/10s. per £100,000, less than half of the taxpayers would have qualified under the proposed plan.[10]

Parsons also depended on the county-convention scheme for the

[9] *The Essex Result*, p. 376.
[10] *The Essex Result*, pp. 391–392.

selection of governor. The delegates chosen by the freemen to select the county's representatives would serve also as the electors for governor, casting as many gubernatorial electoral votes as the county had representatives. The candidate winning a majority of the 100 votes would become governor. To assist him and to serve as a check upon him as well, Parsons provided for a privy council. Its seven members were to be chosen by the lower house out of the forty men elected as senators, leaving an upper house of thirty-three members.[11]

The third branch of government, the judiciary, was to be appointed by the governor, to hold office during good behavior, removable only by the legislature with the lower house impeaching and the upper judging. In addition, judges' salaries would be fixed and independent of any possible tampering on the part of the legislature or the executive.[12]

Qualifications for office-holding had of course long been in force in colonial Massachusetts. Parsons departed from this principle in one regard only: since the lower house of the legislature was to represent the people, any free resident was entitled to serve as county representative. On the other hand, a senatorial candidate had to have paid a state tax in the ratio of £6 per £100,000 levied, and gubernatorial aspirants had to meet a £16 per £100,000 ratio. Parsons strongly believed that wealth and position guaranteed political dependability.[13]

The Essex Result's proposed form of government carefully separated the political powers among the several branches. Each house of the legislature had the right to initiate legislation, with the other holding a negative. The one exception was in the case of money bills, which could originate only in the lower chamber, with the Senate required to accept or reject without amendment. The executive branch also involved a system of checks and balances, inasmuch as the governor had to consult his privy council in the matter of appointments of the various officers of his executive branch, and could veto legislation only with the council's consent.[14]

[11] The Essex Result, pp. 395–396.
[12] The Essex Result, pp. 400–401.
[13] The Essex Result, pp. 390, 392–393, 398.
[14] The Essex Result, pp. 394, 396–397.

Parsons introduced several other provisions to his plan designed to protect the public from power-usurping officials. All terms of office (except those of judges) were of but one-year duration. No man was permitted to be governor for more than three years in every six and the senators were subject to similar restrictions. To assure the selection of experienced officials Parsons established special qualifications. Senatorial candidates were required to have been members of the Senate, the house, or the privy council in the year preceding election. The gubernatorial candidates likewise had to have been either former governors (or lieutenant-governors), senators, or privy councillors. The governor's salary was to be fixed by law, and, like all other officers' salaries, including those of representatives and senators, was to be paid out of the public treasury.[15]

The effect of *The Essex Result* in rallying opposition to the constitution of 1778 cannot accurately be measured. What the authors intended, however, is clear. Jackson indicated to his brother-in-law, Oliver Wendell, that 200 copies of the convention's report would soon be sent to Boston for distribution among some of the gentlemen of the town, including all the members of the war board and the house, and to influential clergymen and others throughout the province. "If they won't attend [to its contents] we hope their *Constituents* will—but if *they* wont I shall . . . dispair of seeing my Country happy in my Day." Jackson took care to point out that the Essex people did not expect the state to endorse *The Essex Result's* scheme of government without alteration, although he thought it was worthy of adoption. The primary purpose of drawing up such a plan was simply to rouse the state into something better than the constitution of 1778.[16]

The Essex Result is historically significant for several reasons. In the first place its author enjoyed an influential career in Massachusetts politics for several decades, beginning with membership on the special committee of thirty-one at the Constitutional Convention of 1779–1780 and culminating with his appointment as chief justice of the state Supreme Court in 1806. Secondly, his docu-

---

[15] *The Essex Result,* p. 399.
[16] Jonathan Jackson (Newburyport) to Oliver Wendell (Boston), 8 August and 28 August 1778, Austin H. Clark Collection.

ment, supported as it was by the merchants and professional men of Essex County, reveals the kind of state government this important group of men wanted. Third, and most important, *The Essex Result* translated political principles long admired by Americans in theory and adopted by other states in their constitutions into a concrete frame of government for Massachusetts: a bill of rights, the principle of separation and balance of powers, an independent judiciary, and a strong executive. Another idea, considerably refined from earlier practice, was that one branch of the legislature should represent the people, the other, property.

The motives of Parsons and his associates in drawing up this frame of government are quite clear. Admittedly representative of the rich and well-born, these men had a strong interest in the establishment of a stable state government, and the proposed constitution of 1778, they were convinced, could not provide this stability. Partly through the influence of *The Essex Result,* an unrestricted electorate rejected the constitution of 1778 by a five-to-one majority of the 12,000 men voting. The town of Newburyport, with 218 freemen present in a meeting especially called for the purpose in June 1778, voted unanimously to turn down the proposed frame of government. Whether or not it was their intention, the merchant-leaders of Essex county spoke for a group of citizens far larger than was included in their own circle.[17]

For nearly a year after the rejection of the constitution of 1778, nothing was done about a new frame of government. Then in the spring of 1779 the General Court asked the towns whether they desired a constitution at that time, and whether they would empower their representatives to summon a special convention for this purpose. At a poorly attended meeting Newburyport voted against having a new constitution but went on to suggest that if a convention were to be called for that purpose, its delegates be selected by some equitable means. Support for a constitutional convention was strong enough in Boston and the western counties to carry the issue, and Newburyport chose five of its leading citizens as delegates: Benjamin Greenleaf, Nathaniel Tracy, Jonathan Jackson, Jonathan Greenleaf, and Theophilus Parsons. Each of these

---

[17] Morison, *History of the Constitution,* pp. 15, 16; Town Records, I, 303.

men was experienced in government, and the last three had been members of the county convention which produced *The Essex Result*. After electing these men to represent it, the town meeting then urged that the resulting constitution be submitted to the towns for ratification.[18]

The convention, meeting as scheduled in Cambridge on the first day of September 1779, delegated the responsibility for roughing out a draft constitution to a committee of thirty-one, among whose members were Jonathan Jackson and Theophilus Parsons. (John Lowell, formerly of Newburyport but recently moved to Boston and serving as a delegate from that town, was also on this committee.) But the draft which was submitted to the convention in late October was virtually the sole handiwork of John Adams. When heavy winter snows prevented many western delegates from getting to the decisive third session in January 1780, the rump convention adopted the Adams plan of government with only a few minor alterations.[19]

Theophilus Parsons, through both his authorship of *The Essex Result* and his membership on the convention's special committee, may have influenced John Adams in several respects, although such influence would be difficult to prove since the Adams constitution rested firmly on principles of government long admired by republicans throughout America. The Constitution of 1780 was preceded by a Declaration of Rights, and there was agreement between Adams and Parsons on several fundamental premises: that all men were born equally free; that the laws of the land ought to be only for the general good; that government by laws meant only those laws which had been consented to by the governed; that all power of the government originally rested with the people and that this power reverted to the people upon its abuse by the government; finally and perhaps most important, that the various branches of government ought to be in balance with each other. Stable govern-

---

[18] Samuel E. Morison, "Vote of Massachusetts on Summoning a Constitutional Convention, 1776–1917," Massachusetts Historical Society *Proceedings*, L (April 1917), 245; Morison, *History of the Constitution*, p. 18; Town Records, I, 314, 317.

[19] *Journal of the Convention*, pp. 28–29; Morison, *History of the Constitution*, pp. 20–21. Jonathan Jackson was detained for a week in Newburyport by the weather conditions. Jonathan Jackson (Newburyport) to Oliver Wendell (Boston), 11 January 1780, Austin H. Clark Collection.

ment was the obvious objective of both Parsons and Adams. The Constitution of 1780 included a strong executive branch armed with veto power and an independent judiciary to serve as a check on the legislature, which was itself bicameral. Membership in the upper house was apportioned among the counties according to wealth, favoring the eastern section of the state, and the advantage held by western towns in the lower house was somewhat reduced. Property qualifications restricting candidates and voters for all offices placed more emphasis on stability than on democracy.[20]

The method of ratifying the proposed constitution was a complicated one. At a meeting in which all adult males were permitted to participate, each town was to vote on the constitution clause by clause, suggesting changes for those parts it disapproved of. The Constitutional Convention, reconvening in June, was then to alter those clauses which failed to gain the support of two thirds of those voting in the towns, so that the finished document would be more in line with the popular will. But the convention was not required to resubmit the constitution to the people for final approval.[21]

Upon receiving copies of the constitution, Newburyport town meeting appointed on May 9, 1780, a committee of three men, not delegates to the convention, to take the proposal into consideration and to report their conclusions. One week later Patrick Tracy, the lawyer Theophilus Bradbury, and Dr. Micajah Sawyer formally presented the document along with a detailed analysis of strengths and defects. More than 300 freemen voted first to approve the Declaration of Rights with but one dissent to the third article, the controversial clause which provided for financial support of the Congregational churches throughout the state. Then the meeting unanimously voted to approve the constitution with the alterations suggested by the committee, except for one article concerning the governor's powers as head of the militia.[22]

The committee's report reveals what principles of government

[20] Samuel E. Morison, "Struggle over the Adoption of the Constitution of Massachusetts, 1780," Massachusetts Historical Society *Proceedings*, L (May 1917), 384; Massachusetts Constitution of 1780, ch. I, secs. II and III; ch. II, sec. III, arts. I and II. See Brown, *Middle-Class Democracy*, p. 394, for a comparison of these property qualifications with earlier ones.

[21] Morison, "Struggle over the Adoption," pp. 359–360.

[22] Town Records, I, 326–327.

were particularly cherished by the men who drew it up and by the freemen who accepted it without dissent. The possibility that the constitution did not sufficiently protect the doctrine of separation of powers caused great concern. It was therefore recommended that the governor be given an absolute veto with the advice of the council over legislative acts, as incorporated by both Parsons and Adams in their original drafts. The Newburyport committee believed that this power would help to preserve the executive's independence from legislative domination. The disastrous effect which would ensue if the balance between branches of government were to be upset was clear:

If ever the legislative body shall become the judicial and executive, also if in other words, the same body of men may make, interpret, and execute the laws, there will be an end to civil liberty.

The annual election of the governor, the committee felt, offered sufficient protection against abuse of power by the executive.[23]

Newburyporters also took exception to several features of the proposed general assembly. They felt that the number of representatives was far too large, making for an unwieldy chamber. And the situation would grow steadily worse as the population of each town increased. In light of this growth of the assembly, the quorum figure, fixed at sixty members, was obviously too low. This criticism was particularly valid since such a number permitted but thirty-one members to enact "laws affecting the property, the liberty, and even the life of every subject." [24]

The articles concerned with the state militia produced similar misgivings among the citizens of Newburyport. "The choosing of militia officers by the people at large has been found by experience productive of disorder and confusion. . . . Very undue measures and improper influence may be used and most probably will in such elections." If this complaint reflects a basic distrust of the military elements of the state, it is an interpretation further borne out by the suggestion that "some of the principle militia officers should be excluded from a seat in the council, senate, or house of representatives" as a safeguard against their abusing the peculiar power which

[23] Town Records, I, 328.
[24] Town Records, I, 329.

they possess. The Newburyport committee then recommended that the governor be granted the power to appoint all militia officers. Since as commander-in-chief he would probably have to lead them in person, he could be counted on to appoint the best officers. Again the committee looked to the governor's annual dependence on the people as protection against his abuse of power. The committee report further recommended that the General Court, or during its recess the governor, be empowered to detach and march out of the state such part of the militia as was required by military necessity, although no man was to be detained in service for a longer term than three months. This was a particularly practical suggestion in light of the wartime conditions prevailing in the spring of 1780. More than one Continental commander was seriously embarrassed by the refusal of his troops attached to the state militia companies to cross into an adjoining state.[25]

The final protest lodged by the Newburyport committee expressed fear that the constitutional provision allowing the legislature to suspend for twelve months the "inestimable privilege" of habeas corpus threatened the citizens' liberty. "The town therefore think that even the legislature ought never to be invested with such a suspending power except in time of actual or expected war, invasion or rebellion, and then they should have power to suspend that right for no longer a space than three months."[26]

The freemen of Newburyport by their endorsement of this report clearly supported many of the theories found in *The Essex Result*. The unanimity with which the town ratified the constitution is surprising in only one respect. At least a few of the nearly 300 men voting in fact approved a constitution which prohibited through property qualifications their own participation in the government it established. Why they still gave it their endorsement is difficult to understand, but such was the case throughout the state. Probably men by deeply ingrained habit accepted the principle that their affairs ought more properly to be handled by the natural leaders of the town and state. Major changes came hard, even during a period of many changes.

The difficult process of tabulating the returns from the various towns began at the fourth session of the adjourned convention in

[25] Town Records, I, 329–331.
[26] Town Records, I, 331.

early June. Because many towns like Newburyport recorded favorable votes for the articles *as amended by town committee,* the convention concluded in one week's time that the constitution had been duly approved by the required two-thirds majority, and the delegates ignored all suggested alterations. But since only two articles failed to gain approval of at least a majority of voters, there was little serious protest to the convention's action, and the constitution went into effect as scheduled on October 25, 1780.[27]

The real significance of the Constitution of 1780 and *The Essex Result* preceding it lies in the conservative republicanism established in Massachusetts Bay. There can be no question that John Adams and Theophilus Parsons shared a faith in the same political principles. If this constitution provided a government more conservative than Massachusetts had known under the revised charter, and this is a debatable point, it was by far the most successful of all attempts during the revolutionary period to find stability midst wartime chaos. The essential principles of this frame of government were overwhelmingly approved by the 16,000 freemen voting. The absence of any sharp clash between elements in the state which in a later time could be labeled respectively "democratic" and "conservative" would indicate that the leading political figures had not as yet divided into these camps.

Writing to Francis Dana, in Paris on Congressional business with Adams, Theophilus Parsons did not spare superlatives in describing the final outcome of the Constitutional Convention:

Our Constitution is settled. . . . The People accepted the Report of the Convention without the alteration of an iota though objections were made to every article. . . . The People discovered themselves to be steady sensible judicious and fond of a respectable Government. Their Votes & Instructions were in general shrewd & generous. The greatest objections were to those articles which were calculated as it was thought to please the People—viz the Governor's Negative—Militia—etc. Had the Convention been wise & united, we might have had a *perfect constitution.* The People would have accepted one, & the palliated articles discovered that many of our wise ones did not know the real sentiments of the People. *There was no danger in proposing too perfect a Constitution.*[28]

Perfect or not, the constitution hammered out by John Adams

[27] Morison, "Struggle over the Adoption," pp. 396–401.
[28] Theophilus Parsons to Francis Dana, 3 August 1780, Dana Papers (MHS).

and the convention served to bring political stability to the citizens of Massachusetts at a time when many felt that stability was sorely needed.

Political differences in Massachusetts under the new government were at first drawn along lines of personal faction, since divisive issues did not exist. Under these circumstances the popular John Hancock had little difficulty winning election to the governorship for five consecutive terms, from 1780 to 1785. So completely did Hancock spreadeagle the field that the existence of two other factions barely attracted attention. Essex County leaders, rallying around James Bowdoin, were no more successful in offering resistance, even in their own backyard, than was a third group, headed by Sam Adams, Elbridge Gerry, and James Warren, who found only modest support among the artisans of the coastal towns.[29]

Election returns from Newburyport in 1780 revealed the strength which Hancock's name wielded even in the heart of Essex County. Although both the Essex and Adams-Gerry factions had nominally endorsed Bowdoin for governor, Hancock outpolled his opponent 181 to 19. Town meeting sent the victor a congratulatory address, and the worst Jonathan Jackson could say of him in a private letter was that he led too active a social life. All told, in the first five elections under the new constitution, Newburyporters gave their alleged candidate, Bowdoin, a *total* of only twenty-nine votes, a trend culminating in 1784 when he received no support at all. Not until Hancock resigned in 1785 did Bowdoin receive a majority in Newburyport, and even then it was by the slim margin of nineteen votes over the former lieutenant-governor, Thomas Cushing. At no time during the period did more than a third of the qualified voters turn out. Obviously it made little difference to the merchants of Newburyport which of the several candidates won the governorship, for no effort was made to turn out the vote for Bowdoin.[30]

[29] Anson E. Morse, *The Federalist Party in Massachusetts to the Year 1800* (Princeton, 1909), pp. 14, 15, 20; John C. Miller, *Sam Adams, Pioneer in Propaganda* (Boston, 1936), pp. 360–364, 368; Herbert S. Allan, *John Hancock, Patriot in Purple* (New York, 1948), pp. 273–274; Oscar and Mary F. Handlin, "Radicals and Conservatives in Massachusetts after Independence," *New England Quarterly*, XVII (September 1944), pp. 354–355.

[30] Jonathan Jackson (Newburyport) to Oliver Wendell (Boston), 29 November 1780, Austin H. Clark Collection; Town Records, I, 337, 341, 352, 382, 403, 423, 442.

Independence and the resultant departure of Loyalist officials gave several Newburyporters the opportunity to assume offices of responsibility on the state level of government. Jonathan Jackson was chosen a delegate to the Continental Congress in 1782, where he joined his old friend, John Lowell, now a resident of Boston. Tristram Dalton, a state senator from the Essex district for several years, found his name being mentioned as a gubernatorial candidate in 1785, but factional strife had become so intense after the resignation of Hancock that Dalton's supporters could make no headway. Rufus King, who had set up his own law practice in Newburyport after finishing his training with Theophilus Parsons, was chosen a congressman in 1784, serving until 1787 when he became a delegate to the Philadelphia convention. On the county level, in such positions as probate judgeships, justices of the peace, and militia officers, other Newburyporters expanded their political activities. At the same time, of course, the merchants and their lawyer allies maintained full control of the local government.[31]

Although the political scene in Massachusetts remained peaceful for several years after the establishment of the constitution, economic disturbances reached unprecedented proportions. The war left both public and private financial affairs in such a confused state that stability did not return for nearly a decade. During the years 1781–1786 in particular government officials desperately searched for means by which to meet the state's heavy war debt.

In brief, the economic crisis came about by a combination of problems whose roots reached far into the past. Chaotic methods of financing the war left the state's finances in sorry condition by 1780. The principal source of revenue remained the traditional direct tax on polls and real property. Commerce was in no position during these years to support any significant taxation even if agreed to by the mercantile interests well represented in the Senate. But the main difficulty came with the collapse of the prosperity enjoyed by the farmers during the war years. Continuing their free-spending habits acquired earlier, farmers soon found themselves saddled not

---

[31] Currier, *History of Newburyport*, II, 220, 261, 266; Elbridge Gerry to Rufus King, in Charles R. King, *The Life and Correspondence of Rufus King* (New York, 1894), I, 76.

only with a ruinous taxation, but with heavy private debts as well. Currency depreciation added to the confusion. Governmental attempts at stabilization deprived debtors of the only benefit which inflation could bring them, the ability to pay back their obligations in cheaper money. The establishment of hard monies for the payment of debts put farmers in an almost untenable position. The only succor received by debtors during this period seemed to be by grace of Hancock's lackadaisical attitude toward the collection of taxes.[32]

Financial confusion, agricultural depression, and heavy taxation all contributed to the economic distress which enshrouded the Bay State in the period 1781–1786. It is doubtful, however, that any governmental fiscal policy could have cured the illness so long as commerce languished. The troubles which beset the Massachusetts merchant, not markedly different from those facing his New York and Philadelphia counterparts, came thick upon him by 1782, when the war had done its full damage. The loss of ships and cargoes alone sufficed to ruin some merchants. When they attempted recovery by increased commercial activities, they found the once-familiar patterns of trade no longer operative. Destruction of the New England fishing fleet had slashed the mainstay of the West Indies trade, for without the sacred cod to export to these rich islands, New England merchants were unable to acquire the produce necessary for resale at home and abroad. What trade there was had to be carried on in worn-out vessels, many of which had been constructed during the war as fast privateers, extremely costly to operate as cargo-carriers. Nor could these merchants afford new construction.[33]

[32] Oscar and Mary F. Handlin, "Revolutionary Economic Policy in Massachusetts," *The William and Mary Quarterly*, 3d ser., IV (January 1947), 25–26, 41–42; Ralph V. Harlow, "Economic Conditions in Massachusetts During the American Revolution," Colonial Society of Massachusetts *Publications*, XX (May 1919), 163–190; Charles J. Bullock, "Historical Sketch of the Finances and Financial Policy of Massachusetts from 1780 to 1905," American Economic Association *Publications*, 3d ser., VIII (May 1907), 6, 15; William B. Norton, "Paper Currency in Massachusetts during the Revolution," *New England Quarterly*, VII (March 1934), 43–69; Robert A. East, "The Massachusetts Conservatives in the Critical Period," in Richard B. Morris, ed., *The Era of the American Revolution* (New York, 1939), pp. 354–358; Handlin, *Commonwealth*, pp. 37–42; Morse, *Federalist Party*, p. 34.

[33] Morison, *Maritime History*, pp. 30–31; See also my article "Nantes to Newburyport: Letters of Jonathan Williams," in Essex Institute *Historical Collections*, XCII (January 1956), 68–69.

In addition to the direct costs of war, however, the very fact of independence at first worked against mercantile interests. No longer could American vessels enjoy the privileges attending the display of the Union Jack. Trade with the British islands in the Caribbean was prohibited outright, and, after the peace treaty, commercial relations with the former mother country were sharply limited. To the new England merchant who before the war had relied on the sale of lumber, ships, and plantation products, these restricted commercial relations with England were clearly not enough to restore prewar prosperity. As late as 1786 the Bay State's exports amounted to only one fourth of the 1774 figure.[34]

Even before the end of hostilities many merchants experimented with overseas markets formerly closed to their direct contact by various colonial regulations of the Empire. On paper it appeared that the freedom to ship plantation products directly to the Continent would result in increased profits for the American merchant. But in practice the effect was far different, for no readily salable return cargo could be found to replace the popular English goods of the prewar period. Furthermore, the opening of American ports to foreign vessels of all flags meant that when American ships returned to their own shores, they faced a market already glutted with the products they themselves carried. Inexperienced in the fine art of selling American goods on the Continent, operating old and inadequate ships, and no longer able to rely on the essential cornerstone of trade with the British West Indies, the New England merchant in the years immediately following the Revolution, with rare exceptions, only added to his previous losses.

Jonathan Jackson's difficulties seemed typical. After 1777, when the firm of Jackson, Tracy & Tracy was dissolved, its senior partner carried on business in association with various local and Boston merchants on single ventures. "My losses be sure have thickned upon me lately," he wrote his brother-in-law Wendell in the spring of 1782. "I made out upon fair computation when I was with you at Boston £6 m Stg. Loss the last year & the three vessels you mention that I have lost this year . . . will make 2 or £3 m more—I'll assure you that I have but little more that is floating to risk . . ." Jackson closed on a grimly determined note: "I am quite at a Loss

[34] Morison, *Maritime History*, pp. 31–32.

what plan to pursue to support the expence my large Family will necessarily call for but I mean not to despond, tho' my commercial Faculties for the present times at least are very small." [35]

After the departure of Jackson the Tracy brothers continued in business on their own into the 1780's. In early 1782 the Newburyport firm established a commercial relationship with Jonathan Williams, an American merchant residing in Nantes. In June of that year the Tracys' ship *Cato* arrived at the Loire with a cargo of tobacco, which Williams expected to bring a high price, but apparently its quality was so poor that several hogsheads did not sell at all. This of course did not prevent Williams from buying at the Tracys' expense a large cargo including tea, brandy, hemp, and window glass for *Cato's* return voyage.[36]

During the same summer another Tracy vessel, the privateer schooner *Success*, arrived with a cargo of indigo, also regarded as rather inferior by the fussy Mr. Williams. It was the Newburyporters' wish that Williams send an order of hemp back by *Success*, but apparently that vessel's capacity was so limited that only part of the amount requested could be stowed aboard. Here was graphic evidence why a privateer made such a poor substitute for a deep-hulled, broad-beamed merchantman. The same letter, incidentally, revealed that the ship *Cato* had still not cleared for home, a three-months' delay which must have proved rather costly to the owners.[37]

Another Tracy voyage revealed additional problems of trade in the immediate postwar period. *Port Packet*, a small privateer, entered the Loire in February 1783 with a little indigo aboard and with a prize she had captured on the trans-Atlantic passage. The indigo was worse than that sent by *Success*, according to Williams. Although its prize brought £26,873 at auction, *Port Packet's* return cargo cost £107,796. Furthermore, some of it got damaged in a gale of wind while being loaded on board, although Williams promised that he would "endeavor to make the Loss to you as light as possible." A letter dated the day following indicated that the balance

---

[35] Jonathan Jackson (Newburyport) to Oliver Wendell (Boston), 28 March 1782, Austin H. Clark Collection; also quoted in Porter, *Jacksons and Lees*, I, 347.

[36] Jonathan Williams (Nantes) to Messrs. Nat. & John Tracy (Newburyport), 3 June 1782, 3 September 1782, Jonathan Williams' Letterbook II (20 January 1782 to 30 January 1783), pp. 125, 308–311 (YUL).

[37] Williams to Tracys, 10 October 1782, Letterbook II, p. 384.

due Williams on account of the schooner *Success* stood at £59,728. And the fall in the price of tobacco at Nantes soon added to the Tracys' discouragement.[38]

By the summer of 1783 the Tracy debt to Williams had reached £206,649, some of which was probably in depreciated currency, but certainly not all. While Williams urged the Tracy brothers to construct a larger ship for their trade with Nantes, the Newburyporters decided to send their next ship to Amsterdam, in hope of a better market for tobacco. By autumn the Tracys had completely abandoned their ill-fated trade with Nantes in favor of other European ports. But conditions were not much better elsewhere on the Continent. The fact that the war for American independence involved the major European nations meant that the Treaty of Paris brought similar conditions of postwar depression to all the commercial powers of Europe. The troubles which saddled the Tracys' relations with Nantes could not be dodged by trading with other ports.[39]

In a desperate move in the spring of 1784 the Tracys ordered from London nearly £5600 worth of linens and other cloths, followed by a similar order later that year. The tightness of commerce at this time is no better illustrated than in the Tracys' letter of instructions to Captain Samuel Tucker of their ship *Cato*, bound to the West Indies with a cargo mainly of lumber. Tracy gave Tucker explicit directions as to the best possible market in the Islands, where he was told to purchase molasses, sugar, salt, and rum. He was then ordered to take these goods into Richmond, to be exchanged for a cargo of tobacco destined for Lane Son & Frazer in London. There the crew was to be paid off and the ship sold if possible. Tracy closed with this warning: "keep this always in mind, that unless the Strictest Frugality is observed, the most successful markets and the best Freight will not support navigation at this time."[40]

Nathaniel Tracy soon came to realize that only the most direct action could stave off disaster. In the summer of 1784 he sailed to Europe in an effort to straighten out his affairs in England, France,

[38] Williams to Tracys, 19 March, 20 March 1783, Letterbook III, pp. 89, 101.
[39] Williams to Tracys, 18 July 1783, Letterbook III, p. 174.
[40] Stock and Invoice Book of Nathaniel and John Tracy, 20 March 1784—8 October 1785, Patrick Tracy Jackson Jr. Collection (Boothbay Harbor, Maine); Nathaniel Tracy (Newburyport) to Capt. Samuel Tucker (Portsmouth), 30 June 1784, Commodore Tucker Papers, II, 250 (HUL).

and Spain, but to no avail. After satisfying as many of his creditors as possible, Tracy retired to his Newbury farm. Jonathan Jackson, who had left Newburyport late in 1783 to enter partnership with Stephen Higginson in Boston, also traveled to England and the Continent to attempt the establishment of a profitable business. Among the new enterprises he investigated were contacts with Sweden and Russia, direct trade with the East Indies for tea and other oriental products, and the slave trade. But he too found it impossible to make a successful comeback, and when he returned in 1787 to live once more in Newburyport, he had retired from mercantile activities entirely.[41]

Precarious enough was the general economic situation in the immediate postwar years; in addition Newburyport particularly suffered from the languishing condition of shipbuilding. Although accurate figures are scarce, one authority doubts that more than one hundred vessels were built in all of Massachusetts in the four years 1784 through 1787, a figure not even equaling the annual rate of prewar years. The importance of shipbuilding to the economic recovery of Newburyport is revealed in a petition to the General Court from a large group of its merchants, traders, and artisans. This group sought relief from the state's Navigation Act, which seemingly prevented them from selling "used" vessels abroad. It had been the custom of Newburyport merchants to purchase and use locally built vessels for a few foreign voyages until they could be sold at a profit abroad, a practice that permitted the shipbuilders to construct vessels with a specific purchaser in sight. But if, as the Newburyporters feared, the new act prohibited them from selling these second-hand vessels to foreigners, no merchant would risk contracting for ship construction. This was a matter which concerned the entire town, as was clearly indicated by the diversity in the signatures of the nearly 150 townsmen who supported the petition.[42]

Economic growth in Newburyport was sharply curtailed during

[41] Porter, *Jacksons and Lees*, I, 338–339, 347–370, 374–375; Letters to Oliver Wendell, July–December 1784, Austin H. Clark Collection; Jonathan Jackson (London) to [Stephen Higginson (Boston)], 2 August 1784, Henry L. and George C. Shattuck Collection, Brookline, Massachusetts.

[42] Petition to General Court from Merchants and Traders in Newburyport [no date], Massachusetts Archives.

the postwar years. Although total population increased by several hundred and more than thirty new dwellings were constructed between 1780–1781 and 1784–1786, wharf footage increased less than 5 percent and shipping tonnage actually declined from 8327 to 7176. Furthermore, difficulty in moving goods on hand accounted for the fact that in the period 1784–1786 merchants had in their warehouses trading stock worth nearly £75,000, up £30,000 from five years before. This figure is especially important because merchants were credited in this column whether or not they had yet paid for the goods. On the other hand, such standard assets like plate silver decreased from over 22,000 ounces to less than 6000.[43]

Newburyport vessels still cleared for the West Indies and southern coastal ports, and occasionally a ship entered from a European venture. Such activity, however, did not imply that these were prosperous voyages; evidence seems to indicate quite the opposite. And as the merchants sent their vessels on an increasing number of ventures, their losses only mounted. If there was a lesson to be learned from the period, it was that the small operator with low fixed costs and only a few vessels to maintain was best able to survive this period of commercial depression.[44]

Newburyporters realized that they could not cure the economic ills of the Commonwealth by their own efforts alone. In May 1786, therefore, the town meeting addressed a long letter to its delegates in the General Court, analyzing the causes of present misfortunes and offering suggestions for improvement.

The letter went directly to the heart of the state's financial problem. Unredeemed state notes representing wartime loans tied up much of the Newburyport merchants' capital. Hence this plea for the creditor:

We conceive there are no promises or obligations more solemn than those entered into for supplies advanced and for the most honorable and hazardous services in defence of the sacred and invaded rights of this

---

[43] Newburyport Valuation, in Hudson Papers (EI) as "1780" and Dane Papers, 1663–1784 (MHS) as "1781"; Newburyport Valuation, 1784, Hudson Papers (EI); and as "1786" (State Library of Massachusetts); [Newburyport] Assessors' Account Book, 1784–1797 (Newburyport City Clerk's Office).

[44] Compiled from Marine List in *Essex Journal*, 9 July to 6 October 1784; "Record of all vessels arriving in [and departing from] Newburyport in 1780," kept by Henry Hudson (EI).

state. . . . The Creditor . . . did not hesitate to accept the solemn pledge of his country's faith, as his only security . . .

Failure to redeem this debt caused other problems as well, for the interest-rate payments accounted for an extraordinary share of the state's annual expenditure. The Newburyporters proposed a rather elaborate arrangement involving the issue of "final settlement" securities and the establishment of a sinking fund of £100,000 annually toward the repayment of the state's obligation.[45]

But more fundamentally, the Newburyporters continued, the entire structure of the new nation's commerce rested on a disastrous economic principle.

We exceedingly lament, that in a country abounding with every [raw] material, the ingenuity and dexterity of whose people are exceeded by none, the practice of exporting unwrought materials, and importing manufactures, should be general, for we esteem it impolitic and uncommercial to export the former, till wrought to perfection or to import the latter, especially when wrought from materials of our own produce . . .

The Newburyporters also recognized the deplorable state into which agriculture had fallen. "It is the basis of manufactures, and both of these are the pillars which only can support a flourishing commerce." [46]

A solution to these problems, it seemed to the authors of the report, could be brought about only through the close attention of government. One thing was sure. "The emission of a paper currency we deprecate as a calamity . . . the integrity of the upright shall guide them to safety, but the injustice of transgressors shall be their destruction." The government should improve the condition of agriculture (no specific method was suggested) and encourage manufactures, ostensibly through bounties. Furthermore, the Congress ought to be granted powers sufficient to permit the establishment of general commercial regulations, enforceable throughout the states. To this end, the Newburyporters therefore exhorted their representatives in the General Court to address themselves.[47]

In addition to resolutions by town meeting Newburyporters freely expressed their frustrations by a barrage of advice-giving letters

[45] Town Records, I, 467.
[46] Town Records, I, 468–469.
[47] Town Records, I, 468–469.

to the press. Particular concern for the revival of commerce set off a virulent discussion of the state's navigation laws. "A Determined Freeman" laid the blame for depression squarely at the doorstep of the British, citing as evidence the high duties, confiscation, and ruinous competition with which they continued to stifle American enterprise. With more optimism than realism "Freeman" seemed to think that the British should have acted more kindly toward their ungrateful former colonies, perhaps even to the detriment of their own rather listless commerce. At any rate this correspondent hailed the enforcement of the Massachusetts commerce act as an effective step toward forcing England into a mutually advantageous commercial treaty. In reply, "An American Whigg" more realistically pointed out that England, "like every other nation pursues what she esteems to be in her own interest." Although denying British actions as responsible for the depression, "Whigg" had nothing to offer as a solution.[48]

But generally public opinion in Newburyport seemed to support the sentiments of "Freeman," that trade with England on her terms should be sharply limited, even if it resulted in the curtailment of luxuries. A regulation reminiscent of wartime already restricted the wearing of mourning at funerals. The newspaper editor, himself badgered by a state tax on advertising which reduced his revenue from that source, saw the scarcity of hard money as a major cause of difficulty. The war produced a shortage of European goods, he pointed out, although the demand remained undiminished. With the restriction of American trade to the British West Indies and England, there remained no means by which to purchase these manufactures except by cash. But the editor concluded that free trade would eventually enable the American enterprising spirit to find a way to prosperity.[49]

On one matter nearly all commentators seemed agreed: the importance of establishing local manufactures. When two Scotsmen moved into town to set up a brewery, they were welcomed on many counts. Not only would their product serve as an export article to the West Indies but the neighboring farmers could profit from the culture of barley hops as well. Oddly enough, the news-

[48] *Essex Journal*, 25 January, 1 February 1786.
[49] *Essex Journal*, 3 August 1785, 6 September, 18 October 1786.

paper editor considered porter to be a superior drink to rum, because
"of the poisonous quality that rum receives from the copper in
which it is distilled." But a single brewery could hardly make a
significant dent on the town's economy. Clearly a more comprehensive plan was necessary. Such an undertaking came in late
1786 with the establishment of the "Society for the Relief of the
Industrious Poor." The idea was that the society would purchase
wool and hire the unemployed to manufacture it into cloth. The
sale of this product would more than compensate the society for
its capital outlay. "Such an institution," wrote the editor, "must
certainly have a tendency to lessen the cry of poverty which is continually heard in our streets." By the following spring voluntary
associations of housewives took to their spinning wheels in an
all-out effort to end the depression singlehandedly. The ladies of
the Presbyterian Society were further encouraged when a visiting
delegation of leading citizens proclaimed their labors to be more
important to liberty and independence than treaties of commerce
"with all the nations on the face of the earth." [50]

By 1786 the merchants of Newburyport realized the full meaning
of independence. Politically they were free, and with the Constitution of 1780 and the recognition of independence in 1783 they
gained an important voice in the administration of their own
affairs. These political responsibilities they accepted without question, for self-government had been their main objective in supporting the revolutionary cause. But they were ill-prepared to accept
the consequences of economic independence. And yet had the Newburyport merchants not lost so heavily in ships and money invested
in the war effort, perhaps more of them would have been able to
survive the postwar depression. As matters stood by the end of
1786, however, the future was bleak indeed.

[50] *Essex Journal,* 11 October 1786, 11 April 1787; East, "The Massachusetts Conservatives," pp. 357, 361; Rufus King to John Adams, 3 October 1786, in King,
Rufus King, I, 190; William V. Wells, *The Life and Public Services of Samuel Adams*
(Boston, 1888), III, 234; Tristram Dalton (Boston) to [Michael Hodge (Newburyport)], 6 November 1786, in Essex Institute *Historical Collections,* XXIV (January
1888), 18.

Chapter IV

DECLINE OF THE COLONIAL MERCHANTS

Few of the merchants who had been prominent in the economic and political activities of Newburyport in the colonial and revolutionary periods ever succeeded in recouping the losses they suffered immediately following the war. During the years 1786–1788 the merchant class made a collective effort to stem the continuing depression by supporting the movement for a strong central government, which they hoped would provide much needed commercial regulation at home and command respect abroad. Partly through their hard work the federal constitution was ratified in Massachusetts, but by that time few of the merchants were still in business. A number of them had already left Newburyport to make a fresh start elsewhere. Some moved to Boston, another to Ohio, while still others obtained positions with the new federal government in New York. When the commerce of Newburyport began to revive in 1789, it was in the hands of a new group of merchants, in many cases men who had bought the wharves, vessels, and even the homes of those they replaced. But in their last years of power the old colonial merchants, by supporting the federal constitution, gave final declaration to the nationalism which had committed them to the revolutionary cause a quarter-century before.

The winter of 1786–1787 seemed bleak indeed to the residents of Newburyport. There was no sign of improvement in the town's commercial affairs, shipbuilding had virtually ceased, and the movement toward developing home industries had made no significant progress. Conditions were even worse in other parts of the Commonwealth, where debtor farmers under the leadership of Daniel Shays opposed the policies of taxation and foreclosure by the threat of armed rebellion. Newburyport made two militia companies available for duty against the insurgents, and gave support to Governor Bowdoin's vigorous suppression of disorders. Although the crisis was met within the Bay State without recourse to the several offers of outside assistance, the episode nevertheless precipitated the movement toward a stronger central government.

When Congress had drafted the Articles of Confederation in 1777 and submitted them to the states for ratification, Massachusetts had asked each town to study the document and to express its views to the General Court concerning adoption. Newburyport town meeting had instructed its representatives to vote for ratification, giving them only general authority "to remonstrate against such particular parts of it as their Prudence shall dictate." There seems to have been surprisingly little excitement over the proposition in Massachusetts and no evidence of serious objection.[1]

But a few years of postwar depression began to give some observers second thoughts. Writing to the English Unitarian minister Dr. Richard Price in the summer of 1785, Jonathan Jackson commented on the gloomy state of commerce and expressed his belief that before long necessity would require a strengthening of the federal government. But an ill-founded jealousy concerning the delegation of power to a central authority and the assumption that the states had few interests in common, Jackson wrote, had postponed serious consideration of change. Lack of regulation led not only to fierce rivalries between ports of different states but also to the importation of useless articles from abroad.[2]

As for the weakness of central government affecting its ability to raise money, Rufus King had nothing but contempt: "the credit of the States is not sufficient to procure loans at home or abroad," he wrote Jackson. "Indeed if the public credit was better, it could not, in my Judgment, be reconciled to the principles of common honesty to borrow, without foreseeing the means of Repayment." King had a gloomy view of the situation indeed. With his usual perception he saw that there was more than just southern opposition to strong commercial regulation. "Every partizan of France or England residing among us, uses his utmost exertions to inspire

[1] Town Records, I, 292.
[2] Jonathan Jackson (Boston) to Richard Price (London), 8 August 1785, printed in Massachusetts Historical Society Proceedings, 2d ser., XVII (1903), 327.

the People of the different States with jealousies of each other; and some of them have even sounded the alarm that the liberties of the People were endangered by the plan of delegating additional powers to congress." Elbridge Gerry had already noted that both Nathaniel Tracy and Jonathan Jackson, on their visits to the Continent in 1784–1785, had been especially struck with the disrespect with which European nations regarded the United States, mainly due to the weakness of its central government but also because of sectional bickerings carried on in the press.[3]

Governor Bowdoin had in fact devoted his inaugural address in the spring of 1785 to the problem of federal government in America, with the result that the legislature of Massachusetts on July 1 recommended that a national convention be called to revise the Articles of Confederation. But when these resolutions were forwarded to the Massachusetts delegates in Congress, Gerry, Holten, and King, they refused to submit the idea to the House, explaining that they did not think the states were ready for such a sweeping action. Any attempt to give the Congress perpetual control over commerce would surely fail, blocking the establishment of even temporary powers of regulation. Furthermore, the delegates felt that a convention, though not prohibited by the Articles, would be regarded by Congress as an infringement on its powers and would consequently draw staunch opposition from that quarter. Gerry and his associates made it perfectly clear that they favored increasing the power of the central government, but such was their concern for the method and timing of the move that they succeeded in persuading the Massachusetts legislature to withdraw the resolutions until a more opportune time.[4]

In light of these events it was not so strange that Massachusetts failed to take part in the commercial convention called at the behest of several southern states and held in Annapolis the year following. The state selected several sets of delegates, but despite the support

[3] Rufus King (New York) to Jonathan Jackson [Newburyport?], 11 June 1786, in Massachusetts Historical Society *Proceedings*, XLIX (1915–1916), 85, 86; Elbridge Gerry (Boston) to Rufus King (New York), 19 May 1785, in King, *Rufus King*, I, 98.

[4] Elbridge Gerry, Samuel Holten, and Rufus King (New York) to Governor James Bowdoin (Boston), 3 September 1785, in King, *Rufus King*, I, pp. 60–66; Morse, *Federalist Party*, p. 32; East, "Massachusetts Conservatives," pp. 369–370.

of Governor Bowdoin, none of these men took part in the convention. This informal boycott stemmed not from a lack of interest
in commercial reform—such merchants as Tristram Dalton and
Stephen Higginson had been among the intended delegates—but
rather from a strong distrust of the southern states which had
called the convention. King summed up the suspicions of his colleagues in a letter to Jonathan Jackson in June of 1786: "This is
certain, that the proposition for the Annapolis convention, which
originated in the Assembly of Virginia, did not come from the
persons favorable to a commercial system common to all the states,
but from those who . . . have advocated the particular regulations
of individual states." As late as the winter of 1786–1787 King was
still chary of a general revision. Writing to Gerry in January, he
warned "If Massachusetts should send deputies [to the Philadelphia
convention,] for God's sakes be careful who are the men; the times
are becoming critical: a movement of this nature ought to be carefully observed by every member of the Community." [5]

By no means were all of the inhabitants of Newburyport of one
mind concerning the future of the Confederation. The editor of
the *Essex Journal,* taking his cue from a southern paper, reported
a suggestion made to Congress that the Confederation be dissolved
in favor of the states into four republics, New England, the Middle
states, the South, and the West. Without specifically endorsing the
scheme, the editor nonetheless took pains to point out its advantages.

The religion, manners, customs, exports, imports, and general interest of
each [region] being then the same no opposition arising from difference
in these as at present would any longer divide their councils; unanimity
would render us secure at home and respected abroad, and promote
agriculture, manufactures, and commerce.[6]

Despite Dalton's refusal to attend the Annapolis convention and
King's suspicions of the southerners, most of Newburyport's mer-

[5] Eben F. Stone, "A Sketch of Tristram Dalton," in Essex Institute *Historical
Collections,* XXIV (January 1888), 7; East, "Massachusetts Conservatives," pp. 373–
375; Rufus King (New York) to Jonathan Jackson [Newburyport?], 11 June 1786,
in King, *Rufus King,* I, 86; Rufus King (New York) to Elbridge Gerry [Marble-
head?], 7 January 1787, in King, *Rufus King,* I, 201.
[6] *Essex Journal,* 25 April 1787.

chant class seemed to favor the strengthening of central government as the only salvation of commerce. The outbreak of violence in western Massachusetts seriously upset the confidence many easterners had in the ability of the state government to preserve order and tranquillity, and the need for a stronger central authority gradually overcame their traditional distrust of the southern states.[7]

Shays' Rebellion had a particularly strong effect on Rufus King, for by the spring of 1787 he had come to favor the wisdom of a general constitutional convention and was in fact chosen one of the Massachusetts delegates to Philadelphia in May. At the convention King laid aside his suspicions of southerners long enough to become an important member of the "nationalist" group which succeeded in winning approval of the Virginia Plan. Whenever possible he supported motions for strong executive and judicial powers. His skill at oratory won him respect from all sides, and as a member of the Committee on Style he wielded considerable influence on the document's final form. Upon finishing his work in Philadelphia, King returned to Newburyport, where he began organizing the campaign for ratification in Massachusetts.[8]

Although Newburyport appeared to be solidly behind ratification, nevertheless the upcoming convention produced a spirited exchange of views in the local newspaper. In early October the editor had published the complete text of the proposed frame of government, and his readers almost immediately obliged with their comments. "A Correspondent" saw the fate of the country balanced between a united nation or a petty anarchy. Rejection of the proposal could result only in "bold usurpers establishing governments for us, pregnant with all the evils of the most abject slavery." Others stressed the importance of commercial powers given the proposed government. One correspondent pointed out that the town suffered more severely from stagnating trade than perhaps any other in the union because of its dependence on shipbuilding and predicted that with ratification, "we may soon expect to see our rivers lined as heretofore with new ships," giving employment to artisans of many trades.

[7] Rufus King (New York) to Elbridge Gerry [Marblehead], 18 February 1787, in King, *Rufus King*, I, 215.
[8] Richard E. Welch, Jr., "Rufus King of Newburyport: The Formative Years (1767–1788)," Essex Institute *Historical Collections*, XCVI (October 1960), 256–268.

The author was careful to point out that benefits would also accrue to the farmer and the woodsman. At times the argument for adoption stooped to the sort of vilification not seen in the Bay State since the last months before the outbreak of the Revolution. One correspondent labeled any opponent of the constitution as "a dangerous member of society," or "a sham patriot." [9]

The ideological basis for the position taken by Newburyport federalists was stated by Jonathan Jackson in a political pamphlet which included an extraordinary plan for continental union. Although not published until 1788, Jackson's *Thoughts upon the Political Situation of the United States* . . . had been written the preceding year, at a time when most of the states had not yet made a decision concerning the proposed constitution. As Jackson explained:

We have tried our separate sovereignties long enough to see to feel, that they are puny governments only while not cemented by one common interest, while not assisted by some higher authority, established equally by all, and common to all.[10]

Jackson felt very keenly the need for a firm government uniting all the states. How else could the high ideas which inspired the revolution continue to be expressed? "[M]y pride will be mortified," Jackson admitted, ". . . if we should be obliged to confess to the world . . . that we had no idea of the object for which we contended." Secondly, Jackson pointed out that although Massachusetts had little difficulty suppressing its recent rebellion, perhaps other states with similar difficulties would not be so fortunate. In such an emergency a national force would be necessary. More important, however, would be the removal of the causes for rebellion, which Jackson saw as "the laxity of government for so long a time past and . . . the injudicious mode of imposing the Taxes, more especially the capitation tax." If the United States could once put an end to its internal quarrels and hold itself free from the politics of the Old World, this nation within a century would match the accomplishments of its European counterparts. First, however, it was

---

[9] *Essex Journal,* 3, 10 October, 21 November 1787.

[10] [Jonathan Jackson], *Thoughts upon the Political Situation of the United States of America . . . with some Observations on the Constitution for a Federal Government . . .* (Worcester, Mass., 1788), p. 45.

necessary to give up Old-World "gewgaws and trifles," the profuse
importation of which had nearly ruined the country, and this could
only be accomplished by strict commercial regulations.[11]

Although recognizing that one of the strongest arguments against
the proposed constitution was that it might lead to an oppressive
aristocracy, he felt that Americans actually faced a much greater
danger from "an highly democratical government . . . in which
they would be guided by no rule but their own will and caprice."
In every government, Jackson admitted, men of fame or ability
would inevitably emerge as leaders. But America had no hereditary
titles, land was held in small portions only, and an aristocracy
dangerous to liberty had little chance of developing. What he hoped
for was that political authority would be bestowed on men who "by
nature, education, and good dispositions" were best qualified to
govern. The success of free government depends on "obtaining the
wisest and best general will of the community" and enforcing it.
"I care not where [these] men come from. . . . Let them be taken
from the plough, from the mechanick's bench, from behind the
counter." [12]

To achieve this goal Jackson devised an intricate and hopelessly
impractical scheme which would distill the people's choice. A ward
of ten voters would choose a delegate to its hundred, which would
send a delegate to the county. After two more selective levels, a
congress of twenty senators and forty representatives would emerge.
Existing state boundaries would give way to a new division and
even town government in its traditional form would disappear.
The president, to serve for twenty years, had to be at least forty
years old, and a man known to have made a leisurely tour through
all the states! Jackson appeared convinced that his scheme would
create in those chosen as delegates a sense of responsibility far
greater than found in the representatives of his time. He even hoped
that eventually his scheme would lead to a government compre-
hending all the world.[13]

Newburyport had one prominent antifederalist, the apothecary
Daniel Kilham, who had oddly enough been elected representative

[11] Jackson, *Thoughts,* pp. 5, 18–19, 51, 96–97, 120.
[12] Jackson, *Thoughts,* pp. 54–58, 70.
[13] Jackson, *Thoughts,* pp. 170, 171, 192, 202.

to the General Court in June 1787. When the House debated whether to call a state ratifying convention, Kilham opposed the measure, fearing hasty action. He also doubted the legality of the Philadelphia convention and believed that the Massachusetts delegates had exceeded their instructions. Kilham received little enough support in the legislature, however, the convention being authorized 129 to 32.[14]

John Quincy Adams, at that time studying law in the office of Theophilus Parsons, boarded at the same house as Kilham and shared his antifederalist views. In October he wrote in his diary:

If the Constitution is adopted it will be a grand point gained in favor of the aristocratic party. There will be no titles of nobility, but there will be distinctions. . . . For my own part I am willing to take my chance under any government whatever, but it is hard to give up a system which I have always been taught to cherish, and to confess that a free government is inconsistent with human nature.[15]

As Adams admitted, however, Newburyport appeared "very unanimous" for the constitution, and in late November the town chose as its delegates to the ratifying convention Rufus King, Theophilus Parsons, Benjamin Greenleaf, and Jonathan Titcomb, all four staunch federalists.[16]

When the ratifying convention first met on January 9, 1788, the antifederalists were superior in numbers but lacked the strong leadership which united those in favor of the new form of government. Although many of the rural delegates sat firmly in the antifederalist camp, enough of them remained uncommitted to make an ultimate federalist victory at least mathematically possible.[17]

[14] Nathan Gorham to Henry Knox, 25 October 1787, Knox Papers (MHS); *Essex Journal*, 31 October 1787.

[15] John Quincy Adams, *Life in a New England Town, 1787–1788—Diary of John Quincy Adams while a Student in the Office of Theophilus Parsons at Newburyport* (Boston, 1903), p. 46.

[16] Town Records, I, 501; Adams, *Life in a New England Town*, p. 64; *Essex Journal*, 21 November 1787.

[17] Samuel B. Harding, *The Contest over the Ratification of the Federal Constitution in the State of Massachusetts* (New York, 1896), p. 61; Theophilus Parsons (Boston) to Michael Hodge [Newburyport], 14 January 1788, in Eben F. Stone, "Parsons and the Constitutional Convention of 1788," Essex Institute *Historical Collections*, XXXV (April 1899), 93; Morse, *Federalist Party*, pp. 42–50; Miller, *Sam Adams*, pp. 376–377.

Both King and Parsons of the Newburyport delegation played important roles in a gradual campaign to present the proposed constitution to the convention in the best light. In a brilliant speech King spelled out the weakness of the old Confederation government, particularly in regard to its inability to raise revenue, by drawing parallels from classical and modern European history. By contrast, of course, the proposed powers of Congress as set forth in the new constitution seemed perfection. Parsons, minimizing the danger of oppression, maintained in his turn that the constitution established "a government to be administered for the common good by the servants of the people with delegated powers by popular elections for stated periods."[18]

Despite the federalists' best efforts to swing the convention to their position by persuasive oratory, many days of carefully reasoned debate still left them short of the necessary majority. "Our prospects are gloomy," wrote King on January 23, "but hope is not entirely extinguished." Meanwhile, Hancock, by remaining absent from the convention, stymied federalist efforts to gain additional converts, greatly enhancing his importance to both sides. It soon became quite evident that only with the governor's support could ratification be assured.[19]

How the federalists won Hancock over was the result of a bargain which the Essex County forces carefully planned and executed. On the 29th ratification seemed lost. Had a vote been taken that day the convention would surely have rejected the constitution. Some scheme was needed by which Hancock could be enticed to declare for adoption. On the evening of the 30th, the federalists caucused to determine what to do. As the meeting was in progress, Tristram Dalton and Theophilus Parsons took time out to dispatch a brief note to their friend, Michael Hodge, back in Newburyport. "If [Governor Hancock] may be depended on, he will give countenance to the proposed Constitution. . . . Mr. S. Adams will [also] come out in favor. . . . All this is scarcely known out of our caucus."

[18] *Debates and Proceedings in the Constitutional Convention . . . of Massachusetts* . . . (Boston, 1856), pp 124–125, 133–134, 141, 149, 154–156, 189, 191.

[19] Harding, *Contest over Ratification*, p. 83; Rufus King (Boston) to James Madison [New York?], 23, 27, 30 January 1788, in King, *Rufus King*, I, 316–318; Tristram Dalton (Boston) to Michael Hodge (Newburyport), 20 January 1788, in Stone, "A Sketch of Tristram Dalton," pp. 19–20.

On the same day Nathaniel Gorham had written to General Knox concerning some "recommendatory amendments" which were being written and would be ready on the next day for presentation if the occasion offered.[20]

Sometime the following day a group of federalists talked Hancock into declaring for ratification. They supplied him with a set of recommended amendments to present to the convention which if accepted were to be appended to the state's resolution of ratification. These recommendations, apparently drawn up by Theophilus Parsons, included limitations on Congressional powers to regulate elections, restrictions on the jurisdiction of federal courts, and most important, the principle later embodied in the tenth amendment, that all powers not expressly delegated to the federal government were reserved to the states. For their part of the bargain the federalists agreed to give full political support to Hancock. As explained by King in a letter to Henry Knox: "Hancock has committed himself in our favor and will not desert the cause. . . . [He] will hereafter receive the universal support of Bowdoin's friends and we told him that if Virginia does not unite, which is problematical, that he is considered the only fair candidate for President." [21]

After having been favorably reported to the convention by a bipartisan committee, the recommendations were adopted, although not before Samuel Adams nearly upset the whole affair by moving a well-meaning amendment of his own. Thus mollified by the recommendations and persuaded by the declaration of Hancock, enough uncommitted or originally antifederalist delegates swung into line to assure ratification on the 6th by a 187–168 vote. "God be praised!" wrote Dalton to his brother-in-law, Stephen Hooper, that night. "With the utmost satisfaction I now announce to you

[20] Harding, *Contest over Ratification*, p. 85; Tristram Dalton to Michael Hodge, 30 January 1788, in Stone, "Parsons and the Constitutional Convention," p. 94; Nathaniel Gorham to Henry Knox, 30 January 1788, Henry Knox Papers (MHS).

[21] Harding, *Contest over Ratification*, pp. 84, 87, 89, 97, 98; George H. Haynes, "Conciliatory Propositions in the Massachusetts Convention of 1788," American Antiquarian Society *Proceedings*, new series, XXIX (1919), 302–304; *Debates and Proceedings*, pp. 83–85, 280; Tristram Dalton (Boston) to Stephen Hooper (Newburyport?), 31 January 1788, in Stone, "Parsons and the Constitutional Convention," p. 94; Rufus King to Henry Knox, 1 February 1788, in King, *Rufus King*, I, 319. See also Jeremy Belknap to Ebenezer Hazard, 3 February 1788, in Massachusetts Historical Society *Collections*, 5th ser., III (1877), 15.

and to my fellow citizens . . . that this afternoon at 5 o'clock the convention consented to ratify the proposed constitution." [22]

To one observer the whole affair was a most unsavory business. John Quincy Adams, who in other entries to his diary showed himself a good loser, could not help resenting the apparent fact that Parsons was a poor winner. "[Mr. Parsons] speaks with pleasure of every little trifling intrigue which served to baffle the intentions of the *anti-federalists,* though many of them to me exhibit a meanness which I scarcely should expect a man would boast." [23]

It is perhaps not surprising that upon Theophilus Parsons fell the task of drawing up the conciliatory amendments submitted to Hancock. After all, as author of *The Essex Result* a dozen years earlier, Parsons was no stranger to the idea of a bill of rights. Although he and the federalists, in opposition to Samuel Adams and others, felt that the state had no right to amend the proposed constitution as such, Parsons had no real objection to suggesting alterations to Congress. To be sure, he compromised with his earlier principle, that man's inalienable rights must be guaranteed "in a Bill of Rights [declared] previous to the ratification of any constitution." But he started, for whatever motives, a movement which not only facilitated the establishment of the constitution but also led to the ratification of the first ten amendments as a safeguard of man's inalienable rights.[24]

When word of the successful completion of the convention's business reached Newburyport, many of the merchant-leader group went over to Newbury Green to meet the returning delegates and properly escort them into town. According to young Adams, "a number of respectable citizens and a number who were not very respectable" took part in the affair, and as they came into town church bells were rung and "the noisy expression of joy continued with some intermission until 8 o'clock in the evening." [25]

With the often-bitter convention over, the defeated antifederalists accepted the verdict and prepared to cooperate with the new government, should enough other states agree to its establishment.

[22] Harding, *Contest over Ratification,* p. 98; Tristram Dalton to Stephen Hooper, 6 February 1788, in Stone, "Sketch of Tristram Dalton," p. 20.

[23] Adams, *Life in a New England Town,* p. 96.

[24] *The Essex Result,* in Parsons, *Memoir,* p. 367.

[25] Adams, *Life in a New England Town,* p. 94; *Essex Journal,* 13 February 1788.

Many of the antifederalist leaders might have agreed with John
Quincy Adams:

for my own part, I have not been pleased with this system, and my
acquaintances have long since branded me with the name of *antifederalist*. But I am now converted if not convinced. . . . as upon the
decision of this question I find myself on the weaker side, I think it my
duty to submit without murmuring against what is not to be helped. . . .
I should view a man who would now endeavor to excite commotions
against the plan as no better than an insurgent who took arms last winter
against the courts of Justice.[26]

The federalists' bargain with Hancock threw politics in Massachusetts into turmoil. Few basic issues existed to separate the politically minded into irreconcilable camps, but the clash of personalities
enlivened both caucuses and elections. True to their pledge, the
federalists swung full support behind Hancock for the gubernatorial
election of 1788. Even before the ratifying convention had adjourned
in February, insiders spread word of the arrangement. Rufus King
told General Knox about it as soon as he could, and Tristram
Dalton wrote a Newburyport friend, perhaps Michael Hodge, in-
forming him of the new situation. "Governor Hancock has hazarded
his whole interests to the support of the Constitution . . ." Dalton
confided. "We must whether successful or not support his interest.
Are you willing that we should pledge yours? Do not say 'I will
be damned first. He shall never have my vote.' Will you not if the
Judge [Benjamin Greenleaf], Parsons and myself pledge ourselves?" [27]

In early April the Essex leaders caucused in Ipswich to draw up
a ticket for the federalists of the county to support. The unusual
situation of men such as Parsons and King endorsing Hancock for
re-election at first mystified outsiders like John Quincy Adams. "The
revolution that has taken place in the sentiments within one twelve-
month past," he wrote in early April, "must be astonishing to a
person unacquainted with the weaknesses, the follies, the vices of

[26] Adams, *Life in a New England Town,* pp. 93–94.
[27] Rufus King to Henry Knox, 1 February 1788, in King, *Rufus King,* I, 319;
Tristram Dalton to ———, 3 February 1788, in Stone, "Parsons and the Constitutional Convention," pp. 87–88.

human nature. The very men who at the last election declared that the Commonwealth would be ruined if Mr. Hancock was chosen have done everything to get him in." But already the seeds for dissension within the loosely organized federalist camp had been sown. The Bowdoinites, fearful of what would happen in Massachusetts if Hancock were elevated to the presidency, took great pains to nominate dependable Benjamin Lincoln as lieutenant-governor instead of Samuel Adams.[28]

Newburyporters backed the ticket with apparent enthusiasm. Hancock received 270 votes to a single ballot in favor of Bowdoin. Lincoln, in turn, won 232 against Sam Adams' 42. Since neither Lincoln nor Adams gained a majority of the votes cast for lieutenant-governor in the state, the contest went to the General Court, where Lincoln was chosen. All federalist factions seemed to be satisfied with the Hancock-Lincoln triumph, King writing Knox in June that Massachusetts was in good hands. "Never has there been more able and honest men in the administration of this state." And the gentlemen of Newburyport did not confine their support of Hancock to the polls alone. When the governor passed through town in August on a journey, he was given full welcome, with bells, cannon, and military escort. On his return Jonathan Jackson entertained him for dinner.[29]

All was not well within the federalist camp, however; Bowdoinites could not be expected to remain associated with the capricious Mr. Hancock for long. Previous political battles had generated too much mutual hatred. By the fall of 1788 those who had favored ratification of the constitution had split into two definite factions. On the one hand were the Bowdoinites, including Stephen Higginson, George Cabot, Fisher Ames, and, most important, Theophilus Parsons. Their standard-bearer, after Bowdoin's feeble appeal had waned beyond usefulness, was the popular General Benjamin Lincoln, who, although a conservative federalist himself, was nevertheless respected by all factions of the party. In opposition to this group was a loosely knit group which included Christopher Gore,

[28] Morse, *Federalist Party*, pp. 58n, 59, 213; Adams, *Life in a New England Town*, p. 119.
[29] Town Records, I, 515; Rufus King to Henry Knox, 16 June 1788, Knox Papers (MHS); *Essex Journal*, 13, 20 August 1788.

Rufus King, Jonathan Jackson, and perhaps Tristram Dalton. These men had no leaders other than Governor Hancock and Samuel Adams, neither of whom seemed to care very much about their supporters.

The deep division within federalist ranks made its first public appearance in the late fall of 1788, when the General Court sat to choose the Bay State's two senators. The House first selected Caleb Strong and Charles Jarvis. The Senate accepted Strong but rejected Jarvis, returning instead the name of John Lowell. Only after several exchanges did the General Court settle on Tristram Dalton as a compromise candidate for the second seat. Rufus King, who had for several years resided in New York while representing the Bay State in Congress, was in fact the favorite candidate of many Boston federalists. But the question of residency was raised by his old mentor, Parsons, whose associates in the legislature supported Nathan Dane, in opposition to both King and Dalton.[30]

The next Newburyporter involved in the factional battle was less fortunate than Dalton. Jonathan Jackson had earlier in 1788 hoped to be appointed collector of customs for the port of Boston, the Newburyport position having already been filled by the staunch federalist merchant Jonathan Titcomb. But when he learned that Benjamin Lincoln also sought the office, Jackson abandoned his own ambitions and supported his competitor's application with magnanimity. His next move was to seek elective office, as representative from Newburyport's district to Congress. But in this attempt he ran headlong into the opposition of Parsons and his faction. Just what issue had originally opened the breach is not known. It must have been a serious one, however, to counteract the good turn which Jackson had previously done Parsons' favorite, General Lincoln. The first trick sprung by the clever lawyer was to leak a rumor, apparently through Tristram Dalton, that Rufus King disapproved of Jackson's candidacy. Gore got wind of the scheme and quickly convinced Jackson that King fully supported his campaign.[31]

Jackson cleared the first hurdle sufficiently well to be included

[30] Christopher Gore to Rufus King, 23, 26 November 1788, in King, *Rufus King*, I, 345–347.
[31] Porter, *Jacksons and Lees*, I, 374–375; Christopher Gore to Rufus King, 14 December 1788, 29 January 1789, in King, *Rufus King*, I, 347, 349–350.

in a special run-off election in January. Between the two elections, however, campaigning became somewhat rougher than Jackson had expected. "Some folks whom you see almost every day," he later wrote his brother-in-law Oliver Wendell, "have tried to propagate . . . that I am without property. . . . This electioneering has grown a vile business," he concluded. Meanwhile a correspondent to the *Essex Journal* attacked Jackson for his authorship of *Thoughts upon the Political Situation*. "An Elector of Essex" came to his defense the following week, praising him for his splendid wartime record of leadership. Throughout those perilous years "he steered the course of an able statesman and a fixed patriot. . . . Offices of profit or honor he never courted and not a little of his own estate was freely spent in his country's service." Despite strong support from his home constituency, however, Jackson finally lost to Salem's Benjamin Goodhue.[32]

Almost immediately after his defeat Jackson teamed with strange associates. Only one political issue in the Bay State during these years cut beneath the level of personalities: the clash between those who had supported and those who had opposed the ratification of the constitution. "Fed and anti are the only distinctions at this day," wrote young Adams in the previous spring. In Newburyport two men stood out as leaders of the antifederalist camp. Daniel Kilham had shown his colors in the fall of 1787 when he attempted to block the calling of a convention to consider ratification. Attacks against him continued from all parts of eastern Massachusetts, including the threat of a coat of tar and feathers for his nonconformity. Behind the scenes of Newburyport's small antifederalist group stood Stephen Cross, shipbuilder and patriot. Cross had served faithfully on many of the town's important committees during the Revolution, owned shares with other wealthy merchants in several privateers, and represented the town in the General Court throughout most of the war. Upon his appointment in mid-1786 as collector of impost and excise for the eastern district of Essex County, Cross resigned his seat in the legislature, creating a vacancy subsequently filled by Kilham. At least until that time he had been strongly allied with other men of the mercantile class in town, even to join-

[32] Town Records, I, 523, 526; Jonathan Jackson to Oliver Wendell, 11 January, 5 February 1789, Austin H. Clark Collection; *Essex Journal*, 17, 21 January 1789.

ing Theophilus Parsons at the Ipswich Convention in 1778 which had drawn up *The Essex Result*.[33]

Jackson had been on good social terms with Kilham for over a year. Ironically, on the very evening that Parsons and his associates planned their bargain with Hancock at the ratifying convention in Boston, Jackson was entertaining Kilham and young John Quincy Adams at dinner in Newburyport. When Parsons' Hancockian opponents in Newburyport decided to contest the election of town representatives in the spring of 1789, they named Jackson, Kilham, and Captain John Fletcher as their candidates. In the state elections this faction strove to replace General Lincoln in the lieutenant-governor's chair with Sam Adams.[34]

When Parsons returned to Newburyport from a stay in Boston, the attack on the Kilham slate took to the newspaper. "That there are men who are opposed to the operation of the federal government no man in his senses will deny," wrote "AN ELECTOR" to the *Essex Journal*, "and that a C——— [Collector?] in this town has been at the head of the party will appear very evident by tracing his conduct from the publication of the federal constitution." "ELECTOR's" harshest words were reserved, however, for Daniel Kilham. In his opposition to the constitutional convention in 1787, he had apparently used the argument that the people were not sufficiently sophisticated to judge the merits of the document, a peculiarly "federalist" position which probably had considerable truth to it. But the doctrine was now thrown in his face, ironically enough, by his federalist foe in Newburyport. It was folly, claimed "AN ELECTOR," to choose a man "who for the most unprecedented abuse of his constituents' most invaluable privilege, viz. the right of private judgment—was justly neglected and for his assumption was treated with that silent contempt which he merited." [35]

Kilham struck back at the opposition the following week, deny-

[33] Adams, *Life in a New England Town*, pp. 119–120; Morse, *Federalist Party*, p. 52n; Currier, *History of Newburyport*, I, 678–679, 679n; Town Records, I, 299. Cross's presence at Ipswich rules out participation there as *prima facie* evidence of Essex Junto membership, as implied by Charles R. Brown, *The Northern Confederacy* (Princeton, 1913), pp. 8–9.

[34] James Bridge to John Q. Adams, 28 February 1789, in Adams, *Life in a New England Town*, pp. 105–106; John Q. Adams to John Adams, 28 June 1789, in W. C. Ford, ed., *The Writings of John Quincy Adams* (New York, 1913), I, 41.

[35] *Essex Journal*, 6 May 1789.

ing that he had abused his constituents while a representative. He defended his opposition to the constitution and charged that some federalists had supported ratification in order to gain a position in the new federal government. Furthermore, Kilham prophetically stated that if the evils of central government which he had feared (unlimited power, financial control, underrepresentation, among others) should in fact materialize, "I doubt not I shall await a constitutional remedy with much more patience than those changeable zealots who were the most clamorous for its adoption." [36]

The Kilham slate lost decisively, however, and Jackson set out for New York in hope of gaining a federal appointment. Christopher Gore gave his mission a helping hand by twice reminding Rufus King, now a senator from New York, that their old friend desperately needed an office. Jackson sought additional support from John Lowell, asking the judge to have letters written to Robert Morris in his behalf. This pressure must have succeeded, for Jackson soon received appointment as United States Marshal for Massachusetts. When Washington made his triumphant tour through the New England states in the fall of 1789, Jackson was on hand in his new capacity to welcome the president to the Bay State. After returning from having guided him safely to Portsmouth, Jackson could not contain his loyal enthusiasm in the next letter to Lowell: "he is great you may depend upon it—and I think he is *greatly good*. . . . Whatever may be my future success, I shall always think of the last fortnight I have devoted to him to have been precious time and almost inestimable." [37]

Despite their failure to gain election for themselves during this period, the politicians opposing Parsons in Newburyport had no difficulty returning handsome majorities for Hancock at each gubernatorial election. In the spring of 1789, for instance, at the same time that Jackson and Kilham lost their bid as representatives, Newburyport returned for Hancock a two-to-one edge over Bowdoin. For lieutenant-governor, Sam Adams even defeated Benjamin Lincoln by a nearly three-to-one margin. Selective voting remained the keynote of the period. As much as the town seemed to dislike

---

[36] *Essex Journal*, 13 May 1789.
[37] Jonathan Jackson to John Lowell, 8 August, 4 November 1789, Henry L. Shattuck Collection (MHS).

Parsons' gubernatorial choices, the voters still preferred his local candidates to the antifederalist Kilham, even when the latter was joined by the respected Jonathan Jackson.

The effort to bring about ratification of the federal constitution in Massachusetts was the last campaign waged by Newburyport's colonial merchant group. By 1790 most of those who had led the town through the revolutionary crisis and the difficult postwar years had either moved away, retired, or died. A comparison of the valuation lists for the years 1767, 1782, and 1790 shows how complete was the decline of this group. Of the wealthiest twenty-five families of 1782 only nine held similarly high rank by 1790. And in the generation from 1767 to 1790 only five families managed to retain ranking among the top twenty-five. Fifteen had fallen from the list by the end of the war; the other five in the period 1782–1790. In fact Nathaniel Carter, second on the valuation list of 1767, was the only merchant who came close to maintaining his wealth throughout the whole period, ranking third in 1790. What made the decline of these men particularly significant was that their families went with them, for few sons of colonial merchants chose to remain in Newburyport. By 1790 an entirely new group of merchants had begun to take over the leadership of the town's political and social activities as a result of a rise to economic power.[38]

Some of the wealthiest colonial merchants, like Robert Roberts and Ebenezer Little, who had stood fourth and fifth respectively on the tax list of 1767, had died before the war began with no sons able to take over their businesses. Others simply moved away. William Hazen and Leonard Jarvis, for instance, disappeared from the New-buryport scene before the end of 1769, only to turn up in Boston during the Revolution as owners of privateers sailing from that port. John Bromfield had also gone to Boston, in a movement which became increasingly popular among the out-port merchants as the colonial years passed.[39]

Many of the older men retired from active business before the beginning of the war. Some, like William Atkins, had no son capa-

---

[38] Valuation List for the Year 1767 (EI); Valuation List for the Years 1782 and 1790, Assessor's Office (Newburyport City Hall).

[39] Gardner W. Allen, *Massachusetts Privateers of the Revolution* (Boston, 1927).

ble of following in their steps, while others were more fortunate. Patrick Tracy, whose wealth gave him first place in the 1767 rankings, turned his affairs over to his sons Nathaniel and John in partnership with their brother-in-law Jonathan Jackson. Tristram Dalton assumed charge of his family's mercantile house shortly before his father's retirement and death. By 1790, however, these men had lost their inherited wealth.[40]

Tristram Dalton's struggle to maintain the position of wealth which he had inherited from his father illustrated the plight of many merchants. Although he was active in privateering, his interest in that business was not extensive, a fact which probably saved his fortune from earlier collapse, for privateering was a source of heavy losses among Newburyporters. Moving to his Newbury seat in 1786, Dalton was in need of a job when he became junior senator from Massachusetts two years later, partly because he could not bring himself to accept the reduced standard of living dictated by his dwindling income.[41]

As a senator Dalton was in his proper element. According to tradition he proceeded to the capital in his four-horse coach, with a full retinue of servants attired in the Dalton livery. He never doubted that his particular constituents were the merchants of Massachusetts, whose interests he faithfully served for his two-year term of office. Writing to his friend and distant cousin Michael Hodge in the spring of 1789, Dalton candidly stated his position on the proposed impost on molasses. "No difficulty . . . shall deter me from performing what I esteem to be my duty . . . remember me to all friends, especially those concerned in the molasses trade." When it came to matters affecting the shipbuilding industry, the senator spoke just as plainly: "This manufacture appearing to me to deserve every encouragement upon *National* principles & the affection I feel for my Native Town adds force to my inclinations to protect a Business which is of so much Consequence." [42]

---

[40] Valuation Lists for the Years 1767 and 1790, Assessor's Office (Newburyport City Hall).

[41] Stone, "A Sketch of Tristram Dalton," pp. 1–29; Currier, *History of Newburyport*, II, 214; Allen, *Massachusetts Privateers*, pp. 80, 81, 108, 186.

[42] Tristram Dalton to Michael Hodge, 30 May, 2, 21 June 1789, in Stone, "A Sketch of Tristram Dalton," pp. 23, 25; Tristram Dalton to [Ballard], 8 March 1788, Ballard Papers (MHS); Morison, *Maritime History*, pp. 164–165.

Dalton, in fact, seemed to concern himself with little else during his brief term. Although a member of the subcommittee on titles, and other *ad hoc* groups during this first session of the Senate, he made his most significant mark in the debates on imports. With the help of favorable decisions from John Adams in the chair, New England senators succeeded in beating down the levy on molasses. During these debates Dalton repeatedly rose to speak for lowered duties, until the issue was finally settled most favorably at two and a half cents a gallon.[43]

Dalton drew the short Senate term, and when the General Court named George Cabot, a Bowdoinite, in his place, he took the reversal hard, although not deprecating Cabot's abilities. From that point forward Dalton fell victim to a series of misfortunes which reduced him to straitened circumstances. His land speculations in New Hampshire had already become a drag. "I wish to sell my interest in the Township [of Dalton]," he wrote a fellow investor, Josiah Little, in March 1790, "Expecting not to meet with any purchasers, my next wish is to render it more valuable by getting on settlers . . . if not," he wearily concluded, "I must jog on—adding charge to charge— having gone too far to retreat." Dalton had even worse luck with speculations in Georgetown, D.C., lands, and when the vessel carrying all his household effects foundered on its passage to the Potomac, the former senator was nearly finished. In his search for relief through government employment the scrupulous Dalton thought it improper to seek any office established while he had been in the Senate. The creation of many attractive positions during his term in that body naturally limited the field. He was not too shy, however, to ask Rufus King's help in late 1790 in seeking the office of post- master general of the United States when the incumbent proved unwilling to move to Philadelphia with the capital. But despite his close association with such influential men as Tobias Lear, Dalton failed to win any federal office until offered a clerkship in the Boston Customs House in 1815.[44]

[43] William Maclay, *Sketches of Debate in the First Senate of the United States* (Harrisburg, Pa., 1880), pp. 60, 62, 65, 71, 72–73; Benjamin Goodhue to Michael Hodge, 14, 17, 26 May, 4, 16 June 1789, Eben F. Stone Papers (EI).

[44] Henry Jackson to Henry Knox, 22 June 1790, Knox Papers (MHS); Tristram Dalton to Josiah Little, 24 May 1790, Tristram Dalton Papers (HSON); Tristram Dalton to Rufus King, 25 September 1790, in King, *Rufus King,* I, 392–393; Currier, *History of Newburyport,* II, 214.

Dalton at least had some funds to tide him over until better times. Others were less fortunate. To Jonathan Jackson, for instance, retirement was out of the question. Although his fortune had never been great, Jackson at least had ranked among the wealthiest half-dozen residents in Newburyport at the close of the Revolution. During the decade of the 1780's his losses were heavy, and by 1790 his name no longer appeared among the top twenty-five property holders in Newburyport.[45]

One scheme by which Jackson planned to shore up his slipping income would have sent him to North Carolina to inspect some lands in which he and a number of other merchants of Boston and Essex County had invested. His terms, however, apparently were too high for the other members of the company to accept: three pounds a week to his family during his absence and horse and chaise plus expenses for himself and sons on the trip.[46]

Meanwhile, Jackson's personal financial position steadily worsened. In late 1788 he wrote his close friend Lowell inquiring about the expenses and procedures for getting his son Charles a college education. "Can I avail myself of any privileges there?" he asked. "It is difficult enough for us to get along from day to day without any extra calls—I must devote some remaining real estate if I can to my maintenance the coming year or I must suffer severely . . . nothing is to be expected as income for this twelve-month to come, if so soon." His bid for elective office having failed that winter, Jackson had to seek appointive office, a quest in which he was ultimately successful in the fall of 1789.[47]

Jackson did not long remain contented with his post as United States Marshal, however. Almost within a month of his appointment he wrote again to Lowell in search of a still more lucrative job. He had to gain the ear of John Adams as well as of Henry Knox for the kind of position he was after, and Lowell's assistance was necessary. Jackson's maneuvers eventually resulted in his appointment in 1791 as inspector of internal revenue for the second district of Massachusetts. Five years later he moved up to become supervisor of internal

---

[45] Valuation Lists for the Years 1767 and 1790, Assessor's Office (Newburyport City Hall).

[46] Jonathan Jackson to John Lowell, 22 August 1788, Henry L. Shattuck Collection (MHS).

[47] Jonathan Jackson to John Lowell, 14 December 1788, Henry L. Shattuck Collection (MHS).

revenue for all Massachusetts. After losing this post in 1802 when the Jeffersonians abolished internal revenue, Jackson turned to a variety of jobs to earn his living. Until 1806 he was treasurer of Massachusetts; relinquishing that position, he became treasurer of Harvard, a job he held along with the presidency of the Boston Bank until his death in 1810.

Jackson's search for more suitable employment was possible only because he had enough income to support himself and his family in fairly decent fashion while struggling to improve his lot. For another family, the Tracys, the descent from heights of fabulous wealth was a precipitate plunge. Nathaniel's fate was probably the most humiliating suffered by any of the Newburyport merchants. Even as late as the valuation of 1785, his distinction as the town's wealthiest inhabitant went unchallenged. By 1790, however, a simple epitaph appearing in the Town Records marked the collapse of his fortune. "Voted that all the Taxes now outstanding against Nathaniel Tracy, Esquire . . . be abated by the Assessors of the Town." [48]

Tracy's downfall followed no unusual path. The partnership through which he and his brother John had continued in business went into debt by the middle of the 1780's. In 1785, while in England attempting to straighten out his tangled affairs, Tracy had to sign over most of his extensive waterfront property in Newburyport to the British firm of Lane Son and Fraser, to whom he owed at that time well over six thousand pounds. After selling or mortgaging most of his other real estate holdings in Newburyport and in Cambridge, Tracy retired to the farm which he owned in Newbury. One of his major creditors, the Boston merchant Thomas Russell, assisted in every reasonable way to ease the burden of debt which dominated Tracy's last years. Unable to find suitable work, partly because of uncertain health, he failed also in a petition submitted to Congress for relief based on his contributions made during the Revolution. Tracy remained helplessly dependent on the largess of his more fortunate friends until his death at the early age of forty-five, in 1796. [49]

[48] Valuation List for the Year 1785, Assessor's Office (Newburyport City Hall); Town Records, II, 8.

[49] *Supra*, pp. 60–62. Deed of Mortgage signed by Nathaniel Tracy to Lane Son and Fraser [1785] (MHS); Currier, *"Ould Newbury,"* pp. 551–557; Rufus King, Elbridge Gerry, and Henry Knox to Nathaniel Tracy, 2 March 1790, Knox Papers

The most persistent struggle for economic survival by any of the Newburyport merchants was that of Nathaniel Tracy's younger brother John. Described by the Marquis de Chastellux in 1782 as "the most considerable merchant in the place," with whom the Frenchman spent a pleasant evening of wine and conversation during his American journey, John Tracy's fortune was lost along with his brother's partly through overextended commercial involvements with several English and Continental houses.[50]

By the fall of 1788 John Tracy determined to investigate the Ohio country around Marietta as a possible place of resettlement for his family and himself, although frontier farming was hardly an occupation for which he had had much experience. With this project in mind he wrote General Knox for letters of introduction and spent the winter of 1788–1789 in Ohio looking over the prospects. On his return trip in the following spring Tracy wrote ahead to his friend Winthrop Sargent that "the Scoundrels from Wheeling . . . were giving us Trouble on account of the Indians [friendly Senecas whom Tracy's party had with them] but we outmaneuvered them and got through without any time being lost." Upon his return to Newburyport, the *Essex Journal* reported Tracy's impressions of the Ohio country in glowing terms. "The accounts he gives of that country are very flattering and encouraging, as well as to new settlers as to those who wish to emigrate." The editor of the *Journal* was convinced that Tracy would not be staying long.[51]

While home, Tracy tried to straighten out his recently deceased father's estate. "My old Creditors will make a push at me to endeavour to get the Estate left to my Children," he wrote Sargent in May. "But you know I can live in the Woods." Apparently Tracy was convinced that his family's future lay in the west, for he wrote Knox in June that his return to Ohio was being delayed only by his father's death. "[My children's] Estate may be exchanged for other real estate, I shall make the Exchange for shares in the Ohio

---

(MHS); Porter, *Jacksons and Lees*, I, 339; Brissot de Warville, in George F. Dow, *Two Centuries of Travel in Essex County, Mass.* (Topsfield, Mass., 1921), pp. 165–166; Adams, *Life in a New England Town*, p. 112.

[50] Porter, *Jacksons and Lees*, I, 339.

[51] John Tracy to Henry Knox, 20 October 1788, Knox Papers (MHS); John Tracy to Winthrop Sargent, 21 April 1789, Knox Papers (MHS); *Essex Journal*, 6 May 1789.

Company. Their personal Property will afford something to put the Wheels in Motion in the new Country." [52]

Despite his own difficulties, Tracy willingly wrote to Knox in behalf of two friends, General Jonathan Titcomb and Stephen Cross, naval and impost officers respectively in the Newburyport district custom house. With the establishment of federal authority these posts were to be transferred to the general government. Tracy's arguments for the retention of these two men show what were considered proper qualifications for federal employment during this period. Titcomb had been a commanding general of the Essex County troops during the war, had served his town as selectman and representative to the General Court, and at one time had been a prominent merchant whose wealth in 1780 had placed him twentieth on the town's valuation list. When Titcomb first undertook the task of organizing the county militia, wrote Tracy, "he was worth a very handsome estate. . . . Misfortunes at Sea, depreciation of our Paper Currency very much injured him." Of Stephen Cross Tracy pointed out that he had been an industrious patriot and "while in Court a great Friend to the Officers & Soldiers of the Army," a comment calculated to attract the admiration of old soldier Knox. As for himself, Tracy reaffirmed his intention to settle in the Ohio country but offered to discharge while there any duties for the United States which would not distract him too much from his task of settling a farm.[53]

But John Tracy never did return to Ohio, probably because he was unable to raise enough capital to begin a new life there on the scale to which he was accustomed. At least he still had a roof for his family as long as he stayed in Newburyport. His affairs had fallen into such a state by the fall of 1789 that Mrs. Tracy herself found it necessary to beg General Knox's assistance in retaining her husband in his inconsequential post as inspector and deputy adjutant general of the Essex County militia, a position apparently given to him by former Governor Bowdoin. Mrs. Tracy was most profusely apologetic for her presumptuous entreaty, but she knew that her husband's pride would have prevented him from taking

---

[52] John Tracy to Winthrop Sargent, 15 May 1789, Knox Papers (MHS); John Tracy to Henry Knox, 15 May 1789.

[53] John Tracy to Henry Knox, 4 June 1789, Knox Papers (MHS).

steps in the matter himself. If he were to lose the position, Mrs. Tracy feared, the family would never succeed in extricating itself from financial straits.[54]

The plea was apparently successful, but Tracy's continuance was of little more than stopgap value. By December 1789, he was reduced to a frank hands-and-knees approach to his good and patient friend General Knox for further assistance. The tragedy of an entire merchant group is woven into the text of this letter.

My friends tell me if I can support myself a year or two here, they have no doubt the times will better for me, and then if I feal [sic] a disposition to settle [in Ohio] I can purchase an Estate in that country under Cultivation. Upon this view my prospect is very slender—into Trade unless their [sic] is a Statute of Bankruptcy takes place I cannot go—an Estate which consists of a large House and ten Acres of land only—will not support me.

Tracy was straightforward in his account of how his fortunes had fallen into such a dismal condition, and he realized that for the most part the causes were beyond his control. He therefore could swallow his pride to seek a vacant post in the custom house, which would at last release him from the limbo-like years of poverty through which he had been wandering.

I must look to my Country—a Country that I neither spared property, Labour or Attention to support, when in my Power, but on the contrary, the confidence I placed was my ruin. I do not reflect on myself or my Country—I was happy in sinking or swimming with them.[55]

Many a patriotic supporter of the Revolution who lost his fortune through depreciation or privateering, or during the chaos which followed, found asylum in federal government posts. But for each one who did, ten others like John Tracy were left to fend for themselves in a strange new world.

The colonial generation of merchants in Newburyport had made

[54] Mrs. Margaret Tracy to Henry Knox, 10 October 1789, Knox Papers (MHS).

[55] John Tracy to Henry Knox, 21 December 1789, Knox Papers (MHS). Not until 1801 were bankruptcy proceedings brought against Tracy. IIe still remained high in his neighbors' affections, serving often as moderator of town meeting. Newburyport *Herald*, 27 February 1801.

extraordinary contributions to its town. The members of this group had provided a quarter-century of political and economic leadership. They had spearheaded the separation from Newbury which led to the incorporation of their town in 1764; they drafted the resolutions and served on the committees which forged Newburyport's increasingly firm stand against what they considered to be a tyrannical Parliament. These were the men who led their town through the Revolution, the men who built, equipped, or commanded the privateers which provided their adventurous townsmen additional means by which to fight for their liberty. These merchants, joined with young lawyers, gave unsparingly of their time to found a state government on sound principles, gleaned from their knowledge of political theory and their experiences of the previous decade. Finally, these men made every effort to win ratification of the new federal constitution by their state because they felt that only through a stronger national government could they prosper as a people.

The adoption of the constitution was in many ways a fitting capstone to a generation of accomplishment. It provided a government that would support the commercial activities to which these merchants had devoted their lives. The economic program of the new administration met with similar approval. Writing to Fisher Ames in February 1790, concerning Hamilton's "Report on Manufactures," Jonathan Jackson commented: "Mr. Hamilton has certainly done himself personally great honour by his report—all agree it is ingenious. . . . I am pleased he has adopted so fully the sentiments of Adam Smith as he has—it will serve to disseminate them more fuly here, and it will create him just applause and our Country deferred honour in Europe—where we have unfortunately lost a reputation it is full time we should repair." [56]

The honor which the new government could bring to the American people played a more important role in the movement for a national government than one might suspect. The mercantile class in particular, those men who constantly dealt with business associates in the West Indies, in England, and on the Continent, keenly felt the disrespect which foreigners had shown for the new nation throughout the 1780's. Jackson had particularly suffered during his visit to England in 1784–1785. With the inauguration of

[56] Jonathan Jackson to Fisher Ames, February 1790, Sedgwick Papers (MHS).

Washington and the establishment of a central, responsible authority which could speak for the nation, the merchants at last had a
government they could depend upon. In George Washington they
had a national leader whose administration, they were confident,
would enhance the name of America throughout the world.

The merchant families of Newburyport in the colonial period
provided economic leadership as well. It was this group which by
the time of the Revolution had made the town at the mouth of
the Merrimack a leading entrepôt. On their vessels plying routes
to the West Indies and to England were employed hundreds of
fellow townsmen. In the shipyards were jobs for shipwrights,
caulkers, mastmakers, and riggers. On or near their wharves were
the shops of other artisans, the sail-lofts and shipsmithies whose
craftsmen kept the fleet of vessels in sound repair. The town's unskilled workers too found employment on both wharf and vessel.
Even less-affluent members of the merchant-leader group depended
on the dozen or so major entrepreneurs whose importations from
England paid for locally built ships and provided stock for the
shopkeepers. As Newburyport prospered and expanded in the
decade before the Revolution, opportunities for lawyers, doctors,
and other professional men increased proportionately.

The town's growing wealth meant also a broadening of its tastes
from the simpler needs of provincial America to the catholic de-
sires of a cosmopolitan community. Newspaper editors, hairdressers,
fashion shops, and of course skilled housewrights and painters all
found the demand for their services expanding with the town. A
new standard of luxurious living was being set along High Street
and at the country seats of Tristram Dalton and others. Although
the postwar depression temporarily halted this growth, the changes
which had taken place in Newburyport since 1764 remained.

The colonial merchants of Newburyport made their greatest
contribution to community and country by their unwavering faith
in the new nation. Their nationalism led them to join the revolutionary cause in 1765–1775 and the movement for a strong central
government in 1787–1788. In both these struggles, the merchants
provided such skillful leadership that the town gave them virtually
unanimous support. The legacy which the colonial merchants left
the people of Newburyport in 1790 was a bright future in a new
nation.

Chapter V

A NEW ERA

By 1790 Newburyport began to recover from the long depression which had shackled its growth through most of the previous decade. With this return to prosperity came a new group of merchants, replacing members of the older generation who had lost their fortunes in the 1780's or who had moved away. These new men at first showed little interest in politics, partly because there were no issues as critical as independence or ratification of the constitution on which to take a stand. With the outbreak of war in Europe, Newburyporters enjoyed the profits of neutral trade while sympathizing with the French. But Jay's Treaty and the capture of their vessels by French privateers soon changed their minds. With typical converts' zeal their animosity toward all Francophiles steadily grew, and by 1798 the new merchants of Newburyport had become active members of the Federalist party.

When the Reverend William Bentley visited Newburyport in the spring of 1793, he found a flourishing town of nearly 5000 people. New houses under construction along High Street and numerous shops opening were responses to a new period of prosperity. In the last decade of the eighteenth century Newburyport enjoyed a boom hardly dreamed of five years before, and yet it was only a foreshadowing of what was to follow.

Among the new merchants were two whose careers illustrate how different they were from the Daltons and the Tracys of an earlier era. William Bartlet was considered the most prominent of the new merchants. With a real estate in 1793 worth £171 annually and personal property assessed at £1560, he was the town's richest individual. Before the Revolution Bartlet had been like his father before him a cordwainer, maintaining a shop near Lower Long Wharf and selling apples and candies on the side. How he made his first step into mercantile business is not known, but before the war ended in 1783 he had acquired his first vessel. By the next year he had purchased two more vessels and had on hand goods valued at £1300, although in the first of several complaints to the assessors he claimed cash debts of about £1000. Three years later Bartlet bought controlling shares in the wharf formerly owned by Stephen Cross and others and made plans for further expansion along the waterfront. In 1786 Bartlet's holdings were assessed at slightly less than £400. By 1790 he had doubled his wealth and three years later had doubled it again.[1]

Moses Brown rose to financial prominence by a similar route, having begun as a chaisemaker. Tradition claims that when Brown was repairing one of Tristram Dalton's several carriages before the Revolution, the merchant showed the chaisemaker around his estate. Carried away by enthusiasm, Brown forgot his place enough to assert that he would one day own the property himself, a prophesy made good in 1791 when he purchased the Dalton mansion for £1400. Brown made his fortune primarily in the importation of sugar and molasses, which he in turn sold to several of the town's ten distilleries. By 1793 he ranked close behind William Bartlet in wealth, with real estate worth £204 annually and a personal property assessed at £1080, having redoubled his holdings in the seven years since 1786.[2]

The best-known though admittedly exceptional change of station was effected by Timothy Dexter. This eccentric entrepreneur had come to Newburyport in 1769 as a leather-dresser. Despite the mental aberrations which soon established him as the town fool (he was honored with the title "Informer of Deer" in this urban community) and his almost total lack of education, Dexter had the good fortune to invest his savings in government notes and depreciated

---

[1] The year 1793 was the last one in which the assessors kept their records in pounds. Figures for this year represented 6 percent of the actual value of the taxpayer's property. In 1793 Bartlet's real estate was worth $9490 and his personal property $86,480, computing the pound at $3.33; Currier, *History of Newburyport*, II, 233–238; William Bartlet to Newburyport Assessors, 6 September 1784, Bartlet Papers (HSON); Vaulation Lists for the Years 1784, 1786, and 1793.

[2] Brown's real estate was worth $11,322 and his personal estate $59,940; Valuation Lists for the Years 1786, 1790, and 1793; Currier, *History of Newburyport*, II, 226–227; Stone, "A Sketch of Tristram Dalton," p. 11.

currency. Other speculations in trade and real estate steadily enhanced his income until by 1793 he was the fourth wealthiest man in town. With a nice touch for the ironic he bought the old Tracy mansion at which Washington had been entertained during his overnight visit two years before. When the town rejected his offer to construct a badly needed market house, he left in disgust. Returning two years later, Dexter purchased the old Jonathan Jackson mansion on High Street, converting it into one of the most extraordinary estates of the period, with statues of world-renowned figures cluttering up the lawn. Alexander Hamilton shared the grounds, according to Dexter's description, with "John hen Cock, Rouffous King, John Jea, and one Yonnecorne." Under his own likeness he proclaimed: "I am the first in the East, the first in the West, and the greatest philosopher in the known world." An era which could catapult an addlebrained glover into great wealth was indeed revolutionary.[3]

The prodigal rise to fortune of these three men, although on a far grander scale, nevertheless symbolized the experience of many other inhabitants of the town. Two of the *nouveaux riches* were sons of the shipwright Eleazar Johnson, who in 1775 won a degree of notoriety by leading a mob to destroy the tea confiscated by the Committee of Safety. Several had been shipmasters employed by the prominent merchants of the colonial period. William Coombs began as a shipwright, Anthony Davenport as an innkeeper, and John O'Brien as a privateersman from Machias, Maine. The Hunt brothers, starting out in the mastmaking business, put their profits into mercantile ventures and by 1793 ranked as the town's fifteenth and sixteenth wealthiest residents.[4]

In many ways this newer group of merchants differed markedly from their colonial predecessors. Only two men on the list of 1793's wealthiest citizens had attended college. One was the lawyer Theophilus Parsons, the other old Judge Greenleaf, but none of the merchants was a graduate. Throughout the revolutionary era, how-

---

[3] Dexter's total estate in 1793 was worth $44,344; Valuation Lists for the Years 1786, 1790, and 1793; Currier, *History of Newburyport*, II, 419–422.

[4] Valuation List for the Year 1793; Currier, *History of Newburyport*, II, 211–212, 222, 241–242.

ever, college-trained men had wielded a strong influence on the affairs of Newburyport. Six of the wealthiest citizens of 1767, including four merchants, had been Harvard graduates. In the second place, members of the younger generation were somewhat less aristocratic in their social lives. Their houses, while large and well-proportioned, were often located on side streets or near the wharves of their owners. Some of the new merchants purchased beautiful homes built by their predecessors along High Street, but few maintained the country seats at which Tristram Dalton, Stephen Hooper, Jonathan Jackson, and the Tracys had entertained distinguished guests so lavishly. Nor did the second generation of merchants seem quite so interested in public affairs, being content for a time to allow Theophilus Parsons and the young lawyers whom he trained to manage the town as they saw fit.

But what the new group of merchants lacked in social graces and education it made up for in wealth. In 1793, before the boom of neutral trade had begun, no less than twenty-six men could boast estates assessed at £200 or more. Just three years before only eleven men had equaled or surpassed this standard. Business had indeed recovered in Newburyport.[5]

The commercial activities of Newburyport in the early 1790's underwent rapid expansion. Total tonnage of vessels registered and enrolled increased by 50 percent, from under 12,000 tons in 1790 to over 18,000 three years later—mostly brigs, schooners, and sloops for the West Indies trade, which was the backbone of Newburyport's commerce. In 1790 half the vessels clearing the Merrimack called at one or another Caribbean port, and by 1793 over three quarters of the entries were from these islands. Newburyport's exports underwent an even more remarkable increase between the years 1791 and 1794, nearly doubling in value from $250,000 to $495,500. Not all commercial activity was confined to the Caribbean, however. Several ventures to the European Continent, including calls at Amsterdam, Copenhagen, and Hamburg, enhanced the earnings of merchants putting together cargoes for these ports. But for the most part, Newburyport's prosperity in this earlier

[5] Valuation Lists for the Years 1790 and 1793.

period depended upon the more conventional routes to the West Indies.[6]

The basic commodities of the town's import trade at this time were as before molasses and sugar. Coffee and cocoa were also popular imports from the Caribbean islands, along with cotton and indigo. The few voyages to Europe returned with cargoes of liquor from France and Amsterdam, small quantities of lead, nails, steel, and twine from the North Sea ports, and of course wines from Spain and the Western Islands. Primarily, however, the cargo-holds of these ships carried manufactured goods, to the value of $32,000 in 1793.[7]

Fish and lumber remained at the cornerstone of Newburyport's export trade. Country provisions such as butter, ham, and cheese found a lively market in the Caribbean along with manufactured articles like hats and shoes. For the most part outgoing cargoes on the European runs consisted of re-exported West Indian goods, although it is clear that this trade was not so important as it became at the turn of the century.[8]

The merchant capitalists of Newburyport did not confine their activities to ocean-borne commerce. As profits rose and needs of the community multiplied, investors risked their surpluses in a variety of undertakings. The problem which plagued the colonial merchant—paucity of avenues for investment—gradually solved itself in the expanding economy of postwar Newburyport. The community constantly demanded new and better services, and entrepreneurs in their desire to invest newly gained moneys willingly provided the necessary capital.

The first undertaking of the federal period brought the incorporation of the Essex-Merrimack Bridge in 1791. A combination of "old" and "new" merchants joined in this venture to construct a bridge across the Merrimack River at Deer Island, about three miles upstream from the center of town. Until this date the only means of crossing the river below Haverhill had been the ferry.

[6] Newburyport Custom House Entry Book, 1790–1792 (EI); Custom House Records for the Port of Newburyport, 1793 (EI); Value of Exports for Newburyport, *American State Papers*, VII, 320; William T. Davis, "Newburyport," in Hurd, ed., *History of Essex County*, p. 1760.

[7] Custom House Records of Newburyport, 1793 (EI).

[8] Custom House Records of Newburyport, 1797 (EI).

Moses Brown, Timothy Dexter, William Coombs, and Stephen Cross joined with Tristram Dalton and Nathaniel Carter in the original petition for incorporation, but before the year was out many other inhabitants of the town took advantage of the opportunity to invest some of their savings in the bridge company shares. Timothy Palmer, a local engineer who was soon to enjoy a national reputation, took charge of the construction in the year following, and by the middle of the decade the bridge was in full operation. To enhance their income, the proprietors of the company erected a tavern on Deer Island, midstream in the river, which quickly became one of the most popular inns in the area.[9]

In 1793 another undertaking began. Thirty-one gentlemen, including virtually all the newer merchants, joined in petitioning the General Court for incorporation of the Newburyport Woolen Manufactory, to be constructed on six acres of land along the Parker River in Byfield parish. The proprietors held their first meeting in Newburyport in February 1794, and within seven months Captain Nicholas Johnson among other retailers offered woolen goods made at the Byfield factory. But the venture never became a financial success. Finally, in 1803, William Bartlet bought out the other owners and subsequently sold it as a factory for the manufacture of cotton goods.[10]

The expanding business community made its own demands for new enterprise. In 1795, William Bartlet and Moses Brown led a group of merchants in the incorporation of the Merrimack Bank, capitalized at $150,000. As Newburyport's first such institution the bank prospered during the ten years of its chartered life, at the end of which period the stockholders were invited to exchange their shares for holdings in the more recently established Newburyport Bank. Marine and fire insurance companies also attracted available capital for investment. Since before the Revolution a few private insurance offices in Newburyport had offered marine coverage, and some of the wealthier merchants occasionally risked small sums in this uncertain business. The first insurance company in

[9] Essex-Merrimack Bridge Papers (HSON); *Impartial Herald*, 1 December 1795; Currier, *History of Newburyport*, I, 368–369.
[10] *Acts and Resolves*, 1793, ch. 27; *Impartial Herald*, 14 February, 14 June 1794, 23 February, 2 November 1795; Currier, *History of Newburyport*, II, 146–147; Arthur H. Cole, *The American Wool Manufacture* (Cambridge, 1926), I, 69.

town, however, was not incorporated until 1799, when William Bartlet and Moses Brown organized at least a dozen other local merchants in the establishment of the Newburyport Marine Insurance Company.[11]

By far the most ambitious and expensive undertaking proposed by Newburyport's merchants involved the construction of locks around the falls of the Merrimack River. Although the original scheme included canalizing these various hazards as far upstream as the New Hampshire border, the company made little progress for the first two years after its incorporation in 1792. Farsighted members of the community, reading correctly the portent implied in the chartering of the Middlesex Canal Company, realized that swift action had to be taken if Newburyport were not to lose control of its own river traffic.[12]

In February 1795 it was reported that the proprietors had raised enough money to continue their work and that the falls of the Merrimack River below those of Pawtucket would soon be passable by boats and rafts. Within two months the *Impartial Herald* joyously announced that a large raft of boards had come through the locks and canals of the river. Although the original investors never saw the completion of their dream, the company ultimately became a fundamental part of the Merrimack River's greatest enterprise—the textile industry at Lowell. For in 1825 the old Locks and Canals Company, reorganized, purchased real estate and mill rights at Pawtucket Falls, where Jonathan Jackson's son, Patrick Tracy Jackson, had joined with other Boston entrepreneurs to found the city of Lowell, named for yet another Newburyport son, Francis Cabot Lowell.[13]

Some of the new ventures in Newburyport came less as the result of profit-seeking than in response to the inhabitants' desire for broadened cultural contacts. Several newspapers were started in addition to the *Essex Journal and Merrimack Packet,* which John Mycall had resumed publishing in 1784 after a seven-year interrup-

---

[11] Currier, *History of Newburyport,* II, 156, 164; *Impartial Herald,* 28 July 1795.
[12] *Essex Journal,* 5 May 1792; *Acts and Resolves,* 1792, ch. 13; Henry Hudson to ———, [no date], Hudson Family Mss. (EI).
[13] *Impartial Herald,* 13 February, 17 April 1795; Currier, *History of Newburyport,* I, 148–149. Neither young Jackson nor his friend Lowell remained in Newburyport beyond childhood.

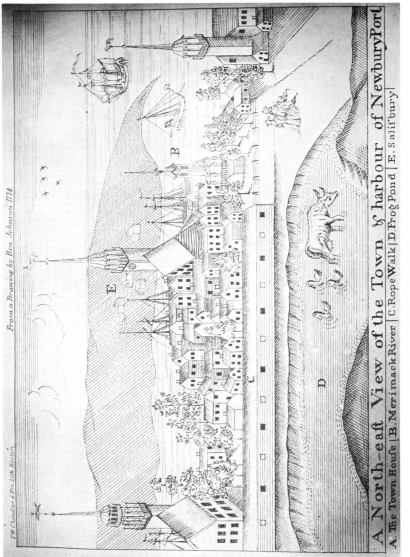

A Northeast View of Newburyport, 1774

Dalton House, 95 State Street, built in 1746

Jackson–Dexter House, 201 High Street, built in 1771

Old Wolfe Tavern, State Street, 1807

Schooner *Lydia* in Marseilles harbor, 1807

Meeting House in Market Square, circa 1800

tion due to the war. In January 1793 Mycall obligingly printed an advertisement announcing the plans of Edmund March Blunt to start a rival paper. In May of that year the first issue of the *Impartial Herald* appeared under the direction of Blunt and Howard S. Robinson. Within a few months, however, Robinson left the partnership and founded a paper of his own, the *Morning Star,* which made its first appearance in April 1794. Meanwhile Mycall's *Essex Journal* steadily lost business to the *Impartial Herald,* perhaps because the editor was a Hancockian in politics, and in April 1794 it folded. A similar fate overtook the *Morning Star* before the year was out. With the opposition temporarily bested, Blunt and his new partner, Angier March, expanded publication to twice weekly. In April 1795 yet another attempt was made to make Newburyport a two-paper town, with the establishment of William Barrett's *Political Gazette.* Although his politics were more acceptable to the town than either Mycall's or Robinson's, his success was not much greater. In October 1797 Barrett merged with Angier March, now the sole publisher of the *Impartial Herald,* and the two began publication of the *Newburyport Herald and Country Gazette.* Within two months March was on his own, and the *Herald* had no competition until after his retirement in 1801.[14]

Not content to rely on the town's newspapers for reading matter, several gentlemen in 1794 proposed the establishment of a library to be run in connection with George Osborne's bookstore. Another bookseller, Bulkeley Emerson, Jr., joined the operation in 1796. In the year following Edmund March Blunt set up his own lending library and by 1798 was able to offer a 1500-title catalogue to his customers.[15]

Other activities occupied the leisure hours of Newburyport's upper classes. Although public entertainment found little encouragement in New England at this time, occasional concerts by local and neighboring musicians had already broken into the sober realities of business life. Horse-racing, not so popular here as in the south, nevertheless offered diversion for those willing to make

[14] Clarence S. Brigham, *Early American Newspapers* (Worcester, Mass., 1947), I, 375–384; Currier, *History of Newburyport,* I, 505 508.
[15] Currier, *History of Newburyport,* I, 518–519; *Impartial Herald,* 25 October 1794, 21 October 1797.

the trip to Newbury Plains or Salisbury. Despite a scolding editorial in the *Essex Journal* agreeing with Governor Hancock that the theater promoted "idleness, extravagance, and immorality," the demand for amusement brought to federalist Newburyport an increasing number of stage performances.[16]

Among the billings were those of Mr. and Mrs. Solomon, offering a concert-and-moral-lecture combination which was a popular attraction of the day. Many performances took place in Union Hall, the second floor of a large building on Green Street, accommodating an audience of 200, where social events from dancing classes to fancy-dress balls were held. Through the next few years of the 1790's sleight-of-hand artists, slack-wire balancers, and waxworks exhibitors followed one another to entertain the pleasure-seekers of Newburyport. Educated pigs, ferocious lions, and a "Bison Imported from Arabia" joined the human entertainers as well.[17]

Club life flourished during the 1790's too. Another lodge of Freemasons had been established after the war and the Marine Society had expanded its membership and activities to keep up with the increased number of deep-sea shipmasters. A host of smaller groups, ranging from private conversational clubs to the more elaborate fire societies and benevolent organizations, provided activities to suit the middle-class appetite for gregarious living.

Other changes altered the physical appearance of Newburyport. The services of the town also needed modernization and development, and now that the postwar depression was at an end, the citizens could give their attention to community needs. A number of new streets were laid down, others extended, and some which had been in existence as private ways for several years were accepted by the town. The amount voted to meet current expenses at each annual meeting nearly doubled in the two years from 1791 to 1793.[18]

The town's greatest problem at this time involved the school system. Since the establishment of Newburyport three schools had been maintained, a centrally located grammar school and two writing schools, one at either end of town. In addition a number of

---

[16] James M. Barriskill, "The Newburyport Theatre in the Eighteenth Century," Essex Institute *Historical Collections*, XCI (July–October 1955), 211–245; *Essex Journal*, 15 May 1793.

[17] Barriskill, "Newburyport Theatre," pp. 228, 231, 337, 339, 349.

[18] Currier, *History of Newburyport*, I, 333–365; Town Records, II, 22, 63–64.

private schools, some for the instruction of young ladies, others offering courses in mathematics in the evenings, made their appearance. But by the decade of the 1790's the original school system, designed to serve a population of under 3000, fell short of providing adequate instruction for a town which by 1800 would grow to nearly 5000. New buildings were needed to replace the original small structures, and more instruction had to be offered, particularly to the children of the town's poorer inhabitants.

With this end in mind a special committee headed by Jonathan Jackson and including the town's ministers examined the entire educational program of the town during the years from 1790 to 1792. The town was divided into school districts, and for the first time provision was made for public education of young ladies. In May 1792 town meeting adopted a series of resolutions to govern the entire system. During the months from April to October, when the number of male students decreased sharply, girls were to be admitted for grammar and reading instruction. The town also resolved to establish two charity schools to enable the children of poorer parents to read words of two syllables. By the autumn of 1793 about 900 children were being educated in nine public schools. In addition the number of private schools had steadily increased so that by the end of the century one could learn everything from accounting and navigation to needlework, French, and dancing. It seemed that all could agree with the *Morning Star's* editor, that "ignorance is the mother of slavery." [19]

Although the town's commitment to a democratic system of education was firmly established, this by no means meant that all of its inhabitants looked with charity toward those they considered beneath them. One citizen under the pseudonym "MINERVA" attacked the presumption shown by ordinary workers who broke off from their toil to discuss topics of public interest which were no concern of theirs. But this bit of aristocratic dogma, although surely shared by others, met with instant and biting retort. Sarcastically restating "MINERVA'S" case to reveal its bitter condemnation of the working classes, "A MECHANIC" suggested that the way for his class to handle such utterances of the "well-born" was

[19] Currier, *History of Newburyport*, I, 315–316; Town Records, II, 30, 49; *Morning Star*, 8 April 1794.

"by presenting him *sans ceremonie* with a genteel suit of *tar and feathers*." Times had changed in Newburyport when a gentleman stooped to criticize his inferiors in the public press, only to be promised a coat of tar in retort.[20]

Newburyport's regained prosperity was shared by almost all the citizens, which meant that more residents could meet the property qualifications for voting in town meetings and state elections. By 1793 86.6 percent of Newburyport's 921 adult males qualified to participate in local affairs, and 73.8 percent could vote in state elections. This broadening of the franchise came as a result of two factors. In 1785 the General Court had reaffirmed a rule of thumb for determining voting qualifications for town affairs. Any resident who paid in a single tax besides the poll tax a sum equivalent to two thirds of the poll tax was a legal voter. As the poll tax steadily dropped to 10d in 1793, almost any property-holding resident could meet the requirement. Although the qualifications for state voters remained unchanged, the growing prosperity of the town's citizens permitted more of them to become enfranchised than ever before. That few of them bothered to exercise their rights was another matter. In 1791, for instance, only ninety-one persons cast their ballots for governor, while in the year following but eighty-one expressed their preference for representative to Congress, about 12 percent of those eligible.[21]

In the first years of the 1790's public affairs in Massachusetts offered little need or opportunity for the development of parties. The only clear issue which distinguished candidates was by 1793 five years old—federalist versus antifederalist. Those who had joined in support of ratification in 1788 agreed on other matters too, but not as yet with the consistency of a party. For one thing the clash of issues upon which partisan politics depends did not exist. For instance, there seems to have been little argument in the Bay State over the Hamiltonian financial program and none whatever in the newspapers of Newburyport. Surely there must have

---

[20] *Essex Journal*, 18 July 1792, 10 October 1793; *Impartial Herald*, 11 April 1794.
[21] Voting figures computed from the Assessors' Valuation List for the Year 1793 (NPL); *Acts and Resolves*, 1785, ch. 75; Town Records, II, 32; *Essex Journal*, 16 January 1793.

been some residents who disagreed with the administration on this issue, but apparently they did not feel strongly enough to discuss the matter in public or make it a political rallying point. Equally important, the Hancockian faction enjoyed during its leader's lifetime such popularity at the polls that no opposition could successfully organize. Even in Newburyport, many of whose merchant-leaders were nominally supporters of the Bowdoin faction, Hancock received the overwhelming endorsement of the few voters taking the trouble to cast their ballots during these years. In 1792, in fact, the Hancockians placed one man on the Board of Selectmen, two others on the three-man delegation to the General Court, and gave a plurality to the old antifederalist chief, Stephen Cross, in a special run-off election for United States representative the following January. When John Hancock died in the fall of 1793, his passing was mourned by many.[22]

The death of Hancock was an important first step toward the development of a party system in the Bay State, but by no means did it bring about immediate change. In the first election after the old patriot's death, 1794, eight names were placed in nomination. In this contest and in the year following the voters at Newburyport supported Samuel Adams, heir to the Hancockian mantle, over the Bowdoinite's favorite, William Cushing, by comfortable margins.[23]

While personalities continued to dominate state politics, the absence of party nominations for federal representatives worked a particular hardship on the well-intentioned voter, since he often was not acquainted with the many candidates' qualifications. The selection of the Fourth Middle District's congressman in 1794, for instance, required three elections before one of the five candidates received a majority. "An Impartial Elector," writing to the *Herald,* had difficulty making a decision. "Mr. Bradbury, from his habits of life has acquired more general political information than Bartlett has, or can," he wrote. "But at the same time I feel very happy that if the election should fall on Mr. Bartlett, I can congratulate the district in having an honest determined federalist for its member." At first the publication of letters in the press and word-of-mouth communication were the only ways to inform other voters that

[22] Town Records, II, 32, 46, 69; *Essex Journal,* 16 October 1793.
[23] Town Records, II, 90, 112.

one or another candidate had received the favor of "all respectable citizens." But even this innocuous method of "nominating" a candidate aroused opposition. "GIDEON" strenuously objected to a letter suggesting that Mr. Bradbury was the people's choice: "I wish, Sir, that our elections may be FREE and that the electors may be left to think and act for themselves and not be imposed on by the publication of falsehoods calculated to serve sinister purposes." [24]

But the main issue in this election, as in others of the period, was which candidates had most vigorously supported ratification of the constitution six years before. No current questions seemed to be involved. Clearly party politics had not yet become firmly established in Newburyport in the middle of the decade. Only the gradual impact of national issues had enough force to demand a consistent position by the politically minded. In the end it was probably the pressure of foreign affairs which did most to polarize the voters into firm party alignments. Until this took place, in the last two or three years of the eighteenth century, Newburyport's political life seemed to follow no easily determined pattern.[25]

While a calm settled over the domestic affairs of Newburyport through the middle of the 1790's, the rest of the world was in turmoil. To a seaport town such as Newburyport, whose men sailed to Europe and its Caribbean possessions, world conditions had long held an importance equal to affairs closer to home. When news of France's declaration of war against England arrived in April 1793, the townspeople took immediate interest in the development. For the first year or so the war had an adverse effect on Newburyport's commerce. Exports dropped in value between 1794 and 1795 by about 17 percent, and losses to British privateers mounted steadily. The promise of fortunes to be made in neutral trade at first seemed rather remote as Newburyporters lamented their "shackled commerce" and the "stagnation of business," but by the end of the century the merchants had adjusted to wartime conditions and a new wave of prosperity was under way. At the same time, however,

[24] Town Records, II, 103, 110; *Impartial Herald*, 7 November 1794; 9, 13 January 1795; *Morning Star*, 29 October 1794.

[25] See Joseph Charles, *Origins of the American Party System* (Williamsburg, 1956), for an appraisal of the significance of foreign affairs in party development during this period.

issues growing out of the war between England and France began to affect the political outlook of Newburyporters.

In Newburyport as elsewhere in America a large residue of friendship for France remained from revolutionary days. No one soon forgot the debt owed the French for their assistance fifteen years before. Coupled with the lingering animosity for the British which was kept alive during the decade after the end of the war by English commercial policies, most Americans overtly hoped that Great Britain would again receive its come-uppance from the old friend and protector, France. This is not to say that the Newburyporters wished to join in open warfare against the British. When Washington led the way with his Proclamation of April 1793, the town supported the presidential policy of neutrality without question. A meeting called in the summer of that year to review the current scene vigorously endorsed neutrality as the best way to advance the interests and happiness of the nation. The town voted unanimously to be on the lookout for any violation of the laws especially concerning the outfitting of privateers. Speedy prosecution was promised any offender.[26]

Although technically neutral, the citizens of Newburyport took every opportunity for the first three or four years of the European war to express their preference for the new republic of France. Fresh news of French victories called for large type and words of praise. "The glorious success of our good Allies," cheered the *Herald* in January 1794, is "the success of Liberty and Mankind." The sins of the British were many, and Anglophobia mounted steadily with each month. Before long absurd charges went hand in hand with more legitimate complaints. In June 1794 a zealous editor reprinted from a London paper an advertisement of manuscript sermons for sale to members of the clergy unwilling or unable to write their own. This offer of eighteenth-century ghost-writing was solemnly published as evidence that "however irreligious the French are represented," religion in England has been reduced to a "complete mechanical system." When two Scotsmen were brutally executed later that year for the crime of treason against "the *humane* and

[26] *Essex Journal*, 17 April 1793; Alexander DeConde, *Entangling Alliance* (Durham, N.C., 1958), pp. 3–30; Charles M. Thomas, *American Neutrality in 1793* (New York, 1931), pp. 13–52; Town Records, II, 74–76.

benevolent King of England," the incident was offered to prove that the English, not the French, deserved the title of "most savage and inhuman people on the earth." [27]

The real issue, however, was British interference with American trade, especially in the West Indies, toward which the Yankee had long taken a proprietary attitude. In April 1794 the *Herald* published fresh reports brought by a local captain of "the cruelty, oppression, and insults of the British in the West India Islands. . . . They add insult to outrage—they laugh at the measures Congress may pursue." Another Newburyport vessel lay "stripped and plundered of everything" in Martinico. By September of that year editor Robinson of the *Morning Star* could print a list of twenty Newburyport vessels carried into various West Indies ports by British cruisers. Most were eventually released but not without costly delay and inconvenience to the owners.[28]

The anti-British attitude of Newburyport's public prints only reflected the sentiments of the people. Although popular demonstrations never reached the proportions of twenty years before, the citizens left little doubt of their feelings toward the former mother country. A peaceful show of strength, which took place in April 1794, revealed the town's state of preparedness. "A large number of jovial TARS with oakum cockades in their caps and the American standard displayed attended by military music paraded the streets in a peaceable and orderly manner," reported the *Morning Star*'s editor. Here was a militant group ready when called upon to repel "those lawless depredations which our insidious enemies—the *British*—have been wantonly committing upon our trade and commerce." The editor invoked the spirit of '76 in his final charge to these "Brave lads," imploring that they show "our haughty foes . . . that AMERICANS are not to be trifled with." A week later a correspondent to the same paper carried the attack still further. Citing the growing reports of British depredations on American commerce, the writer called for an assertion of American rights. "Peace we believe to be the wish of Americans in general," he agreed, "but to have this at the expense of our sovereignty and independence is repugnant to . . . a people who have so lately *fought, bled,* and

---

[27] *Impartial Herald*, 13 January, 21 November 1794; *Morning Star*, 10 June 1794.
[28] *Impartial Herald*, 4 April 1794; *Morning Star*, 22 April, 2 September 1794.

died in the cause of FREEDOM." This appeal to former hatreds was continued two months later by the editor of the *Impartial Herald*. "No doubt the *American* sailors have still their *old feelings* alive," he stated.[29]

Despite the belligerent spirit of those forced to submit to the humiliations of seizure and confiscation, not all the citizens of Newburyport shared the current view that Great Britain was the scourge of the world. One "LUCIUS," addressing several communications to the *Impartial Herald,* dared to defend the former enemy. Editor Blunt, however, felt called upon to explain the appearance of such arguments with a short prefatory note: "Although the following sentiments are opposed to the prevailing opinion, yet as an *Impartial Herald* we esteem it inconsistent with our duty to suppress them, merely because unpopular." In his first letter "LUCIUS" carefully pointed out how the continuation of American trade with French West Indian islands had provoked the British to countermeasures. Shipmasters thought nothing of swearing that the French property they carried was American, he related. Far worse, Americans had made no real effort to maintain the neutrality toward each of the belligerents asked for by Washington. "If we have never publicly espoused the cause of either party in feasting, rejoicings, and congratulations at their successes," Americans may then with justice complain about harsh treatment. But neutrality of thought as well as of deed was as always an impossible expectation. It was difficult for any American to condone British attacks on the vessels of his country, and "LUCIUS" soon switched his line of argument. In examining why Americans complained so much against the British, he considered one cause the most important: "that personal and illiberal antipathy which many of us bear to whatever is English—or rather that bigoted attachment to every thing, which is the least degree adapted to the meridian of Paris or Versailles." Why else would merchants who grew rich on the fat Anglo-American trade protest so vehemently?[30]

A more important question, why the merchants willingly suf-

[29] *Morning Star,* 8, 15 April 1794; *Impartial Herald,* 4 April, 20 June 1794. One shipmaster seemed ready, after being harried by the English, the French, and the Algerian pirates, to go to war against all three.

[30] *Impartial Herald,* 18, 25 April, 2 May 1794.

fered the deprivations of neutral commerce at all, was answered by the promise of immediate profits accruing to the venturesome and to the lucky. Furthermore, to him with a long eye to the future a French victory would result in a commercial revolution whose principal benefactor would be the United States. "If the French overrun all Holland," editor Blunt speculated, "the Spice Islands will be thrown open to American navigators." French conquest of Spain would of course open her American colonies and Brazil as well to Yankee ships. The European manufacturers presently exporting to the Spanish colonies would naturally prefer to carry on their business in the United States, nearer to Latin American markets. The impact of all this upon the British possessions of the West Indies would be catastrophic. "The whole commercial world," predicted the editor, "stands on the brink of great revolution." [31]

As much as Newburyporters may have been convinced that they should support France against England on economic grounds, an equally strong reason was couched in more idealistic language. Most of the communications, editorials, and resolutions seemed to imply that the French were engaged in a struggle for liberty in many ways suggestive of American efforts twenty years before. French military victories were hailed as advances for Liberty; the events of 1794 marked the progress "of that ethereal flame, which was first kindled at the altar of American freedom," as the *Herald*'s editor commented. Robinson of the *Morning Star* saw each French triumph as a blow in behalf of "mankind in general." Even as late as the middle of the year following, Newburyporters felt the existence of a kindred spirit binding them to the French. At several banquets held throughout town to celebrate July Fourth in 1795 toasts were raised to "our brethren in arms in France," "the heroes who have fallen in the Cause of Liberty in France," and "The Republic of France—Success to her Armies and Navy." For a time some inhabitants rather self-consciously addressed each other as "Citoyen," and the women in town idolized Madam Corday.[32]

Although Newburyporters and other New Englanders clearly favored a French victory in the early years of the Anglo-French

---

[31] *Impartial Herald*, 21 November 1794.

[32] *Impartial Herald*, 2 May, 25 August, 21 November 1794, 9 May, 7 July 1795; *Morning Star*, 9 September 1794; *Political Gazette*, 9 July 1795.

war, there was little inclination at home for active involvement. The most convincing proof of the merchants' sincere desire for peace lay in their acceptance of the temporary embargo placed on commerce with Great Britain in late March 1794. A special town meeting called in mid-May resolved that "the embargo ought to be continued . . . as long as the public exigencies require it." [33]

As the year 1794 drew to a close, talk of war with England gradually gave way to hopes for an amicable settlement of differences. With the departure of John Jay on his mission to England belligerent spirits cooled still further. Even Newburyport's most ardent Anglophobes mustered mild enthusiasm for the negotiations, although the editor of the *Morning Star* insisted that only by continued French military success could the American emissary expect a cooperative reception at St. James.[34]

The first word received in Newburyport of the Jay Treaty came in February 1795, and its reception was favorable. Blunt of the *Herald* thought that it effectively placed American commerce "on an equal footing it stood before the Revolution," at least as far as the carrying trade with the British West Indies was concerned. But within a few months the editor and others eager to gain a peaceful settlement of the nation's commercial disputes with England found defense of the treaty increasingly difficult. When a number of "respectable Gentlemen" gathered to celebrate the Fourth of July that year, a toast to John Jay was qualified by the hope that the treaty's twelfth article would be satisfactorily amended. With growing consternation the editors of Newburyport's newspapers dutifully published accounts of protest meetings held in Portsmouth, Boston, New York, Philadelphia, Baltimore, and Charleston, South Carolina. Not until mid-August could the editor find much material to print favoring the treaty. Commencing with the issue of August 11, however, Hamilton's essays over the signature of "CAMILLUS" began regular appearance in the *Herald*. Within a fortnight word came from Philadelphia that the president and the Senate had ratified the treaty, and the issue was apparently settled.[35]

[33] Town Records, II, 94–95; Thomas, *American Neutrality*, p. 246.
[34] *Morning Star*, 9 September 1794; Samuel F. Bemis, *Jay's Treaty* (New York, 1923).
[35] *Impartial Herald*, 10 February, 7, 21, 25 July, 1, 4, 8, 11, 18, 25 August 1795.

Not until the fall of 1795, when the House of Representatives showed reluctance to implement the ratified treaty, did Newburyporters in general begin to support it. To a traveler just returned from a journey through the Merrimack Valley in early September, the whole country seemed to favor the agreement. A group of gentlemen gathered to honor Washington's birthday in 1796 offered an unqualified toast to Jay and his treaty. By late spring Newburyporters were bold enough to contend that opposition to full implementation of the treaty was confined to "disorganizers" and those southerners required by the treaty to settle their long-outstanding debts to British creditors.[36]

Finally on April 23, 1796, the inhabitants of Newburyport took their long-delayed stand on Jay's Treaty. Assembling in the town house without other previous notice than the ringing of church bells, a large group met "to deliberate and decide on measures properly to be taken at the present very critical and important crisis of our national affairs." After hearing an address by Theophilus Parsons, the meeting drew up a petition, modeled after those adopted by similar meetings in New York and Philadelphia. With only one dissident voice the town prayed Congress that the commercial treaty be carried into effect, in order "to preserve the faith, the honor, and the interest of our young and rising republic." Within a few hours a committee acquired the signatures of more than 400 inhabitants, and the document was dispatched to Theophilus Bradbury, the district's representative in Congress. When news of the House's favorable action reached town in early May, "the friends of order and good government received it with a tranquillity highly honorable to them," as though there had not been the slightest hesitancy in Newburyport's support of the treaty. To William Barrett of the *Political Gazette,* in fact, the final triumph of the treaty was nothing less than a victory of "THE PEOPLE. Their voice has been heard, and has had its due influence."[37]

As soon as the issue of Jay's Treaty was settled, the attitude of Newburyporters toward Great Britain began to change. No longer did the editors publish anecdotes purportedly demonstrating British

---

[36] *Impartial Herald,* 1, 26 September 1795, 23 February, 23 April 1796.
[37] *Impartial Herald,* 26 April, 10 May 1796; *Political Gazette,* 12 May 1796.

A NEW ERA 113

barbarity or despotism, although there were still occasional expressions of Anglophobia, as in the demand that the British lion be removed from the Wolfe Tavern sign. (The critic apparently had no objection to General Wolfe's likeness, however!) As early as April 1796 the *Political Gazette* reported the capture of two Newburyport vessels by the British without spicing the account with provocative adjectives. By the spring of 1797 Newburyporters began to agree that the British were not such a bad lot after all. With each issue of the newspapers came fresh reports of English respect for American commerce. When the merchant William P. Johnson learned that the Board of Commissioners had favorably decided the case of one of his confiscated vessels, the whole town seemed to share his elation. Meanwhile merchants in Salem and Boston received similar cheerful news from their London agent, George Cabot. "Another effect of the Treaty!" crowed the *Herald*'s new editor, Angier March. In August 1797 he rejected a letter attacking the treaty, publicly announcing that he would no longer publish such communications. Perhaps the greatest stride toward a reconciliation with England during these years came late in the summer of 1797, when Captain Woodman of the brig *Trial* returned from the West Indies with the extraordinary report that an English vessel had helped him ward off an attack by a French privateer and had conveyed him safely out of range.[38]

At the same time Newburyport's flirtation with republican France was rapidly waning. As early as mid-1795 some local commentators began to express concern over the mounting number of incidents of French depredations on American commerce. Prudence ruled at first, however, as in the case of a Wiscasset schooner captured and burnt by the French. "From our allies we have a right to expect better treatment," cautiously observed the *Herald*'s editor. "We are confident . . . that such conduct is as abhorrent to the present Rulers in France as they are to the citizens of the United States." But March's confidence began to ebb as more reports flowed in. "This almost equals some of the British piracies," he commented on the capture of an American ship by a French frigate. By the spring of 1797 the editor's patience had reached its end. In May

[38] *Impartial Herald*, 8 January 1796, 29 April, 2, 13, 23 May, 12, 22 August 1797; *Political Gazette*, 12 April 1796.

of that year two Newburyport vessels fell into French hands in
the West Indies. Several crew members were taken in irons and
severely mistreated. Captain Johnson, of the brig *Sally,* who two
years before had been captured by the British, was forced to submit
to similar insults. Already impatient with the antics of Genêt and
Fauchet, Newburyporters became indignant at these attacks, and
the editor of the *Herald* shed all his earlier caution to denounce
the French actions.[39]

Although talk soon turned to the possibility of war, most Newburyporters hoped for a peaceful settlement of differences with
France. In fact, as late as April 1797, the *Political Gazette* continued
to hail French military victories on the Continent with evident
approval, while editor March of the *Herald* ardently hoped for an
end to all Europe's embroilments. When Adams dispatched three
commissioners in 1798 to seek accommodation with the French
Directory, Newburyporters followed the events with great interest.
Gerry's nomination to the group was one issue on which the Hamiltonian Junto had strongly disagreed with the president, and both
of the Massachusetts senators had voted against their fellow Bay
Stater without success. Newburyport had given little support to
Gerry whenever he ran for elective office, but his appointment to
an important diplomatic mission did not evoke any protest, although
Theophilus Parsons and other high Federalists could hardly have
approved. Editor March welcomed the choice, in fact. "Mr. Gerry's
Americanism is well-known, and his firmness and independence
have been tried and found not wanting." With more optimism than
accuracy the *Herald* announced in late November that the Americans had been received in Paris "with every mark of respect and
politeness," and that there was no doubt of their impending success. Within three days, however, fresh advices convinced the
editor that the negotiations were not going smoothly. "We *wish*
to be able to announce a favorable termination of our differences
with the French republic," he hoped aloud in January 1798.[40]

But all hopes were dashed later in the month when Newbury-

[39] *Impartial Herald,* 5 May, 16, 30 June 1795, 29 April, 6, 20 May, 14 October
1797.
[40] *Political Gazette,* 7 April 1797; *Impartial Herald,* 1 July, 23 September, 21, 24
November 1797, 19 January 1798.

porters first learned of the XYZ Affair. Although the full text of the papers was not released for several months, the "true nature" of the French government had already been revealed, editor March insisted. From now on one need have no doubt that "the object of the usurpers of French government is to bring all nations to their feet and they will treat as an enemy every nation which they cannot govern either by force or by intrigue." Even though negotiations had collapsed, war was still not regarded as a feasible means of countering the French threat. In fact the editor of the *Herald,* despite his growing Francophobia, willingly republished the series of letters signed "junius" from the Boston *Chronicle.* Here the argument ran that war with France would not only be the ruin of America, but would be unjust as well, since France was a republic, like the United States, and had helped the colonies win their freedom from Great Britain.[41]

Meanwhile Newburyporters began to flock to the support of Adams's beleaguered administration. One citizen countered the criticism of the president's recall of Monroe and received support from the editor, who obligingly reprinted "scipio's" blistering attacks on Monroe's conduct from the *Gazette of the United States.* Another correspondent, "columbus," submitted a lengthy and impassioned defense of the principle of majority rule. In words which he would probably forget a decade later, he reasoned that the minority in government was but the voice of a minority of the people. "By the very nature of a republican government," he concluded, "the majority must constitute law. Let it be respected and submitted to as law, however it may cross our own particular opinions." To "an american," however, the problem was less complicated. In the struggle against France the nation's sole defense was union, he insisted. "Those who do not join us must be considered and treated as Frenchmen, and traitors, for on this question we can admit no neutrals." [42]

In late April came the strongest statement of public opinion in Newburyport since the endorsement of Washington's neutrality proclamation five years before. At the behest of a small group of leading merchants and lawyers, a town meeting assembled on the

[41] *Herald,* 26 January, 2, 6 February, 20 April 1798.
[42] *Herald,* 9, 30 March, 24 April 1798.

30th to endorse without opposition an address to President Adams giving his administration of the nation's affairs full support. After expressing their deep regret at the repeated failure of negotiations with France and their full confidence in the president's wisdom and integrity, the inhabitants took their stand. The people of Newbury-port "duly appreciate the blessings of peace and neutrality but they will never complain at the loss of these blessings, when constrained to sacrifice them to the honor, the dignity and the essential interests of their country." In language recollective of that found in town resolutions of twenty-five years before, the Newburyporters con-cluded their address with the pledge of "their lives and fortunes to support the measures judged necessary by the President and Con-gress." [43]

Over 400 citizens signed the address to Adams. Theophilus Parsons expressed the willingness of the Essex Junto members to back up their nation's president (now that the negotiations they had opposed in the first place had broken down) by serving on the committee to draw up Newburyport's resolution of praise. Independence Day toasts supported Adams and his cabinet with manifest enthusiasm. Such unity on important national issues was soon to become a rarity in Newburyport, but in the summer of 1798 the inhabitants stood firmly behind the president. [44]

As the months of 1798 wore on, public exhortations of all sorts urged the citizenry to muster their defenses against the French. Let no man sleep at this time of crisis or slavery will be the result, cried one correspondent. Another was more specific in his suggestion that each able-bodied male should equip himself in uniform, with forty rounds of cartridges, "fit for the field of battle." At the Fourth of July festivities that year a large procession of young men led a parade through town, joined by their elders "whose hearts were warmed with the recollection of former times." To the editor reporting the proceedings two days later the faces of the participants seemed animated by an enthusiasm seen only in men determined to main-tain their hard-won freedom. The younger set drew particular praise. "A number of them had procured a 24-pound canon . . . and opened the way with a Federal discharge. They uniformly appeared in that

[43] Town Records, II, 177–179.
[44] Herald, 20 April, 6 July 1798.

best of badges, the American Cockade, and displayed the same spirit which had animated their fathers in '75." Many young men hastened to join Newburyport's Independent Volunteers; others, wishing to serve their country on the seas, had only to enlist on board the United States brig *Pickering,* which was about to leave on a four-months' cruise "against the enemies of the United States." [45]

While the younger men of Newburyport devoted themselves to learning the military art, their fathers embarked on a more concrete project. A committee of local merchants, headed by William Bartlet and Moses Brown, was apparently the first such group in the country to suggest the private construction of ships-of-war to be turned over to the government for enhancement of the nation's navy. In the proposal presented on June 1 to the district's Congressional representative, Bailey Bartlett, the subscribers agreed to raise about $30,000 to construct a 20-gun ship of about 350 tons burthen. On accepting the vessel the government was expected to arrange for payment of 6 percent interest on the net cost and a final reimbursement of the loan at its convenience. It was the Newburyporters' further hope that such an undertaking would lead "to proportionate exertions in larger and wealthier towns," such as Salem and Boston. By such a method the government could quickly procure a number of stout vessels for defense, without the necessity of advancing funds, letting out contracts, and working through cumbersome official channels.

The committee must have received the go-ahead from the Navy Department prior to the Act of June 30th which set up machinery for similar agreements, for by mid-June construction began on the ship *Merrimack.* [46]

On October 12, just four months after her keel was laid, the 360-ton ship was launched into the river for which she was named. A company of Boston's finest musicians, already in town on an engagement, offered a special concert for the occasion, including "The New Federal Song—Hail patriots all." After the evening's concert a ball was held to complete the day's celebrations. *Merrimack,* equipped with twenty nine-pounders and eight six-pound cannon, received her complement of seven officers, mostly from Newburyport or vicinity, before sailing in mid-December, eventually to join Commo-

[45] *Herald,* 15 May, 15 June, 6, 10, 17, 27 July, 19 August 1798.
[46] *Herald,* 19 June 1798; Currier, *History of Newburyport,* I, 111–113.

dore Barry's squadron in the West Indies. With the commissioning of *Merrimack* Newburyport had in effect issued its own declaration of war against France.[47]

The French crisis of 1798–1800 revolutionized the politics of Newburyport. The mild federalism which had permitted the town to support Sam Adams for the governorship in 1796 at the same time that it endorsed the presidential candidacy of John Adams gave way in these years to a more rigid political outlook. Perhaps the first sign of a hardening of lines had come in the fall of 1797, when editor March prophetically dropped the adjective "Impartial" from his paper's masthead in absorbing the rival *Political Gazette* to make Newburyport once again a one-paper town. By the following June his political bias gave new significance to the change. In response to criticism that his was a party paper, publishing only one side, editor March retorted: "In the name of liberty, what two sides can there now be in this country but those of America's friends and foes." It was abundantly clear, he continued, that the French regularly made use of foreign agents and other corrupt means to force America to submit to their domination. "And yet there are found men base and weak enough to say publically that [the French] are justifiable in their demands, and that Editors . . . who refuse to publish their base and traitorous scurrility *'publish only one side.'* If this is publishing only one side they may rest assured that on that side only I publish—on the side of my country." [48]

The first attempt to identify Jeffersonians with the French in the Newburyport press came with the Griswold-Lyon affair in early 1798. Taking the part of the Connecticut Federalist, editor March labeled the irascible Lyon as the agent of the French-Americans who were plotting the downfall of the nation by secret intrigue. Writers to the *Herald* accepted as gospel that Federalists held an absolute monopoly on patriotism. Jacobins, in addition to being "friends to anarchy," were "fortune seekers" as well. No Republican was exempt from attack, even the kindly General Heath, who was put up for

[47] Currier, *History of Newburyport,* I, 113–114; Gardner W. Allen, *Our Naval War with France* (Boston, 1909), p. 81; Barriskill, "The Newburyport Theatre," pp. 346–347.
[48] *Herald,* 22 June 1798.

governor in 1799. Newburyport Federalists joined in the scurrilous
campaign against the old patriot, labeling him a "jacobinic partizan,"
and hailing his defeat as a setback for "disorganizing agents." At
the same time Federalist triumphs in local elections signified the
"abhorrence with which Jacobinical principles and practices are
viewed" in Newburyport.[49]

Although by 1800 most of the merchants had become active Federalists, and their hatred of Jeffersonians grew almost daily, as yet they
were not ready for the extreme politics espoused by Alexander
Hamilton and Timothy Pickering. The subtleties of the Adams-
Hamilton feud seemed to go unnoticed, and even the dismissal of
Pickering in May 1800 did not shake the confidence of Newburyporters in the president. Editor March casually explained that the
incident had resulted from "general political motives." In June
Hamilton twice stopped off in Newburyport while touring New
England in search of support for his presidential ambitions. No
public demonstrations greeted his arrival, however, and his embarrassed hosts had to explain that the visits were "unexpected." [50]

As far as Newburyporters were concerned the issue was between
Federalists and Jeffersonians, and the stage was therefore set for a
showdown in the fall of 1800. For by that time most of the town
believed that a vote for a Republican candidate was a vote for France,
and only by undeviating support of the Federalist party could one
advance the interests of one's country.

[49] *Herald,* 9 February, 9 March 1798; 15 March, 2 April, 10 May, 30 August 1799.
[50] *Herald,* 3, 24 June, 1 July 1800.

Chapter VI

FEDERALIST NEWBURYPORT

In the first years of the nineteenth century Newburyport reached its zenith as a Federalist seaport. Beginning with the elections of 1800 a large majority of its citizens rallied around most of the merchants in an unremitting battle against the Jeffersonians, convinced that the issue at stake was whether the atheism and mobocracy of revolutionary France would come to the shores of America. Jefferson had some defenders in Newburyport, but they were few in number and were subjected to constant attack by the Federalist majority. By 1807 Newburyport outwardly symbolized the best of the Federal period, for nearly all its citizens shared in the profits of neutral trade, and its many merchants added daily to their fortunes. But at the same time the Federalists of Newburyport grew steadily more bitter as their party lost strength throughout the nation. Suddenly, with the passage of the Embargo Act in December 1807, they found themselves isolated with other New Englanders in a strange new world dominated by the planters and farmers of the south and west.

The political warfare of 1800 opened in Massachusetts with the gubernatorial election in April. The Federalists counted on Caleb Strong to carry on in place of Increase Sumner, who had died in office the year before after three consecutive victories. The Republicans, in a move demonstrating their political astuteness, nominated Elbridge Gerry, a choice designed to take advantage of his pro-Adams record of the past several years. In fact the old Marbleheader made note of his steadfast support of the president's foreign policy during the campaign, representing himself as the "personal and confidential friend" of Adams. For his part the president pointedly made no move to endorse Strong, a conservative Federalist toward whom he felt little obligation.[1]

[1] Morse, *Federalist Party,* pp. 178–179; William A. Robinson, *Jeffersonian Democ-*

To most of Newburyport's Federalists Gerry's support of Adams seemed to make no difference. He was the candidate of the "disorganizing Jacobins," and that was enough. To one correspondent the world appeared on the brink of collapse. "When the adversaries of our Government and Independence are *active, organized,* and in the *field,*" he warned his fellow Federalists, "is it in character for *you* to be found in your beds? . . . The *Republics* in Europe, it is true, are overturned," he continued, "but the *American* fabric yet stands. Suffer the enemy, by *influencing your State elections* to undermine the Federal Government and the work is done." The United States was about to fall victim of a conspiracy and only the sharpest vigilance could turn the tide. That was not enough, however. "Let all Federal Printers prefer *judicious, weighty, patriotic* communications to juvenile essays and unimportant advertisements. All who love their Country more than *private* gain will cheerfully acquiesce; and those who do not," he concluded, "though they may call themselves *Federalists,* are not true *Patriots.*" And in his concluding clause the correspondent threw down the gauntlet to the moderates in his party wavering toward Gerry.[2]

The fact that Angier March's *Herald* monopolized journalism in town gave the Federalists a distinct advantage. The editor's refusal to print unfavorable material extended even to excluding a list of the Republican candidates for office, while issue after issue carried the Federalist slate in his boldest type. It is difficult, therefore, to evaluate the nature of Republican sentiment in the town during this critical election since no letters favoring Gerry appeared in the *Herald*. But as the results showed, their number was small.[3]

Gerry's fine showing across the state, although in a losing cause, shocked the staunchest Federalists. Winning in Boston and in the eastern part of the state, he nearly made up the 6000-vote plurality which the three western counties of Berkshire, Hampshire, and Worcester gave to Caleb Strong. Obviously a number of voters who had previously supported Increase Sumner crossed party lines to favor Gerry, despite his endorsement by the Republicans. This clearly was

racy in New England (New Haven, 1916), p. 32; Stephen G. Kurtz, *Presidency of John Adams* (Philadelphia, 1957), p. 390; Manning G. Dauer, *The Adams Federalists* (Baltimore, 1953), p. 246.
[2] *Herald,* 1 April 1800.
[3] In 1803 William Bentley reported that the Republican Salem *Register* had only twenty subscribers in Newburyport. Bentley, *Diary* (Salem, Mass., 1911), III, 2.

the case in Newburyport. Contrary to the trend in other parts of eastern Massachusetts, the town gave Strong overwhelming support —236 to 106. But the Republican gubernatorial candidate ran more than sixty votes ahead of the leading senatorial nominee on his ticket, while Strong was twenty-two behind the most popular Federalist senator. Between these two figures is the number of Federalists (or independents) who endorsed Gerry for his pro-Adams record. Newburyport voters nevertheless failed to overcome their rapidly deepening prejudice against the Jeffersonian label, no matter who wore it for whatever reasons. The two-to-one majority they gave Strong set the pace for the rest of the year.[4]

Campaigning resumed in the autumn with the Congressional elections. Political tension mounted steadily throughout the Bay State. In Newburyport's district, the Fourth Middle or Essex North, the retirement of Federalist Bailey Bartlett left a gap in the party's defenses. Choosing a successor proved to be a knotty problem, since none of the regulars showed a willingness to forsake a lucrative law practice or mercantile business for the squabbles of an active political life. The Republicans turned as usual to a member of the Andover Kittredge family. In the middle of the campaign month of October occurred that rarity of political events in Newburyport, the appearance of a pro-Republican letter in the columns of the *Herald*. It was from a correspondent in Andover taking exception to some of the editor's early insinuations that Dr. Kittredge was not a man of "sound political principles." Fearful lest his largess in publishing the criticism should stir up interest in the Republican candidate, March immediately expanded upon his earlier remarks. Kittredge had, in short, opposed the politics of Washington and Adams and held a "cordial coincidence of opinion" with Jefferson, Burr, Gallatin, and company. Imploring his readers to "lay aside prejudice," the editor urged support of the Federalist candidate, despite the fact he had not yet been named.[5]

As election day aproached, the Federalists scrambled about frantically for a standard-bearer. A committee of prominent Newburyport merchants suggested Asa Andrews of Ipswich, while a *Herald* correspondent offered the name of Colonel Josiah Little. "We are

---

[4] Morse, *Federalist Party*, p. 179; *Herald*, 8 April 1800.
[5] *Herald*, 14, 17 October 1800.

authorized to say," assured the writer, "that he is neither a Jacobin nor a *high-toned* Federalist, neither a dupe to the diplomatic skill of Talleyrand, nor a hireling of Pitt." But such moderation was not what Newburyporters wanted, and after Andrews withdrew his name, the local Federalists settled on Manasseh Cutler, minister, land speculator, scientist, and currently member of the General Court from Hamilton. Cutler was the eventual winner, handily defeating Kittrédge in the district and turning in a resounding 284-to-54 victory in Newburyport. Taking the latter figure as the number of hard-core Republicans in town, we can conclude that the Federalists outweighed their opponents by a better than five-to-one margin. Gerry's total in April, twice the normal Republican poll, therefore included some fifty moderate Federalists and independents.[6]

The choice of presidential electors in Massachusetts as in several other states was in a sense anticlimactic. In June the General Court, after a lively debate, voted to alter the method of naming electors. Instead of the voters of each district choosing an elector, the legislature decided to appoint the state's electors itself. One reason for this change, of course, was to eliminate the probability that the two districts which had chosen Republican representatives in the past would select Jeffersonian electors and tip the scales in what everyone expected to be a close election. Another possibility, feared by the Hamiltonian Junto, was that some electors would throw away their votes for Pinckney to assure Adams a first-place position if the Federalists won again. The Junto knew this game well, since they were plotting with southern allies to discard a few Adams votes. Whatever the inspiration for the change, it meant that the real battle for presidential preference in Massachusetts had come in the spring of that year, when the towns chose their representatives to the General Court.[7]

In Newburyport the Federalists had no difficulty controlling the town's new delegation. But sensing the importance of the election a correspondent to the *Herald* cautioned the voters of other towns of the evils ahead should Jefferson win the presidency. "You need not doubt that such alterations will be made," he warned, "not only in the administration of our federal government but in our excellent

[6] *Herald*, 21, 24, 31 October 1800; Town Records, II, 236.
[7] Robinson, *Jeffersonian Democracy*, pp. 34–35; Dauer, *Adams Federalists*, p. 250.

Constitution itself as will throw everything into the utmost distraction." War with England and war at home seemed imminent if the Virginian came to office. But unquestionably the most serious danger came from the character of Jefferson himself, "an open contemner of the Christian religion." There followed a venomous assault on Jefferson the infidel in a vein soon to become familiar in the public prints and private correspondence of New England.

It is absurd to talk of tenderness for a man who has no tenderness for himself. We may, and we *must* detest as well as despise, the base hypocrisy of a man who is daily putting his name to the acts of a government of which he is known to be a malignant enemy. It is forever too late to think of keeping terms with one who keeps none with decency— who has roundly declared his opinion that laws against irreligion and Atheism are a religious slavery, and that it is a matter indifferent to society whether a man say there are twenty Gods or no God!

The writer closed with the direct warnings of the consequences of a Jeffersonian victory. Within a month vice and atheism would stalk the land. The triumph of infidelity would destroy the United States as a Christian nation.[8]

Optimists in Newburyport, as elsewhere in New England, had figured out the mathematics of an Adams victory, despite the foregone conclusion that New York's twelve votes would go to Jefferson. In a breakdown reprinted from the *Columbian Centinel* the *Herald* showed Adams the victor by a 72-to-66 margin. But the editors had not reckoned on the strength of the Republicans in the Carolinas. Their mistake was to expect eleven out of twenty votes from those states to support Adams. Even as late as December 5 the *Herald* editor confidently announced his belief that Adams had won the election.[9]

But before the end of the month, a totally different complexion had come across the political scene. The triumph of Jefferson and Burr was conceded; only one straw of hope remained and some of Newburyport's staunchest Federalists clutched at it. Noting that the tie between Jefferson and Burr called for a settlement in the House of Representatives voting by states, the *Herald*'s editor reasoned that neither candidate would win a majority of the states,

[8] *Herald*, 13 May 1800.
[9] *Herald*, 21 October, 5 December 1800.

if New England save Vermont voted for Burr. "Thus," concluded the ever-hopeful March, "neither of them can be President until after another choice of Electors is made by the People." Before the end of the year, then, at least one Newburyporter had already endorsed the scheme of denying the Republicans their fairly won prize.[10]

All this talk about Aaron Burr confused "A CONSTANT READER." "I wish you, or some of your correspondents would inform me through the medium of your paper who this Mr. Burr is," he pleaded. "What service has he performed, or what talents does he possess, to entitle him to so distinguished an office?" He knew all about Mr. Jefferson, flattering him in fact as a man of superior talents except for his "atheistical sentiments of French philosophy." "But I do wish to know more of Mr. Burr," he concluded.[11]

Some of the leading Federalists found the situation a bit puzzling too, although they must have known a little of Burr's reputation in New York. Writing to Harry Otis in January 1801, shortly after he had moved to Boston, Theophilus Parsons could do no better than to lay down a rather wavering party line for the young representative. In Burr's favor Parsons wrote that "he has no political theories repugnant to the form of the constitution or the former administration." That "his own state is commercial and largely interested in the funded debt" assured Parsons that Burr would be satisfactory on matters of commerce and fiscal policy. Furthermore, "his election will disorganize and embarrass the party who have given him their votes." But Parsons did not quite trust the New Yorker and seemed to sense that he was himself playing a dangerous game. "I am glad that I was not called upon to give my voice on [the] question, the reasons on both sides are so nearly equal, & the consequences . . . are to be anticipated by conjecture only. Were I to decide *today*," he concluded, "probably I should vote for Burr." Otis held firm to the wishes of the Junto this time, along with the other Federalists from New England, including the Newburyport district's representative, Bailey Bartlett. For thirty-five ballots the House was deadlocked. Not until James A. Bayard, casting Delaware's vote, had decided that Burr could not win did he

[10] *Herald*, 26 December 1800.
[11] *Herald*, 26 December 1800.

agree to submit a blank ballot. When the Federalists in Maryland and Vermont followed suit, the Republicans in their delegations put those states in the Jeffersonian column, and the Virginian was named president.[12]

Life under the Jeffersonian regime gave Newburyport editors and letterwriters plenty of ammunition. Laying aside earlier pronouncements concerning the duty of the minority to support its government, local Federalists examined each act of the Jeffersonian administration for evidences of wrongdoing or false principles of government. Despite the triumph of the Republicans the nineteenth century opened on a note of optimism for most Newburyporters. In reviewing the momentous events of the past one hundred years the *Herald*'s new editor, Ephraim W. Allen, could congratulate his fellow townsmen on numerous developments. "Our armies have triumphed over the veterans of Britain; Independence has been established; our fleets visit remotest climes, our national flag commands the respect and excites the envy, of the most haughty powers of the world; and Europe is dependent, to some extent, on the New World for bread." The editor then continued his catalogue of America's accomplishments, including the careers of its most eminent citizens. But dark days were ahead, if the Jacobins were to be given their way. Allen particularly deplored the withdrawal of "the best men in public offices" from the government, "exhausted by their unremitted struggle against secret and open attempts of foreign emissaries and domestic traitors." A complete revolution in government was ahead.[13]

The case against the Jeffersonians had many facets, as it developed in the arguments of Newburyport's Federalists. The Republicans' first sin stemmed from the alleged sectional nature of their party. As early as 1798 "southern democrats" had come in for vituperative abuse in Newburyport. "The planters . . . are generally extremely ignorant, excessively idle, and addicted to all the low vices of drinking, gambling, etc. . . ." a writer claimed. "Supported entirely by the labour of his slaves, under the direction of an overseer, the

---

[12] Samuel E. Morison, *The Life and Letters of Harrison Gray Otis* (Boston, 1913), I, 208–214.
[13] *Herald*, 2, 27 January 1801.

planter reclines at his ease and can live in luxury without any personal exertion." If their slaves should rise in rebellion, "these preachers of anarchy" would be helpless, he continued, "a despicable vagabond with nothing left but his vices, with all the inclination without the means of indulging them." An analysis popular in the Northern press after Jefferson's victory showed that he had gained his office only by the influence of slavery. Editorial writers pointed out that if three fifths of the slaves had not been included in the constitutional basis for Congressional representatives (and thus electoral votes) then Adams would have won 65 to 63.[14]

Many Federalists were simply disturbed by the change of administrations. To them the Jeffersonians were innovators, but perhaps any new party would have been so accused. One annoying aspect of party politics was the idea of turning good Federalists out of lucrative offices in favor of loyal Republicans. Although the same fate had come a decade earlier to Stephen Cross, the antifederalist collector of customs, the Federalists of 1801 acted as though the Republicans had invented the practice. Concrete charges accused the Republicans of promoting southern naval officers ahead of their northern counterparts, with dire predictions of what would happen should the navy fall entirely under the southern interest. To one editor Jefferson's "making births [sic] unconstitutionally for his sychophants" was only one of several charges against his administration. But the Federalists left little doubt about how they would correct these evils when they returned to office.[15]

Perhaps the most hated of all Jeffersonian doctrines among Newburyport Federalists was the idea of democracy. "Why should we be forced to try a Democracy so often tried to the ruin of liberty?" asked a correspondent. "Has it been found practicable to establish the plan of government . . . that the people should rule the rulers?" Federalists of course denied with good reason that the constitution had established a democracy in the first place. As one commentator on the American form of government explained it, "the majority *wisely* give up the government of themselves to the *wiser* minority." This chosen aristocracy then ruled for the people. The case against

[14] *Herald*, 13 March 1798, 6 March 1801.
[15] *Herald*, 6 March, 9 June, 18 August 1801, 16 July 1802; *Repertory*, 31 August, 7 September 1803.

democracy seemed clear enough. Wherever it has been in power, Federalists asserted, corruption shortly followed, by which "the rights of free citizenship are bartered for the beastly enjoyment of a day's debauchery." By the end of 1803 editor Park of the high-Federalist *Repertory* did not take the trouble to dilute his feelings: "We hate democracy—we have opposed it and we will oppose it with all our heart, with all our soul, and with all our strength, and with all our mind; . . . We will never submit to be governed," he concluded, "by a *scape-gallows* rabble." [16]

Probably no event during the first year of the Jeffersonian regime angered the Federalists more than the repeal of the Judiciary Act of 1801. Republicans had not supported the act when it was passed, and they did not hesitate to repeal it soon after they took office. In doing so they struck at the heart of the Federalist power, since Adams had filled the newly created posts with party regulars. The Judiciary Act was the first law to be repealed by Congress, and the Federalists were understandably shocked. Their immediate response was that the action was unconstitutional because it implied an end to an independent judiciary, a principle especially dear to the Federalists since their retirement from the capital. To the editor of the *Herald* repeal was nothing short of "criminally daring." According to one correspondent, then in Washington, the move so greatly disturbed the public there that the sale of land was affected. "Many sober-minded men of Virginia are endeavoring to sell their lands and slaves, and contemplate removing to New-England," he asserted. "From the violation of the Constitution, disunion must, they think, issue [*sic*], and when it shall they mean to be on the safe side of the boundary." Although the turmoil eventually subsided, Federalists ranked repeal of the Judiciary Act as one of Jefferson's most serious offenses.[17]

An even greater storm came two years later with the purchase of Louisiana. Not until July 1803 did news arrive that France had ceded Louisiana to the United States. In a subsequent issue Allen of the *Herald* obligingly supplied his readers with a long geo-

[16] *Herald*, 10 November 1802, 15 March 1803; *Repertory*, 20 August, 19 October, 26 November 1803.

[17] Edward Channing, *A History of the United States* (New York, 1927), IV, 277–279; Morison, *Harrison Gray Otis*, I, 201–202; Dauer, *Adams Federalists*, pp. 324–325; *Herald*, 29 January, 2 February, 5, 23 March 1802.

graphical description of the territory devoid of any editorial comment. By the 15th, the editor could no longer constrain himself from commenting on the treaty. The acquisition of Louisiana was an unquestioned blessing. "It will give to the union the monopoly of the supply of the West Indies with provisions, insomuch that the powers which hold possession in those parts will be obliged from their own interest to cultivate our friendship." The territory would also supply the nation with needed raw materials such as sugar, cotton, and rum. "The possession of Louisiana," he continued, "will render us independent of all the rest of the world in war and in peace." But most important, Allen predicted with well-meaning but unreliable powers of prophesy, "it will afford the means of associating and uniting the hitherto disjointed and sometimes discordant branches of the union." After pouring out his enthusiasm for all the benefits soon to accrue, the editor left for himself a small but fortuitous out. "But then the grand question comes," he ended. *"What are we to pay for it?"* [18]

A correspondent to the town's other Federalist paper, the *Repertory,* was quick to condemn the whole business as a squandering of millions to buy wild lands, or "to purchase a veil for the secret and destructive schemes of a dominant party," as he darkly suspected. By early August Allen began to find his earlier reservation concerning the cost of the purchase a welcome line of retreat. He worried that interest on the $11,000,000 debt was to be paid abroad; he feared that the debt would open us to the aggrandizement of Europe; he concluded that the annual payment of the debt would seriously stunt the growth of his country. But at no time did the *Herald*'s editor paint a picture quite so gloomy as did many of his Federalist colleagues in the press and in letters.[19]

One correspondent wrote the whole operation off as an unwarranted aid to Napoleon and as a political stunt. Others feared that emigration to the new territory would disperse America's population over so great an area as to render protection and government ineffectual. By and large, however, the criticism waned rather quickly in the Newburyport press. Even the scurrilous *Repertory* willingly published in late November part of a letter

[18] *Herald,* 22 February, 24 May, 1, 12 July 1803.
[19] *Herald,* 5, 9 August 1803; *Repertory,* 16 July 1803.

from a member of congress to a gentleman in town: "If we obtain a quiet possession of the Province and a good title, I am disposed to think the price not very extravagant." [20]

The year 1804 was indeed a sad one for Federalists of Massachusetts. For the first time the party of Washington failed to deliver the state's electoral vote to its presidential candidate. Victory in the gubernatorial campaign brought brief comfort in a year which would end with the re-election of the hated Jefferson. So strong had party enmity against the Republican president grown in Newburyport that the *Repertory* by the beginning of the year could actually give preference to Aaron Burr. Quoting from a Washington correspondent's letter, editor Park claimed that "Mr. Burr is certainly a man of great talents and of a clear discriminating intellect. He presides in the Senate with great ease, propriety and dignity." Perhaps Mr. Park was privy to Timothy Pickering's audacious plans for a northern confederacy.[21]

Essex County remained safe for Federalism in the spring, returning a good majority for its senatorial candidates, despite defections in both Salem and Marblehead. Newburyport remained the only seaport firmly in the hands of the Federalists, who maintained a better than 2-to-1 margin for Governor Strong and their senatorial slate. They even looked to a national triumph in the fall, for the Federalist legislature had again altered the method of casting the electoral vote. Each party submitted a list of nineteen electors, and the voter cast his ballot for an entire slate, rather than only for his district elector. With nineteen electoral votes at stake, therefore, the presidential campaign took on new excitement, as Federalists in safe districts strove to get out the vote to balance Republican strength in other parts of the Commonwealth. "Let every Federalist on [election] day quit his shop, his farm, his office, or his counting house, and make everything subservient to the great duty he owes his country." To assist the Newburyport voter, Federalists formed a committee of over one hundred members, including twenty-seven persuasive shipmasters, to distribute ballots in support of the Federalist slate of electors. The outcome, while a victory for the Federalists, was somewhat disappointing. With a 398-to-241 margin over the

[20] *Herald*, 5 August 1803; *Repertory*, 10 August, 26 November 1803.
[21] *Repertory*, 7 January 1804; Brown, *Northern Confederacy*, pp. 25–45.

Jeffersonians, the old guard had lost their once-overwhelming ratio of better than two-to-one. The Republicans, meanwhile, had run up their highest total yet.[22]

When the dismal news arrived that the Republicans had at last won the Bay State's electoral votes, Newburyport's Federalists were crestfallen. The defeat could be explained only by the "unceasing efforts, foul as well as fair, of our opponents." With less than good grace the figures were published. "It is not a very pleasant task to record the triumph of Democracy in this Devoted State," the *Herald* editor admitted. "But it is our duty . . . and we must submit to the degrading task." The Federalists were able to return substantial majorities only in Suffolk, Hampshire, and Worcester counties. Even old Essex went to the Jeffersonians. The bitterest pill was yet to come, for Dr. John Kittredge, son of Andover's oft-defeated candidate and a Republican now resident in Newburyport, won the honor of carrying the news of his party's victory in Massachusetts to Washington.[23]

Newburyport merchants dismayed at the news of Jefferson's re-election could at least find solace in the prosperity which had come to their town in the years since the outbreak of war in Europe over a decade before. By 1807, when neutral trade reached its zenith, Newburyport had achieved a standard of living which all but a few of the colonial generation would have found unbelievable. Population now stood at 7500, a 50-percent growth in the fifteen years since neutral trade began, and the town's total valuation increased fourfold in the same period.

The source of almost all this wealth lay in the expanding business of Newburyport's merchants and of those men who constructed and supported the town's extensive fleet of vessels. From the outbreak of the European war the port's commerce became increasingly concentrated in the transportation of foreign goods, mostly French, to European markets in Holland, Denmark, Sweden, and Russia. This carrying trade operated in two stages: smaller vessels ran down

[22] *Political Calendar*, 16, 23 April 1804; *Herald*, 20 April 1804; Town Records, II, 297, 300, 309; *Herald*, 8 May, 31 August, 2, 4 November 1804; *Political Calendar*, 17 September 1804.

[23] *Herald*, 13, 16 November 1804; *Political Calendar*, 26 November 1804; Bentley, *Diary*, III, 126.

to the West Indies with fish, lumber, and miscellaneous New England manufactures, to be exchanged for the three principal products of the islands: molasses, coffee, and especially sugar. In 1807 ninety-three voyages were made to the Caribbean area. These imports were then entered at Newburyport, duties paid, until enough had accumulated in a merchant's warehouse to make up a cargo for one of his ships or barques to Europe. In 1807 thirteen vessels cleared Newburyport with West Indies produce, to be exchanged in the ports of northern Europe for a variety of European goods, cloths, spirits, and hardware. Only rarely did a vessel return with the full profits from the sale of its outward cargo invested in Continental products. Much of the gain came back in the form of bills of credit drawn on London or Amsterdam. Out of the proceeds from these European voyages, the merchants then purchased more New England goods for shipment to the West Indies, starting the cycle over again.

A typical West Indiaman carried exports worth about $5000 to the Caribbean and returned with sugar and molasses worth in Newburyport around $8000. But when shipped to European markets these goods doubled or tripled in value. By 1807 Newburyport was re-exporting annually to Europe products worth $1,500,000 in American prices. Out of these earnings the merchant had a handsome profit left over after meeting his operating expenses and allowing for such hazards of wartime trade as capture and confiscation by the British and French.[24]

But the rewards from neutral trade did not go entirely to the merchants. In the period 1793–1807 the average adult male's worth tripled to over $5000, while the median value of the inhabitants' holdings rose even more rapidly, from $440 to $1600. In short, almost all the inhabitants of Newburyport had a share in the extraordinary prosperity of the period. Artisans and laborers as well as merchants and professional men realized a revolutionary change in their standards of living, as an examination of the assessor's records will show. The blacksmith Nathaniel Noyes, for instance, near the median in 1793 with a $385 estate, by 1807 was worth $5000. John Libbey, laborer, kept just about even with the general gain, his modest holdings increasing from $165 to $500 during this period.

[24] Compiled from Custom House Records (EI).

Ropemaker John Akerman did almost ten times as well, starting at the same level as Libbey but earning an estate worth $4000 by 1807. Some artisans dabbled in mercantile ventures on the side. Zebedee Cook ran up a fortune worth $30,000 this way from a start of $1665, while still operating his mast yard. One has to search hard for a man whose worth actually declined during the period, though Daniel Johnson, shipwright, was apparently unaffected by the wave of prosperity, his estate dropping slightly from $1650 in 1793 to $1600 in 1807. Had he kept pace with his fellows, he would have been worth about $5000.[25]

The merchants of course gained the most during the period. William Bartlet had increased his worth fivefold since 1793 to just over a half-million dollars, while Moses Brown's wealth nearly quadrupled to over a quarter-million dollars. Several other merchants were newcomers to the list of the town's wealthiest twenty-five citizens. John Peabody, brother of the more famous philanthropist George, had come to Newburyport at the turn of the century and within seven years increased his wealth tenfold to become the town's third richest inhabitant. Even more impressive was Abner Wood's good fortune. By 1807 he had amassed an estate worth nearly $100,000, forty times his 1793 holdings. Altogether over 100 Newburyporters were worth $10,000 or more when neutral trade was at its peak.[26]

One significant effect of this economic growth was a broadening of the franchise. By 1807 92 percent of the town's adult males could fulfill the property qualifications for voting in state elections, in contrast to about 74 percent for 1793. And only a handful of residents could not meet the requirement for participating in town affairs.[27]

Another result was to be seen in the town's physical appearance. Hardly a traveler passed through Newburyport whose journal did not note the grace and charm of its private architecture. High Street, running the town's full length along the ridge behind the wharves and parallel to the river, displayed an elegance unmatched in any

[25] Compiled from Valuation Lists for the Years 1793 (NPL) and 1807 (Assessors' Office, Newburyport City Hall). A 25-percent rise in the price of commodities during this period only slightly modified these gains.

[26] Compiled from Valuation Lists for the Years 1793 and 1807.

[27] Compiled from Valuation List for the Year 1807.

other port save Salem's Chestnut Street, just now beginning to flower. Timothy Dwight in 1800 found that Newburyport's houses made a better appearance than those of any other town in New England. After speaking of the air of "wealth, taste and elegance" which he felt permeating the town, Dwight concluded that "few places, probably in the world, furnish more means of a delightful residence than Newburyport." The Reverend William Bentley, from nearby Salem, was perhaps more critical in his judgment. But even he admitted in 1803 that the Merrimack town deserved the nod when it came to private residences. In fact Bentley conceded that the steeple of the First Religious Society, traditionally ascribed to Timothy Palmer, was among the best in New England.[28]

Kind words for Newburyport's other public buildings were less common. None of the older churches could match the graceful lines of Palmer's designs, and the town's school buildings hardly merited favorable comment. But one new building, the Court House constructed on High Street opposite the head of Green, had a more distinguished pedigree than most, for Charles Bulfinch drew the plans. The Boston architect executed a handsome edifice with an open portico on the ground level, graceful columns and arches supporting the upper story; the structure was capped by a pediment with the figure of Justice. Classical Rome had come to Newburyport and apparently was welcome, for the town willingly shared the building with the county, using it for town meetings and a school for girls.[29]

The Court House was located in a part of town which had just recently been renovated by several civic-minded inhabitants. For many years one of Newburyport's eyesores was the area around Frog Pond, on the westerly side of High Street opposite Green Street. Here a windmill, powderhouse, ropewalk, hay scales, and other buildings had at various times crowded in together without plan or care. A dispute over the title to the ground had raged for years between the selectmen of Newbury and the Port. But in the spring of 1800 Captain Edmund Bartlet, son of the merchant William, went ahead with a donation of $1400 for the purpose of filling up a deep ravine,

[28] Timothy Dwight, *Travels in New England* (London, 1823), I, 400–407; Bentley, *Diary,* III, 44.
[29] Currier, *History of Newburyport,* I, 130–132.

planting trees, and making other improvements in the area. Over the next several years other benefactors gave funds, and the town voted in 1802 to maintain the area, including a tree-lined mall named for the principal donor. Gradually the unsightly buildings came down, the ropewalk to make room for the start of the turnpike to Boston, and the others as new school buildings, a jail, and a keeper's house were constructed. These improvements of course met with great praise from all sides.[30]

Similar innovations changed other parts of town as well. During the first few years of the new century Newburyport spent several thousand dollars leveling streets, constructing sidewalks and gutters, and planting regular rows of poplar and other shade trees along the residential streets. There was even promise that street lights would soon be introduced. The numbering of buildings in the business district had already become a commonplace, although this convenience had not yet spread to the residential areas of town. Generally both individual philanthropists and the taxpayers collectively in town meeting gave a share of their commercial profits to beautify the town.[31]

Inhabitants undertook business projects on an increasingly grand scale. In addition to the operation of corporations earlier established, such as the Essex-Merrimack Bridge and the locks and canals, local merchants combined to launch new schemes. By far the most ambitious during the period was the Newburyport and Boston Turnpike, incorporated in the spring of 1803. Many of the town's prominent businessmen joined together, and stock at first sold widely through the area. The idea of the proprietors was to lay as straight a road to Boston as possible, an ambition which, although successfully accomplished, was one of the turnpike's ultimate disadvantages. This course required extraordinarily expensive construction for the roadbed, with bridges to be built and ravines filled up. When completed in 1806 the pike was an engineering triumph, but within a few years it became a financial embarrassment. Construction costs mounted so rapidly that with the inclusion of toll houses and two hotels the total bill reached nearly $500,000. The route followed,

---

[30] Currier, *History of Newburyport*, I, 124–128; Emery, *Reminiscences*, p. 76; *Herald*, 11 July 1810.

[31] *Repertory*, 10 October 1803.

although seemingly advantageous because of its directness, bypassed all of the larger settlements lying between Newburyport and Boston, such as Ipswich, Beverly, and Salem. Travelers to and from these towns therefore found the new turnpike of little use and kept to the established routes. When Bentley had occasion to use part of the new highway in 1809, he recorded that he found nobody traveling upon it. Stockholders had skimpy returns after annual maintenance costs and tollkeepers' salaries had been deducted. Before mid-century, after ruinous competition from the Eastern Railroad, the turnpike folded as a private operation and its road ultimately became a public way.[32]

Somewhat more successful was the turnpike and bridge to Plum Island. This company, which again brought William Bartlet, Moses Brown, and other wealthy merchants together, was incorporated in 1806, and included the construction of a small hotel on the island for those seeking rest and relaxation by the sea. Those preferring fresh-water baths of warmer temperature in any season of the year had the opportunity to join "The Proprietors of a Bathing House in Newburyport," incorporated in 1807. This group erected a bath house on Unicorn Street open to members every day but Sunday for their refreshment. The usual associations establishing fire societies continued to be popular, four new ones being organized between the turn of the century and the commencement of the War of 1812. The banking facilities in town underwent a change in 1803 with the incorporation of the Newburyport Bank, eventually succeeding the earlier Merrimack Bank. Three new insurance companies appeared on the scene during this same period, including the Phoenix Marine and Fire Insurance Company, incorporated by James Prince and other Republicans in town to compete with the Federalists' Newburyport Marine Insurance Company, established in 1799.[33]

A number of voluntary associations to care for the needs of the distressed and poor were founded during the first decade of the nineteenth century. The most significant was the Merrimack Humane Society, organized in 1802 to reward acts of heroism in aiding

---

[32] H. Follansbee Long, "The Newburyport and Boston Turnpike," Essex Institute *Historical Collections*, XLII (April 1906), 113–128; Bentley, *Diary*, III, 448.

[33] Currier, *History of Newburyport*, I, 378, II, 67–68, 156–159, 164–165.

mariners shipwrecked on Plum Island. Two years later the society erected several small shelters on the outer beach and provided rescue equipment for the town's waterfront. Several ladies formed in 1803 the Newburyport Female Charitable Society for the protection and training of young orphan girls. In 1807 a benevolent association similar in purpose to the Marine Society was organized to aid the town's artisans under the name of the Newburyport Mechanick Association. The incorporation papers of 1810 stated as the group's purpose the encouragement of inventions and improvements of a mechanical nature, financial assistance to young artisans getting established, and relief for indigent workers and their families. Although restricted apparently to working-class members, the society depended upon the professional ranks for its direction. This fact kept the association strictly to business, no political activities diverting its members from economic and social aims. Such was not the case with the Washington Benevolent Society, formed in 1811. However innocuous its title, it became a vehicle for extreme Federalist politicking during the War of 1812. A number of the clergy, financially supported by several merchants and lawyers in Newburyport, formed the Merrimack Bible Society in 1810 for the distribution of Bibles among the poor. Finally, in 1810 also, several of the town's leading citizens joined in the establishment of the Newburyport Athenaeum "for the purpose of promoting learning and diffusing useful knowledge." To this end the proprietors soon put together a library of over 10,000 volumes for the edification of members.[34]

Investment of profits continued to be an important part of the merchants' life—the search for safe and rewarding ventures never ceased. Diversification seemed the wise policy, and Newburyport's capitalists took care not to become too deeply involved in any one corporation. In 1800 William Bartlet owned eighteen shares in the old Merrimack Bank, ten in the Newburyport Marine Insurance Company, and five more in the Essex Bridge. Moses Brown held a similar distribution, plus $6500 in public securities. Timothy Dexter had also found public securities a worthwhile investment, but for the most part Newburyport merchants preferred to keep their money closer to home. Jonathan Gage was one of the few who risked supporting corporations in other parts of the Commonwealth,

[34] Currier, *History of Newburyport*, II, 17, 128–136, 172–173.

with shares of the Portland Bank and a marine insurance company in Boston among his holdings. Many members of the mercantile class from time to time made private loans, and some, following the practice of the Crowninshields in Salem, in effect underwrote the insurance on their own vessels by setting aside the cost of premiums in the event of a loss. But the general pattern by the turn of the century was for these men to pool at least some of their resources under the protection of a state-chartered incorporation to ease the burden of risk and to relieve them of the task of becoming banking and insurance experts themselves.[35]

Progress was by no means a monopoly of the merchants. One of the most distinguished of Newburyport's citizens at the turn of the century was Jacob Perkins, inventor of machines for making nails, for milling coin, and for engraving counterfeit-proof bank notes. His stereotype plates brought him a fair turn of business when banks first appeared, but soon he removed to Philadelphia and later London in hope of greater success. Timothy Palmer, another resident with a bent for engineering, gained a considerable reputation with the construction of the Essex-Merrimack Bridge in 1792, for the design of which he soon after obtained patents. Mariners navigating the river found the bridge a considerable nuisance, however, and Palmer was forced to take a secondary role in the construction of the chain suspension bridge replacing the original span in 1810. In the field of navigation the printer Edmund M. Blunt made two significant contributions with his publication of Captain Lawrence Furlong's *American Coast Pilot* and Nathaniel Bowditch's *New Practical Navigator,* while Michael Walsh earned considerable renown as a mathematician. The art of shipbuilding gained steady improvement in the yards along the Merrimack with one major development coming from the inventive mind of Orlando B. Merrill. His water-line model of each vessel under construction gave the exact dimensions to guide the shipwrights. Newburyport probably contributed no more to the techniques of a gradually awakening industrialism than any other town its size, but at least not all its citizens made their reputations on quarterdecks or in countinghouses.[36]

[35] Valuation List for the Year 1800 (Assessors' Office, Newburyport City Hall).
[36] Currier, *History of Newburyport,* I, 368–370, 493–494, II, 363–368; Morison, *Maritime History,* p. 102.

The range of social activities continued to broaden in the first decade of the nineteenth century. The inveterate clubman had yet another Masonic lodge to join, and those interested in passing their leisure time more informally could blend their voices in good company at one of Samuel Holyoke's singing schools. For the less talented, traveling entertainers increasingly made Newburyport a stop on their tours. The usual educated pigs and philosophical fishes came to town, along with ventriloquists, acrobats, and dramatic readers. But performers of loftier skills also appeared, among them John Bernard with his program of light drama. Unquestionably the high point of public entertainment in the period before the War of 1812 was the arrival of Messrs. Cayetano & Company's circus. For two glorious weeks in the spring of 1811, Newburyporters could at the cost of one dollar for a box seat or fifty cents for the pit witness feats of horsemanship, clowning, tumbling, fireworks, and the rest. Opening night had offered the additional excitement of two young Newburyporters riding disguised in place of two missing members of the company. Some of the old-fashioned members of society frowned on the performance, but "as seat after seat and box after box filled with the wisdom, wit, beauty, and fashion of the town and vicinity," one member of the audience could finally sit back secure in the knowledge that she was in respectable company.[37]

Prosperous though it was, life in Newburyport during the first decade of the nineteenth century had its ugly side. For the divisive scar of partisan politics separated the town into two irreconcilable camps, slashing through business associations, social groups, and sometimes even families. To a good Federalist, any Jeffersonian supporter was at best a fool, at worst an atheist, an enemy to the constitution, and a slave to France. These sentiments were returned in kind by the Republicans, who saw in their political adversaries shades of toryism, monarchy, and aristocracy of the vilest sort. Almost all of the most prominent merchants and professional men supported the Federalist cause, with William Bartlet, Moses Brown, Jeremiah Nelson, Abner Wood, Samuel A. Otis

[37] James M. Barriskill, "The Newburyport Theatre in the Federalist Period," Essex Institute *Historical Collections*, XCIII (January 1957), 1–35; Emery, *Reminiscences*, pp. 259–260.

(Harrison Gray Otis' younger brother), and Edward St. Loe Livermore leading the list. On the Republican side stood the Cross family, joined by Josiah Smith, Benjamin Pierce, James Prince, the Marquands, and the O'Brien brothers. Of the town's twenty-five wealthiest citizens in 1807 at least sixteen were Federalists, while only two are readily identifiable as Republicans.[38]

The Federalists used the fact that almost all the "respectable people" in town supported their cause as a strong argument in their favor, while the Republicans, of course, saw it simply as proof of the aristocratical nature of a party dedicated to the "overthrow of the Constitution" and the establishment of a "hereditary monarchy." When in 1804 the Federalists lost control of Massachusetts, Jeffersonians took great delight in labeling them a "faction," a term particularly annoying to the local Federalists, who were still very much in the majority.

The contrast between Federalist and Republican candidates was often marked. In the contest for state representatives in 1808, for instance, each party offered a full slate. The eight Federalist candidates had had an average wealth the previous year of $44,900, their adversaries but $17,675. The fact that four of the Federalists ranked among the twenty-five wealthiest inhabitants of course pulled the average way up, but even the median worth of the Federalist slate topped the Republican, $29,400 to $12,800. All the Federalist candidates were merchants of considerable prominence save two—a gentleman and a shipmaster. Half the Republican ticket, however, was composed of captains, while three lately arrived "Esquires" and a man of unknown occupation filled out the group. The Federalists won handsomely that year by a margin of nearly four to one. It should be noted, of course, that the Republican candidates were hardly men of low estate. Few working artisans had the time or the hope of success to enter active politics during the period. The line between the office-seekers was rather one between established merchants, lawyers, and their associates, and those still working their way up from the quarterdeck to the countinghouse. This is not to say that all of the Republican candidates were younger but only that the Federalists had generally "arrived" first. Exceptions were the Marquands and the Crosses, whose wealth came during the

[38] *Herald,* 11 November 1804; Valuation List for the Year 1800.

Revolution. Few enough of the Federalists active in politics during this period had attended college, but as far as can be known none of the Jeffersonians had the benefit of higher education.[39]

One can only speculate on the general differences between rank-and-file members of the two parties. In the gubernatorial election of 1807, 600 voters supported the Federalist candidate while 250 voted Republican, altogether about 70 percent of the qualified electorate. This ratio between the parties is typical of most elections during the period, although Federalists had even greater strength in local contests. Some of the shipmasters were Republicans, and a number of merchants too, but most of the mercantile class were staunch Federalists. Just what line divided the large artisan group between the parties unfortunately cannot be known. Apparently most of the shipyard workers in Newbury and Salisbury were Republicans, suggesting that the Federalists were to be found among the more skilled, prosperous, and self-employed artisans, leaving the few marginal laborers and perhaps younger artisans to the Republican ranks.[40]

The split between partisans of the two parties ran through almost every facet of life in Newburyport at the turn of the century. Social fraternization was kept at a minimum; ladies of the opposite factions avoided calling on each other, while their husbands could only with difficulty muster up a civil word for members of the opposition. Theophilus Parsons had once stated that he would never drink wine with a *Jacobin,* and when one of his wife's relatives (a Cross from Portland) came to dinner, the judge was greatly relieved to learn that he was not a French spy as suspected. The divisiveness of party seemed to have a lesser effect on the younger generation, however. Josiah Smith's daughters shared the social limelight with the Misses Wood, Brown, and Tracy. Young Marquand vied for the ladies' favors along with the sons of old Joseph's staunchest foes.[41]

In business the line was even more sharply drawn. Although

---

[39] *Herald,* 10 May 1808; Valuation List for the Year 1807; John Q. Adams and Daniel Kilham had both graduated from Harvard, but had long since moved from Newburyport.

[40] Town Records, II, 347.

[41] Parsons, *Memoir of Theophilus Parsons,* p. 108; Emery, *Reminiscences,* pp. 239–243.

many Federalists originally invested funds in the Newburyport Turnpike, within a few years that project seemed to take on a particularly Jeffersonian aspect. James Prince was one of its Newburyport directors, a position held by no local Federalists. Furthermore, at a Republican Independence Day celebration, a participant saw fit to give the company "the turnpike, may it answer the expectation of the proprietors." Most significant, Salem's Republican minister, William Bentley, seemed to take a paternal interest in the undertaking, praising the directors and lamenting the lack of traffic. Perhaps its financial difficulties partly resulted from a political boycott.[42]

A clearer manifestation of political rivalry in the business community was the establishment of the Phoenix Marine and Fire Insurance Company, under the presidency of James Prince. Prince had been head of the Union Marine and Fire Insurance Company, founded in 1807, but was replaced in an obviously political move by Federalist Stephen Holland in January, 1809. Housed in the four-storied Phoenix Building, the Republican company made a brave effort to compete with the older firms established by Federalist merchants a decade earlier. Under the same roof Ralph Cross moved his custom house and Caleb Cross the Post Office, when those sinecures went to good Republicans. And the fourth-floor assembly room was appropriately named "Madison Hall."[43]

Potentially more serious was the split between the town's "Washington Light Infantry" company, Federalist to the core, and the Republicans' artillery company. Fortunately for all concerned, a pitched battle between the two forces never materialized. But at the annual muster day ceremonies in 1802 Captain Somerby's artillery refused to participate because his group was assigned to a position in line inferior to that which he considered proper. Rather than take any insults from the officer-in-charge, staunch Federalist Colonel Greenleaf, Captain Somerby simply marched off with his troops. By the following spring, however, the dispute had been settled, and the two companies shared the honors at a special

[42] *Herald,* 19 April 1803; *Political Calendar,* 5 July 1804; Bentley, *Diary,* III, 188, 448.
[43] Emery, *Reminiscences,* p. 229; Currier, *History of Newburyport,* II, 158–159; *Herald,* 17 November 1812.

exercise. But throughout the rest of the period before the War of 1812 the artillery remained firmly Republican and the infantry just as strongly Federalist.[44]

Each year the parties faithfully celebrated the Fourth of July at separate banquets. At the Federalist affairs, generally held at Washington Hall, "a large number of gentlemen, consisting of the officers of the Newburyport Regiment, Clergy, and other Citizens of the Town," regularly appeared. The Republicans could hardly match this array of talent at their functions, although the artillery company was on hand to give a salute. In addition to these regular dinners, the Federalists usually appropriated Washington's birthday for a mid-winter fete, while the Republicans countered by celebrating the anniversary of Jefferson's inauguration of March 4, 1801. Toastmasters and other enthusiastic participants at these banquets never missed an opportunity to make a jibe at the opposition. Most of the sentiments were of a particularly sober nature—in support of Strong, Hamilton, Pickering, and other luminaries of the one camp, or to the health of Jefferson and the future of Louisiana for the Republicans. Occasionally a more original toast would be made. One year the Federalists offered "a hard trotting horse, a thin pair of breeches, and porcupine saddle and a long journey to the disorganizers of America." The prickly animal came back at the Federalists when a Republican, not missing the reference to William Cobbett's *Gazette,* volunteered the following: "May those who sicken at the return of this day [July Fourth] have raw hides and cartridge boxes to eat, small beer to drink, and a Porcupine's skin to wipe their mouths." When the Federalists praised both Adams and Hamilton, the Republican editor of the *Political Calendar* chided them for exposing the ex-president to his bitterest enemy. For the most part, however, the celebrants took their politics soberly, and friendly rivalry was a rarity.[45]

Caleb Cross, Republican editor of the *Merrimack Gazette,* wasted no time employing his press to answer the charges made by the Federalists against Republican policies and actions. His first quarrel was with the Federalist press itself. Sadly he reported the conviction

[44] *Herald,* 6 July 1802, 10 May 1803.

[45] *Herald,* 5, 8 July 1803, 4 July 1804; *Merrimack Gazette,* 19 July 1803; *Political Gazette,* 5, 9 July 1804.

and jailing of William Carleton, editor of Salem's Republican *Register,* as the result of a libel suit with Timothy Pickering. Noting with disgust that Federalist editors escaped with impunity "when every column of their papers exhibit a libel upon the general Government," Cross recalled the days of the Adams' administration, when Republicans were prosecuted for statements in opposition to the government no worse than now published by the Federalists. Quoting from an earlier Federalist declaration to the effect that "a good citizen will ever respect his rulers," the Republican editor wondered what had happened to the scripture.[46]

Republicans saw Federalists as plotters against the "American" way of life just as clearly as the Federalists viewed the Jeffersonians in similar garb. "There is a faction in this country that want to prostrate our present form of government," warned "A Republican Gazetteer," "and establish one that . . . would finally reduce them down to the situation of the most abject slave." To the Republicans of Newburyport United Columbia was the best of all possible nations. They seemed almost to feel that Republicans had invented Independence, as they invoked the memory of Hancock and the services of Samuel Adams. Jefferson, of course, collected the highest accolades, not only for his "benign and judicious" administration, but for having saved from ruin what Washington had won in battle. In advancing themselves as the true ideological heirs to the patriots of '76 the Republicans did all in their power to label the Federalists as Tories. "Toryism—never let us forget that those who were once the bane of society, are now the chief pillars in the temple of federalism," ran an 1803 toast.[47]

Even the pulpit was not exempt from the broils of partisan battle. The Congregational clergy had long since established itself as a bulwark of conservatism throughout New England, and Newburyport ministers were no exception. The region had one particularly violent spokesman for the Federalists in the Reverend Elijah Parish. Although his church was in Byfield, town folk often made the short journey to enjoy his harangues against the atheistic Jeffersonians. Country people, for their part, just as often came into town to hear the Reverend John Giles lambaste the Federalists from his

[46] *Merrimack Gazette,* 30 April, 11 June 1803.
[47] *Merrimack Gazette,* 9 July 1803.

pulpit in the Second Presbyterian Church. When political pressure mounted during the Embargo, Giles found his situation nearly untenable. Fifty families left his parish, and he was virtually ostracized by all respectable Federalists for his preachments. By this time, however, many of the citizens had even begun to tire of Parish's extremes, though it was many years before politics left the pulpit in Newburyport.[48]

The Jeffersonians continually complained about the evil political influence of the town's clergy. At their Independence Day celebration in 1803 they exhorted the ministry never to place "their Religion in a party Cockade." In a long letter the following month, a Jeffersonian showed his annoyance further. Admitting that there was probably no plot afoot to unite church and state, he nonetheless strongly objected to the obvious partiality which the clergy showed for the Federalist party. Making use of professional influence to promote the interests of party was culpable. "When they impose party essays on persons, who have paid for religious discourse, I think it an insult," he complained. A more dangerous plot was seen by another correspondent. The aristocrats were endeavoring to stir up civil strife wherever possible, he felt, in order to excite the peaceable into supporting a stronger government. "We venture, then, to assert that we already have all the evidence that there is a powerful combination formed for the establishment of monarchy in America as well as in Europe," he concluded.[49]

One thing that gradually became obvious in the publications of the Republicans was that a number of their party members had been fairly recent converts to the Jeffersonian banner, some at least because of the Hamiltonian betrayal of John Adams. The Republicans' hatred for Hamilton knew no limit, and the editor of the *Gazette* did not hesitate to take full advantage of the split in the opponents' ranks caused by the New Yorker. The result seemed to bring at least some new supporters to Jefferson. "G.S.," on the other hand, switched allegiances apparently because of the Federalist tax policy, which he concluded was unfair and extravagant. The Republicans, he felt, had taken steps to correct these evils and to bring about a policy of equality. Another Republican pointed out that

---

[48] Emery, *Reminiscences*, p. 217; Bentley, *Diary*, III, 417, 427.
[49] *Herald*, 7 July 1803; *Merrimack Gazette*, 13 August 1803.

Adams and Jefferson shared the honors of having made a peaceful settlement with France, the one for the convention of 1800 and the other for implementing it. "These two great Statesmen, (though widely differing in some parts of their policy) are doomed to be honored by the hatred of this abominable sect [the Junto] because they were about equally concerned with depriving it of its darling objects of war and confusion." [50]

As bitter as Newburyport's political wranglings had become by the middle of the decade, the rank-and-file Federalists seemed to be completely oblivious of the more extreme measures advocated by members of the Essex Junto. The first whispers of a secessionist plot appeared in the Republican *Political Calendar* in the spring of 1804. Roundly denouncing the scheme of a northern confederacy, the editor launched a spirited attack on its advocates. The Jeffersonians continued the pressure at their annual Independence Day celebration, at which two toasts specifically urged the continuation of the union "which a Washington recommended and a Jefferson would strengthen." The Federalist press remained silent in the face of these insinuations until January 1805. At that time the editor of the *Herald* did his best to rebut the Republican accusations. Without attempting to deny or defend the plots of Pickering, Burr, and other supporters of a northern confederacy, Allen pointed out that it was in Virginia that threats of secession were first bruited about, during the Adams administration. No evidence has appeared to indicate that any resident of Newburyport took an active part in the scheme, although so much of the Junto's correspondence was destroyed that proof would be hard to find. At any rate, by 1804 the only active member of the Junto from town, Theophilus Parsons, had moved to Boston. The failure of Newburyport's Federalists to endorse the Essex Junto's plan for secession is not surprising. Local politicians had given fairly consistent support to John Adams at the same time that the Junto was scheming with the Hamiltonians against the president's peace efforts. Although some of the town's extreme Federalists went along with the plot to place Burr in the presidency in 1801, not even Theophilus Parsons could muster more than lukewarm enthusiasm. [51]

[50] *Merrimack Gazette,* 9 July, 6 August, 17 September, 10 December 1803.

[51] *Political Calendar,* 28 May, 5, 9 July 1804; *Herald,* 4 January 1805; Brown, *The Northern Confederacy,* pp. 25–27.

A far more serious problem than divisive partisan politics at home had been slowly developing on the high seas during the period of neutral trade. As this trade expanded, more and more vessels were captured by privateers or condemned in admiralty courts, and an increasing number of American seamen were impressed into service aboard the ships of the British fleet. The Federalist press in Newburyport made no attempt to condone these depredations on the part of the English, party politics as yet not stretching that far. The only partisan note interjected charged that Jefferson was not doing enough to defend American commerce from British insults. When the administration finally ordered the construction of a fleet of gunboats, two of which were building on the Merrimack, the editor of the *Herald* roared with laughter. "We may soon expect [the gunboats] to take their flight on the ocean and carry terror and destruction among our enemies. . . . By some it is supposed that they will take some commanding station on the coast of the U.S. to oppose the approach of the British fleet," he snickered. "Some of our good and honest citizens think they are designed to sail on land to keep the Federalists in awe." The editor sarcastically concluded that "the reign of universal peace" was surely about to commence. For their part, the Jeffersonians tried to reap political advantage by playing up the acknowledged Anglophile sentiments of the opposition.[52]

Relations with England became considerably more strained as news of the *Essex* decision trickled into the New England seaports. The *Herald* editor was dismayed. Labeling the principle handed down by Sir William Scott as "unjust, arbitrary, and tyrannical," he objected strenuously to the decision that French colonial goods carried by American vessels were not "neutralized" by being laid on shore in the United States. The doctrine of "continuous voyage," if enforced by the British admiralty courts and fleet, would soon ruin the prosperity which Newburyport and other towns had enjoyed so fully. Newburyporters were made particularly aware of the decision's effects with the seizure of a locally owned ship. *Huntress* had cleared Newburyport on June 15, 1805, bound for Denmark with 1052 gallons of New England rum and 229,352 pounds of brown sugar, a cargo worth about $27,500, American

---

[52] *Herald*, 30 September 1800, 20 September 1803, 26 November 1805; *Merrimack Gazette*, 24 September 1803; *Political Calendar*, 11 February 1805.

prices. *Huntress*'s owners had followed the standard practice of a "broken voyage." The brown sugar had been imported into Newburyport on three different vessels, the brigs *Amazon* and *Juno* from Martinique, and the schooner *Sally* from Guadeloupe, all three islands being in the possession of the French at that time. Altogether the importers received drawbacks totaling $5531 when their sugar was re-exported via *Huntress*. Before the ship could reach Copenhagen, however, it was taken into Yarmouth, England, by a British frigate. As Captain Chase wrote his owners, the reason for the capture given by the frigate commander was that "the greater part of the cargo was the produce of an enemy's colony, and that purchased and imported by an American into the United States did not neutralize the property." Chase reported that at least twenty other American vessels had been carried in under the same directive.[53]

As the crisis deepened, most Newburyporters of both parties closed ranks. Jefferson's Message to the Congress in December 1805 took a strong stand in behalf of American commercial rights. When the address reached town, editor Allen of the *Herald* printed it entire, accompanied by that Federalist's first public words of praise for the Republican president. Although he hastily added that no reader should conclude that the editor approved of all of Jefferson's assertions, he welcomed the stand taken by the president, which "Federalists will view with pride," since they so much resembled those recommended by Adams in May 1797.[54]

The real test for Newburyport and other centers of Federalism came with the British ship *Leopard*'s attack on the American frigate *Chesapeake* off the Virginia capes. When a communication from the Norfolk Committee of Correspondence arrived in town in mid-July, the solidly Federalist board of selectmen immediately called for a special town meeting. Convening on the 17th, the freemen proceeded to appoint a seven-man bipartisan committee to draw up resolutions for consideration. Federalists Enoch Titcomb, Samuel A. Otis, Daniel A. White, and Jeremiah Nelson sat

---

[53] *Herald*, 13, 17, 24 September 1805; Newburyport Custom House Records (EI).
[54] *Herald*, 13 December 1805; Claude G. Bowers, *Jefferson in Power* (Boston, 1936), pp. 330–331; *Herald*, 28 February, 17 March 1807.

down with their Republican adversaries Ralph Cross, Josiah Smith, and William Cross.[55]

The meeting first denounced *Leopard*'s attack as "a violation of our national rights and an insult to our national dignity, no less humiliating than unwarrantable." After praising Jefferson for his "firm, dignified, and temperate policy," the town pledged all-out support in language reminiscent of prerevolutionary days.

Resolved that we unite with our Government in wishing ardently for the continuance of peace on just and honorable terms: yet we are willing and ready to co-operate in the support of any measures, *however serious,* which may tend to secure the honor and safety of our country and *we pledge our lives and fortunes to support the same.*

The resolution then closed with special praise for the patriotic actions of the Norfolk committee.[56]

The political truce started to crumble within two weeks when calmer (and more partisan) heads began to realize how serious was the threat of war with England. In early August "PLAIN DEALING" wrote to the *Herald* that a catastrophe would befall the nation (or at least New England) should war break out. It was the fault of the United States that the incident occurred in the first place, he admitted, for American vessels readily signed aboard mariners known to have deserted from British warships. Had Jefferson not allowed the nation to fall into a defenseless state, perhaps a stronger position could be taken against the British. But the suggestion of a voluntary embargo was foolhardy. Such a scheme, he concluded, could only have been devised by "a disciple of the French school." "PLAIN DEALING's" communication so annoyed the Republicans that one of them, perhaps Stephen Cross, stormed into the *Herald* office to demand the blackguard's name. This, retorted "PLAIN DEALING," forgetting in his anger the main issue, was a bald-faced violation of liberty of the press, "the height of arrogance, insolence, and impudence." [57]

Meanwhile the editor of the Republican Newburyport *Gazette* did not hesitate to take advantage of the Federalists' uncomfortable

[55] Newburyport *Gazette*, 6, 16 July 1807; Town Records, II, 351.
[56] Town Records, II, 351.
[57] *Herald*, 4 August, 11 August 1807.

position. Self-righteously advocating unity in time of crisis, the editor chided those Federalists who showed reluctance to support preparations for war. He singled out one of the recent *Herald* correspondents, IMPARTIALIS, who complained that his fellow Federalists had been duped into passing the recent resolutions of the town. Against him the *Gazette*'s editor employed the effective if unfair "guilt by association" technique. "It would perhaps be considered too illiberal to impute to this and other writers *the crime of advocating the British interest, knowingly, to our own destruction,*" he purred, "but certain it is that *the most devoted servant of the Court of St. James could not utter sentiments more detrimental to the welfare of the U.S.*" [58]

The palmy days of Federalist Newburyport were nearly over. Second-generation merchants had in fifteen years taken advantage of their commercial opportunities to build a rich community on the solid foundation of the past. But they had come to regard prosperity as theirs by right, forgetting that much of their good fortune resulted only from unusual conditions of world trade. In the lean years ahead this attitude would combine with their continued hatred of the Jeffersonians to turn the merchants of Newburyport to embittered and desperate opposition.

[58] Newburyport *Gazette*, 24 August 1807 [italics the editor's].

Chapter VII

TWILIGHT OF FEDERALIST
NEWBURYPORT

For nearly seven years Newburyport's Federalist merchants continued to hate Thomas Jefferson, even though his actions as president had given them less cause for opposition than they had first expected. But with the passage of the Embargo Act in December 1807 and the commercial restrictions which followed its repeal, their worst fears were confirmed, for these policies soon put an end to the profits of neutral trade. Suspecting that the Jeffersonians were motivated by sectional prejudices against New England, the merchants of Newburyport grew more sectional in their own outlook. In the years from 1808 to 1812 they became increasingly isolated from their national government, regarding it by the outbreak of the war with England as a remote authority to which they owed little more than token allegiance.

American merchants had easily survived the rigors of blockade and counterblockade which had been decreed by the belligerents at regular intervals since the spring of 1806. Losses by confiscation and impressment sometimes ran high, but profits ran far higher. The procedure of laying French colonial goods on American shores before transshipment to north European ports had effectively avoided the strictures of Fox's Blockade of April 1806, which had tacitly ignored the principle of the *Essex* decision. The "broken voyage" dodge was back in business. Napoleon's Berlin Decree of November 1806 had no practical effect, since the French navy was no longer a power. And the British Order in Council of January 1807, which prohibited neutral vessels from trading directly between one French-held port and another, had no serious effect on the Yankee's "broken voyage" trade in French colonial goods.[1]

But the British Order in Council of November 1807 was a different matter. All trade in the products of France and her colonies was prohibited, and vessels coming from French-held ports were liable for seizure, along with their cargoes. Only by stopping at a British port, paying duty, and receiving a new clearance could a shipmaster proceed to any port from which the British flag had been excluded. To meet this violation of neutral rights Jefferson turned to commercial retaliation. In his message to Congress on December 18 he requested that body to consider prohibiting the departure of American vessels as a safety measure as well as a means of applying economic pressure on the belligerents, particularly England. Congress acted almost at once, and on the 22nd Jefferson signed the Embargo Act. As amended by two supplementary acts in January and March 1808, the legislation prohibited the export of any American produce or the re-exportation of foreign goods by land or sea. In fact no American vessel was allowed to depart for any foreign port. With the exception of the coastal and fishing trade and voyages abroad in ballast to bring back American property, all maritime activity was summarily halted.[2]

Reaction in Newburyport to news of the Embargo Act came slowly at first. In his December 29th issue editor Allen of the *Herald* published the text of the act and appended his own comment. "This measure has been expected; and although the necessity of it is deprecated by our exporters, yet all things considered," he calmly concluded, "the existing state of things undoubtedly require it." How quickly would this tune change! The merchants in town, as the *Herald* item implied, were somewhat more concerned. Official notification of the Embargo Act did not reach the custom house until the 29th, giving shipowners several days' grace in which to get as many as possible of their vessels to sea with whatever goods they had on hand. Nearly a dozen made it out of harbor before

---

[1] Channing, *History*, IV, 374–375; Alfred T. Mahan, *Sea Power in its Relations with the War of 1812* (Boston, 1905), I, 100–109.

[2] Channing, *History*, IV, 363, 380–381; Louis M. Sears, *Jefferson and the Embargo* (Durham, N.C., 1927), pp. 59–60; *Herald*, 29 December 1807.

the deadline to join about half the Newburyport fleet still at sea on uncompleted voyages.[3]

Embargo affected Newburyport in several ways. By the end of 1808 all but fourteen of the town's vessels had returned home, bringing with them $763,347 worth of imports (in terms of 1807 values), including 2,000,000 pounds of sugar. The town's warehouses were full to overflowing with commodities temporarily worthless to their owners and to the town's inhabitants as well. With the ending of export trade the economic system of the Merrimack Valley ground to a halt. Merchants no longer had any need for lumber, fish, and other domestic articles formerly shipped to the West Indies for sugar and coffee. Nor did they have the cash from the sale of European goods with which to meet their fixed costs such as taxes and maintenance on buildings and vessels, as well as payment of duties on cargoes still coming into port. The collection of unpaid debts owed by town and country storekeepers became an unpleasant necessity. Although rum could still be manufactured, who had the money to buy it? And so this liquid currency, so often used before as a medium of exchange for exportable country products, no longer had a large market.[4]

Much as the Embargo affected the valley people, the act bore heaviest of course on the Port itself. Most of the merchants had a large enough backlog to get them by, but the smaller fellow was trapped. Owners of the many West Indian schooners who made a living by their twice-yearly runs to sugar islands were in serious trouble. Some could go into the coastal trade, but many could not afford the triple bonds which soon were required. A fishing fleet of nearly fifty sail, giving seasonal employment for perhaps 500 men, had similar difficulties. Not all of the owners could post the necessary bond equal to four times the value of the vessel and cargo, and if they did go to the grounds, there was only the domestic market for their catch. At least another 750 mariners who shipped out on the vessels bound on foreign voyages lost their jobs. Of course not

[3] *Herald*, 29 December 1807, 1 January 1808; shipping records compiled from Marine List in *Herald*, 1807.

[4] Compiled from Newburyport Custom House Records (EI); *Herald*, 12 July 1808, 1 February 1809.

all of these men, or the fishermen either, had made Newburyport
their home; many were from neighboring towns and villages. But
with the cessation of commerce, maritime artisans whose trades
involved the construction, rigging, and maintenance of vessels had
little business. Unskilled workers, the stevedores, truckmen, and
common laborers of the waterfront, were thrown out of work.
"Our wharves have now the stillness of the grave," wrote the
Herald's editor. "Nothing flourishes on them but vegetation." As
the town's collective earning power declined, domestic artisans faced
a decreasing demand for their services. The tailor William Vickery,
for example, offered clothing at a 12-percent discount and tailoring
"one quarter cheaper than before the embargo." [5]

The assessor's list did not accurately reflect the stagnation of
business because it evaluated property holdings rather than income. Even so, the growth of the town's collective wealth, which
had increased at the annual rate of $600,000 since the turn of the
century, came to a sudden halt. By 1807 each inhabitant was worth
more than he had been just a few years before, but this fact gave
little comfort to men out of work. In an urban community, dependent on other towns for its food, wholesale unemployment had
more serious consequences than in the country areas. Lacking the
means with which to purchase food, some of the poorer inhabitants
of Newburyport went hungry during the long winter weeks. By
early February 1809 emergency measures had to be taken, and the
town established two kitchens where "good and wholesome Soup"
was made available to the needy. By one expediency or another the
citizens of Newburyport got through the period without mass
starvation.[6]

Newburyporters seemed at first almost paralyzed by the reality
of Embargo, and it was several months before protests began to
be voiced in the public press. But when Timothy Pickering addressed an open letter to Governor Sullivan in March, hinting that
Massachusetts should consider nullification, editor Allen of the
Herald reversed his earlier stand. He urged his readers to study

    [5] *Herald,* 13 May, 15 July 1808.
    [6] Valuation Lists for the Year 1808; Town Records, II, 378; *Herald,* 14 February
1809.

Pickering's letter carefully, not as Republicans or Federalists, but as "Independent Americans," for, he explained, "the party distinctions which have obtained among us, weigh light in his [Pickering's] comprehensive mind." From the middle of March on, opposition to the Embargo Act mounted steadily in Newburyport. In an early editorial designed to arouse his readers' sectional jealousies, Allen called attention to "the undue influence which the Southern states have acquired over the hardy, honest, and industrious people of New England. Look at the comparative insignificance of Massachusetts—and then ask your own hearts, is there not cause for alarm? Is there not real danger?" [7]

One of the first points of friction was the Republican Governor Sullivan's favoritism in granting clearances for coastwise transportation of flour and other commodities essential to survival but also tempting cargoes for surreptitious export. All Newburyport watched when the schooner *Little-Dick*, belonging to the Republican Joseph O'Brien, cleared for Philadelphia to pick up a cargo of flour for Newburyport. "A YANKEE" was infuriated: "I have determined to imitate the example of our Fathers, in refusing to use Tea during the continuance of the duty imposed by the British Parliament," he wrote, "and am resolved that I will consume only the produce of the New England States rather than to purchase a barrel of Flour of any known supporter of Mr. Jefferson's administration." If O'Brien's schooner ever did return with his cargo (no notice of his entrance was listed in the Ship List that year), here was one inhabitant he could not count on for a customer. "A YANKEE" had invited other "friends of our liberties and the enemies of presidential oppression" to join him in the boycott, but the movement received little public attention.[8]

Throughout the year correspondents to the *Herald* attempted to place their opposition to the Embargo on a broader footing than that of the oppressed merchants, whose obvious self-interest might dull the effect of their arguments. "Unexampled distress is felt by every class of citizens; and most severely by those whose 'mouths of labor' stand yawning in vain for the accustomed supply of daily industry," "INQUIRER" pointed out. Not only did merchants and

[7] *Herald*, 15 March 1808.
[8] *Herald*, 10, 20 May 1808.

sailors, joiners, blacksmiths, ropemakers, and truckmen suffer, but the businesses of all artisans were embargoed. "Ask the farmer why his hay brings him but *eight dollars* instead of *twenty four* per ton, which was the price two years ago," he continued. These were the sweeping results of Jefferson's Embargo. "A NEW-ENGLAND MAN" also appealed to the farmer for support of the merchants. "While commerce was flourishing, there was not a spear of grass, nor a hill of potatoes in all the country, but might in some form find a profitable market," he stated, establishing the "we're-all-in-it-together" approach.[9]

Another correspondent widened the appeal for opposition still further. Addressing "MECHANICKS AND FARMERS" as the people who had voted the supporters of Washington and Adams out of office, "MARCUS" asked them why they should believe, as they had been told, that Federalists were their enemies. "Do not they [Federalists] pay as much for your work, and as punctually, as any class of men —do not they *very* often help you when in distress—and are they not as worthy of your confidence as the Democrats?" Striking to the root of Jeffersonion strength in the region, "MARCUS" asked the shipbuilders of Salisbury and Amesbury, "who are so much enamoured of Mr. Jefferson, whether they build more ships now and if they bring higher prices than they did under the Adams administration . . .? Mr. Jefferson would see them *all* starve," he concluded, "before he would have another vessel built on the banks of the Merrimack."[10]

Needless to say, the Republicans were hard-pressed to defend a policy so oppressive to the pocketbooks of local constituents. In Newburyport Republican Nathaniel Cogswell, in a Fourth of July address to his fellow Jeffersonians, labeled the Embargo a wise and necessary measure, "the *only alternative* between us and a war." No act, he bravely concluded, "had done more honor to his [Jefferson's] head and to his heart." It was the same Cogswell who optimistically wrote the president a week later that there was some hope that voters in Newburyport, "the cradle of the Essex Junto and which has been emphatically called the political Algiers of America," would eventually support Republican candidates "in

[9] *Herald,* 12, 22 August 1808.
[10] *Herald,* 26 August 1808.

preference to those who are the open and avowed advocates of Monarchy." [11]

One of the common arguments used by the Republicans to defend the Embargo Act was that Jefferson was simply trying to protect the American merchant from losses and seamen from impressment or worse. The Embargo was really harmless, this line of reasoning concluded, since there were no areas of the world in which the Americans could safely trade because of the combination of the British Orders in Council and the Napoleonic Decrees proscribing neutral commerce. To this assertion the Federalists had a justifiable retort. A letter reprinted from a Norfolk paper pointed out numerous areas of the world still open to neutral shipping, listing among others the Swedish West Indies, Africa, the Atlantic Islands of Portugal, Spanish colonies in America, most ports in the Orient, and Near East ports of Turkey, the Levant, and Egypt. The original writer estimated that trade with these areas had before the Embargo Act amounted in value to nearly twenty-five million dollars. Another reprinted article, this one from the Salem *Gazette,* noted that at least ten vessels would soon sail from that harbor by "special permission" to foreign ports. "This, by the way, gives the lie to the executive reason for laying an embargo—the danger of being captured. It is evident the President thinks there is no danger," the Salem editor concluded. The fact that ten of the eleven vessels to clear Newburyport at the last moment before the Embargo had returned safely home gave the opposition still more evidence.[12]

The Federalists' argument that neutral trade could flourish and still avoid the clutches of the belligerent powers gained great momentum with the startling news of Spain's revolt against Napoleon. When Britain lifted her Orders in Council as to Spain and Portugal, the Federalists suddenly saw their opening. Wrote one correspondent to the *Herald,* "Were it not for Mr. Jefferson's 'strong, wise measure'—not only our fish, flour, and corn, but all kinds of colonial produce might be brought to a ready market. But while America is oppressed with such politics and politicians,

---

[11] Nathaniel Cogswell, Esq., *An Oration Delivered before the Republican Citizens of Newburyport on the 4th of July, 1808;* Nathaniel Cogswell to Thomas Jefferson, 11 July 1808, Jefferson Papers (LC).

[12] *Herald,* 26, 29 July, 6 September 1808.

as now afflict our land," he gloomily concluded, "we can only look on, and behold other people reaping the fruits of the folly of our rulers!" [13]

The merchants of Newburyport, calling a town meeting for August 9, could not let slip by this opportunity to argue the lifting of Embargo. As its first step the "unusually numerous" meeting at Newburyport appointed three Federalists, Daniel A. White, Joseph Dana, and Enoch Titcomb, to draw up a petition for presentation to President Jefferson. The resolution, unanimously adopted by the voters, including many "heretofore styled democrats," opened with a respectful account of the onerous effect of Embargo on the prosperity of the town. Citing their large interest in shipping, the townspeople's dependence on commerce, and the perishable nature of their principal exports, the authors wrote that they could not contemplate the Embargo's continuance without the most serious apprehensions. With less than complete accuracy the petitioners put themselves in the best possible light: "they flatter themselves," it was claimed, "that they are and ever will be ready to manifest their patriotism in making every necessary sacrifice for the good of their country and they have yeilded [sic] to these laws unlimited respect and submission, whatever differences of opinion may have existed as to their expediency or constitutionality." Noting that the law empowered the president to suspend the Embargo in whole or in part whenever he thought changing events in Europe had made such action safe and expedient, the memorialists came to the point:

Spain is emancipated . . . and an immediate peace of course takes place between that nation and Great Britain, and Spain with her immense colonies to which we may also add Portugal and her dependencies, will now invite to a commerce interdicted by no decree or orders of the belligerents, a commerce beyond example important to Americans.

The resolution then closed with magnificent nobility: "Your petitioners cannot deny themselves the pleasure of congratulating your excellency on the pleasing opportunity which you now have of restoring to your suffering countrymen the blessings of commerce." [14]

[13] *Herald,* 9 August 1808.
[14] Town Records, II, 368–369; *Herald,* 19 August 1808.

At the end of the meeting, the town appointed a committee of correspondence to communicate the proceedings to other towns, to confer with their committees, and to request their concurrence "on such measures as may seem calculated to effect a removal of our embarrassments." In addition to the three men who drafted the petition to Jefferson, the merchants William Bartlet, Moses Brown, Abner Wood, William Coombs, and lawyers Jeremiah Nelson and Ebenezer Moseley stepped out to lead the town during the present crisis.[15]

The inhabitants of Newburyport continued their attack on the Embargo while waiting for a reply from the president to their petition. A strong note of impatience, implicit in the town's appointment of a committee of correspondence, crept into many letters to the *Herald*. In answer to his own question asking what must be done, "CIVES" walked a dangerous tightrope. "We must be loyal to the extent of loyalty. But we must obey God, rather than rulers, when they manifestly depart from the line of conduct pointed out by God in the bill of rights." Without hesitation "CIVES" continued: "if administration says we must wage war with Britain to gratify France, we have an inviolable right to demur." After a long passage in which he explained that God had intended his country for commerce, as evidenced by its extended coastline, "CIVES" asked those Americans who preferred connections with France rather than with England "to examine whether it be best to be found fighting against God." His conclusion was ominous: if petitions, entreaties, and beggings for relief are denied, "we can submit, if it be not strictly constitutional, to do something more. But it is needless for me to hint at appropriate measures. The wisdom of the public mind when aroused and collected, will easily concert proper measures." [16]

To others the Spanish revolt was the signal for renewed invective against France, and by implication of course the Jeffersonian administration. "AN OLD WHIG" warned that the United States would be next on the "PRINCE OF MONSTER'S" list, while several other correspondents took pride in an alleged similarity between the American Revolution and the Spanish. "The real friends of the American

---

[15] Town Records, II, 368.
[16] *Herald*, 9 August 1808.

Revolution must cordially wish that the Spanish people may be successful," asserted one. The editor of the *Herald* denounced the Republicans for their apparent disapprobation of the Spanish cause: "They wish the subjugation of Spain by Bonaparte; in hopes he will be the better able to conquer Great Britain," he stated. Allen in fact claimed that the Jeffersonian administration had planned to go to war with England in alliance with France. Bonaparte was to guarantee Canada and Florida in return for a Franco-American alliance. This "daring scheme of the Cabinet had been frustrated [only] by this untimely opposition of the Spanish patriots." [17]

On and on went the protests, three, four, and sometimes five letters in each issue of the *Herald*. It was not just the catastrophic economic issue which angered the Newburyporters; the restrictions on freedom rankled every bit as bitterly. The utter waste caused by the Embargo, in manpower, wealth, and national resources, was an immoral violation of the first principles. And the law's enforcement by government officers, without any authority derived from the Embargo Act, was in direct violation of all justice—"wanton tyranny." But what infuriated the trade-conscious citizens of Newburyport more than any abstract issue of liberty as such was the continuing existence of a tantalizing, profitable trade with the nonbelligerent areas of the world. If Jefferson's only reason for the Embargo was to protect American vessels, seamen, and merchandise, why then had Congress passed four acts to prohibit domestic as well as foreign commerce, "not only from one state to another, but from one port to another in the same state, and even from one port of the same river and lakes to another. . . . Are our sloops and boats on the lakes of our country . . .," a correspondent asked, "in such jeopardy, either from England or France, as to require such Bonapartean 'protection?'" To this observer the conclusion was obvious. Jefferson's design in laying the Embargo was to bring about his "long cherished, and darling object, the utter destruction of our northern commerce." [18]

The president would not consider a partial suspension of Embargo. This he made clear in his reply to the Newburyport petition, which arrived in town at the end of August. "To have submitted our

[17] *Herald*, 12, 16, 22 August 1808.
[18] *Herald*, 12, 16 August 1808.

rightful commerce to prohibitions and tributary exactions of another would have been to surrender our independence," he stated. Jefferson made it clear that one reason for the Embargo was to force a change in the belligerents' policy toward American commerce. "[The Embargo] has the peculiar advantage of giving time to the belligerent nations to revise a conduct as contrary to their interest as it is to our rights." Jefferson carefully stressed that Congress ("those delegated to exercise the power of legislation for you") had enacted Embargo and that only Congress could remove it. Since no suspension of hostilities or change of measures affecting neutral commerce had come about, Jefferson concluded, he was powerless to suspend the law.[19]

Although they could hardly have expected anything different, Jefferson's reply came as a great disappointment to the petitioners of Newburyport. "WE asked for bread and, alas! he has given us a stone," lamented "BRUTUS." Discounting the president's arguments as "trivial," the correspondent thought he knew the real reason why the town's petition was so ineffectual. "Is it possible," he asked, that "there are miscreants among us who have endeavoured to counteract the wishes of the people. . . . It has been said that such there are in this town and that a counter-representation was sent by them to the President." With all the fury of a frustrated partisan, "BRUTUS" then thundered a warning to his unknown tormentors. "Hide your heads, at least conceal your names, you fraticides [sic], lest the vengeance of your injured country overwhelm you!" Nor did he have any doubt as to the origin of the Embargo. "Bonaparte dictated the measure, or at least, something for which this was substituted." With a rare realism ironically directed to Jefferson, "BRUTUS" concluded: "Could he expect that we should forever reap the golden harvest of commerce without difficulties and dangers. . . . For many years we have grown fat on the blood of Europe, guiltless of shedding a single drop of it; but we must expect and prepare for harder times," he warned.[20]

One of the most frequent arguments advanced by the Federalists, especially during the latter half of the year, claimed that the Embargo was unconstitutional. "HAMPDEN" asserted that no one in the

[19] Town Records, II, 370–371.
[20] Herald, 13 September 1808.

Massachusetts convention would have voted for ratification of the constitution had it been known "that some Southern party at a future day, feeling envious of our greatness . . . might acquire a majority in Congress, and by means of this power might immediately drive us from the ocean." To "ARISTIDES" the proof of unconstitutionality was somewhat more difficult. In fact he opened his communication to the *Herald* with an interesting discussion of who had the power to annul laws of Congress. Dusting off a clause of Jay's Treaty which made permanent the right of free crossing of the border between Canada and the United States, he pointed out that the Embargo violated this treaty. But since treaties were the supreme law of the land, "ARISTIDES" concluded the Embargo Act was therefore unconstitutional. At about the same time, however, the Federalist Judge Davis ruled the law constitutional at the September session of the Massachusetts district court in Salem. Federalists throughout the state were dismayed but not convinced.[21]

The fact that 1808 was an election year intensified the issue of Embargo as autumn approached. The Federalist campaign opened officially on September 30 with a testimonial dinner for Timothy Pickering, whose open letter to Sullivan the previous spring first suggested the doctrine of nullification to the New Englanders. According to editor Allen the occasion expressed "our veneration of [Pickering's] pure and unshaken patriotism; patriotism which Rome in her proudest days would have delighted to honor." Perhaps the Federalists of Newburyport were unaware of Pickering's plan of 1804 to take New England and New York out of the union to form a separate northern confederacy. More likely, they defined "patriotism" as loyalty to New England, rather than to the union. While the Federalists honored Pickering with a banquet, the Republicans marked the occasion by hanging him in effigy, "accompanied by all the usual appendages and embellishment."[22]

Some of the leading Federalists worried that they would suffer at the polls unless steps were taken to counteract the growing image of their party as the advocate of disunion. Although the Newburyport *Herald* never breathed a word of secession during Embargo,

[21] *Herald*, 23 September 1808; Walter W. Jennings, *The American Embargo, 1807–1809* (Iowa City, 1921), pp. 123–124.
[22] *Herald*, 4 October 1808.

other Federalist papers had, and for the benefit of its Republican readers, the Newburyport *Statesman* compiled a handy sample of disloyal sentiments from other towns. From the Boston *Gazette* came the most damning of all: "It is better to suffer the amputation of a limb than to lose the whole body. We must prepare for the operation." He might also have included from the Salem *Gazette* the question: "What charms can a *union* have for New England, if all her commerce by land and water . . . must be sacrificed? She wishes to preserve the Union, she wishes also to preserve her own rights." [23]

Essex Federalists had already taken a first step to improve their party's reputation. George Cabot and other moderates called for a party convention to adopt some sort of resolution stressing "the importance of maintaining the Union inviolable under every trial." What the moderates got when the delegates convened at Ipswich in the autumn of 1808 fell far short of this mark. "We firmly rely for relief on the wisdom and patriotism of our STATE GOVERN-MENT, whom the people have placed as sentinels to guard our rights and privileges. . . . We trust that *they* will take care that the Constitution of the United States be maintained in its spirit as well as in its letter." This implicit suggestion of nullification of the Embargo Act probably came from Pickering, who was unofficially present at the convention, and most likely had the endorsement of the Newburyport delegation, the largest sent by any town.[24]

The election for representative from Essex North could hardly have been in doubt (Newburyport's Edward St. Loe Livermore was standing for re-election against the perennial loser, Republican Thomas Kittredge). But the opportune arrival of a rumor from New York to the effect that France had declared war against the United States further aided the Federalist cause. "We cannot but believe the news to be substantially correct . . ." announced the *Herald*. "We firmly believe that War at this moment exists between France and America." In the same issue that he published the war rumor the editor bore down relentlessly on the local Jeffersonians. "It is a pitiful expedient our democrats have hit upon to do away

[23] Harvey P. Prentiss, "Pickering and Embargo," Essex Institute *Historical Collections*, LXIX (April 1933), 126; Newburyport *Statesman*, 13 October 1808.
[24] Prentiss, "Pickering and Embargo," pp. 126–127; *Herald*, 11 October 1808.

the truth of the important news of Bonaparte's having declared war against us in saying it is an 'electioneering trick.'" If Allen was playing a game, he played it well, for he concluded his chastisement of the Republicans with the expectation of Bonaparte's manifesto by the "first arrivals." "That will be a precious document, and we mistake if it does not make some long faces."[25]

Choosing Federalist representatives and casting electoral votes for Pinckney was not enough to save New England from the oppressive Embargo, and the Federalists knew it full well. When Jefferson dismissed the protests of New England towns with the comment that only the Congress could lift the law, the Federalists were at first slow to react. But when one of their own judges could find no grounds for ruling the Embargo Act unconstitutional, appeal to Congress was the next logical step. In November, shortly after Election Day, the Federalists of Essex North circulated through their district a petition to Congress requesting repeal of the odious legislation. Newburyport's 803 signatures topped the list, and it was forwarded to Edward Livermore for action. Relief could not come fast enough. Hatred for Embargo and its administrators mounted daily, enflamed by letters to the press and the circulation of anonymous handbills. One of these, apparently published in November, proclaimed that "the day of political probation is fast verging to a close." The tract continued: "Let every man who holds the name of America dear to him, stretch forth his hands and put this accursed thing, this *Embargo* from him." Be resolute, the writer urged. "Nerve your arm with vengeance against the Despot who would wrest the inestimable germ of your independence from you—and you shall be *Conquerers!!!*"[26]

When the anniversary of the Embargo Act came in December, towns throughout New England publicly mourned the occasion. In Newburyport was held one of the most expressive demonstrations. Church bells tolled at intervals throughout the day, accompanied by the firing of minute guns, a signal of distress, with the flags of the mercantile fleet at half-mast. A procession of sailors, each the "bloodless image of despair," with mourning bands on their arms

[25] *Herald,* 28 October 1808.
[26] Baltimore *Evening Post,* 1 December 1808, quoted in Jennings, *Embargo,* p. 153.

paraded through the streets to muffled drums. Following along behind was a "ship dismantled. Her yard a cock bill, a bell tolling in her bows, and her masts capped by inverted cans, denoting the want of grog." A flag inscribed *"Death to Commerce"* between her main and mizzen shrouds symbolized a ship in dry-dock. On the bow was the inscription "O grab me" and at the helm stood an old sailor who inquired in the words on her stern: "Which way shall I steer." The vessel and convoy came to a halt opposite the custom house, from which a flag was flown representing a terrapin, its head drawn into its shell "in *most dignified retirement.*" There a sailor delivered an address, written by himself, which went to the hearts of the crowd of spectators on hand.[27]

The gloomy nature of the proceedings depressed editor Allen, he reported in the next day's *Herald*. But the event also made him even more embittered against those who had approved Embargo. Apparently angered by taunts from the town's Republicans that the parade had rather few spectators, the editor exploded. "It is too much, for those who have ruined us by their oppression, to insult us with their malevolence. Let not those who have hurried us to the precipice," he warned with measured words, "complain that we tremble on its verge; and those who have stretched us on the rack accuse us of writhing under its tortures." [28]

As each winter day passed without word of repeal from Washington, the tension in Newburyport became almost unbearable. On January 12, 1809, a meeting was called to draw up resolutions expressive of the town's sentiments and to memorialize the General Court. Although the resolutions spelled out the town's opinion of Embargo, they were moderate in nature and even concluded with the assertion that redress should be sought by "legal and constitutional" means only. Adopted by a meeting described as the largest ever assembled in town, these orderly resolutions were communicated to the inhabitants of other towns for their concurrence.[29]

At the same meeting, however, a committee of nine Federalists drew up a far different document for submission to the General Court. After reviewing the glories of commerce under the benevo-

[27] *Herald*, 23 December 1808.
[28] *Herald*, 23 December 1808.
[29] Town Records, II, 372–373; *Herald*, 13 January 1809.

lent administrations of Washington and Adams, the memorialists denounced the Embargo as a measure "produced by foreign influence, by a dishonorable subserviency of our own government to France." In their present distress the Newburyporters turned to their state legislature as a last resort. "To your honorable body our constitutional sovereign, the depository of all the powers not expressly delegated to the general government, we make our earnest and solemn appeal." With the basis for a doctrine of nullification thus laid the memorial came to the heart of its plea. "The constitution and the people have invested you with the authority and imposed on you the obligation to afford them relief, protection, and redress. We therefore implore your honorable body to interpose in our behalf and to adopt such measures for our relief . . . as may be compatible with the honor and dignity of the commonwealth, and with the Constitution of the United States." [30]

Newburyporters had petitioned the president to permit trade with the nonbelligerent world. They had memorialized Congress to lift Embargo. They had begged the General Court to nullify the act in Massachusetts. And still their trade stagnated, their ships rotted, and their inhabitants went hungry. With the disclosure of the administration's latest attempt to make Embargo more effective, the Enforcement Act of January 1809, their patience snapped. Editor Allen gave hint to the temper of his fellow citizens. "Eternal heavens! Where is the Yankee . . . who could bear to be abused and ridiculed by Virginian boys? Being suckled by slaves, pampered in indolence, and effeminate by indulgence! Can New England, rich in intellect, and knowledge, and wealth . . . support this forever?" No, was his resounding answer, "the time will come if these grievances are not redressed when a spirit, daring and uncontrollable, will burst out in a just and powerful resentment." [31]

For Newburyport that time nearly came on January 20, 1809. At a fully attended meeting of the town called three days prior to a similar protest session in Boston the inhabitants resolved not to assist in any way the execution of the Embargo laws and to consider those who did "*violators* of the Constitution of the United States, and of this Commonwealth, and that they be considered as

[30] Town Records, II, 373–374.
[31] Herald, 17 January 1809.

unworthy of the confidence and esteem of their fellow-citizens." Four days later more than 200 of the men exempt from military duty, those over forty-five, met to organize themselves into an armed guard. Those joining the "Silver Greys," as the company soon came to be called, agreed to provide themselves with musket, bayonet, and twenty-four cartridges and to be ready "to support the Constitution of their country and defend their rights and privileges." At the same meeting the merchants labeled as enemies to their country all those who offered for charter or served aboard vessels which the thirteenth section of the act empowered the president to hire for enforcement purposes.[32]

The similarity between these proceedings and the preparation for revolution thirty-five years earlier was not lost on the citizens of Newburyport. The editor of the *Herald* wrote of how town meeting on the 12th had spoken with the "spirit of '74." In keeping with the analogy Federalists began referring to those who sympathized with the government as Tories, reserving the Whig label for themselves. Wrote Allen in February, "The Tories of Newburyport have had a nightly caucus to plot and plan against the *Federalists,* the genuine Whigs of the present day." [33]

With evident nostalgia for the good old days one correspondent wrote of the "electric spark . . . [which] passed with the rapidity of lightning through every link of union, and filled a battery, which stunned the British lion." May a similar spirit animate the men of New England, "OLD WHIG" fervently wished. "Let us leave no possible legal method untried," he cautioned, "but if *force* to *force* must be the dreadful result . . . [may] our hands possess a nerve, and our hearts be inspired with a spirit that shall not shrink, so long as the last vestige of tyranny defiles our land." When on February 10, 1809, the town appointed a twenty-man committee of safety and correspondence "to watch over the interests and safety of the inhabitants," the analogy was nearly complete.[34]

While some were preparing to use force if necessary to resist the

[32] *Herald,* 24 January 1809; Jennings, *Embargo,* pp. 56, 58; Bentley, *Diary,* IV, 454, declared that the Silver Greys armed "in a most menacing attitude to their country." A list of 204 names, with neither title nor date, in the Essex Institute apparently bears the original signatures of the subscribers.

[33] *Herald,* 17 January, 21 February 1809.

[34] *Herald,* 27 January 1809; Town Records, II, 380.

execution of the Embargo laws, at least one inhabitant laid the theoretical basis for secession as a last desperate measure to preserve citizens' liberties. Writing to the *Herald* in February and March, "CONSTITUTIONALIST" explained the evolution of the present form of national government. The government under the Constitution of 1787 was not an association of the people but of states. The people had had no need for a general popular government; they had their recently adopted state governments. As proof of its federative nature, he described how the constitution had been adopted. "By states it was accepted in convention, and by the states it was finally ratified." Whatever popular features were included came simply as the result of compromise, he explained. "From this view of the constitution . . . it follows, that whenever its provisions are violated, or its original principles departed from by a majority of the states or of their people, it is no longer an effective instrument, but that any state is at liberty by the *spirit of that contract* to withdraw itself from the union." "CONSTITUTIONALIST" fervently hoped that separation would not be the result, but the doctrine was there if needed.[35]

Embargo ended more abruptly than it had begun. The first inkling for most Newburyporters came when the *Herald* under the heading "WORSE THAN EMBARGO," published the text of the Non-Intercourse bill, then in Congress, on February 24. Oddly enough the Non-Intercourse Act provided almost precisely those conditions of trade for which the Newburyporters themselves had pleaded the previous summer: throwing open the ports of the world to American vessels, with the exception of the belligerents England and France. Even more ironic was that the congressman from Essex North, Newburyport's Edward St. Loe Livermore, was one of only two Federalists to cross party lines in support of the new measure. No celebration marked the end of Embargo, no grudging admission in the press that things would now be better. In his annual Fast Day sermon the Reverend Samuel Spring labeled the "partial repeal" of Embargo "a mere snare to commerce." But the merchants took what was offered them, and by March 15, when repeal became effective, several vessels were ready for sea.[36]

[35] *Herald*, 3, 24 February 1809.
[36] *Herald*, 24 February, 24 March 1809; Sears, *Jefferson and Embargo*, pp. 190–196;

A month later the *Herald* editor had better news for his readers, publishing the correspondence between David Erskine and President Madison in which the British minister promised the withdrawal of the Orders in Council in respect to the United States. This announcement and the president's proclamation of April 19, permitting the renewal of trade with Great Britain as of June 10, was greeted in Newburyport with ringing of bells. At last the Republicans had come to their senses. Allen could even find words of praise for the new executive. "There is hope, that through Mr. Madison, the wounds of our country, from party spirit, may be healed." Lawyer Daniel A. White rang the same note in a letter to a friend. "Mr. Madison to be sure thus far manifests a disposition which deserves the praise of federalists, and seems calculated to amalgamate the parties." But White was not so optimistic about the president's prospects of success in ending partisan strife. Nothing but a "bitter party president" will satisfy the Republican leaders, he feared. "No sooner, therefore, does Mr. Madison merit and continue to receive the praise of federalists (which by the way I have little expectation will be the case) than he will be denounced by the Democrats." The Federalists' Fourth of July orator took the same line. While approving the president's candor as an "earnest of his independence and promptitude," he considered it the duty of all Federalists to guard against sinking "into easy credulity and deception, negligence and ruin." [37]

Other Federalists were even more begrudging in their praise of Madison's action. One correspondent to the *Herald* allowed that had the president not accepted Erskine's offer "he would have exhibited the absurdity, the criminality of Jefferson and have been perjured by every line of his inauguration oath." Americans have been so used to "every species of villainy" in the executive department that they begin to regard any example of "common honesty as a miracle." Although admitting Madison to be a man of integrity, "a saint if not a sage" when compared with Jefferson, the

---

Two Sermons Addressed to the Second Congregational Society in Newburyport, April 6, 1809, by Samuel Spring (NPL).

[37] *Herald*, 28 April, 19 May 1809; Daniel A. White to James Richardson, 19 May 1809, White Papers (EI); *An Oration Delivered at Newburyport on the 34th Anniversary of American Independence . . . by William Bannister, Esq.* (NPL).

correspondent cautioned his readers against letting the enthusiasm of the moment persuade them that Madison was really a Federalist without foreign partialities. "We were deceived . . . [if we believe] that he is anything more or less than the same James Madison, who opposed the British treaty, and advocated a system of commercial restrictions." [38]

On the evening of June 9 the town let go the accumulated frustrations of the previous eighteen months with a resounding celebration to mark the end of the Non-Intercourse Act in respect to Great Britain. The Blunt building on State Street was illuminated with more than 300 lights while on the roof a large sign proclaimed "TRADE AND COMMERCE RESTORED," topped off by an American eagle and flag. Another transparency, hung across State Street from the custom house building to the one opposite, depicted the auctioneer knocking off "the whole posse of gunboats, piled up in a heap . . . in lots, to suit purchasers." Some two thousand spectators enjoyed the scene, and the next morning the town's bells were rung. As the *pièce de resistance* a federal salute was fired from one of the wharves, "the last gun wadded with Jefferson's embargo acts and proclamations." Newburyporters and the nation's merchants would go on, deluded but happy, for just six weeks more before learning that Canning had disavowed Erskine's Agreement.[39]

When Madison announced the re-establishment of Non-Intercourse in mid-summer, Newburyporters were at a loss to understand what had happened. At first they were willing to blame the British. "Either Mr. Erskine must have mistaken or misconstrued his instructions or Mr. Canning has sacrificed the faith of the British nation," concluded editor Allen in July. Three weeks later the editor was still trying to determine what had gone wrong, and he continued to resist laying all the blame on Madison. The Federalists in town for the most part accepted the news with good grace. "Many seem not merely content with bestowing praise upon the President for his cool, dignified and temperate conduct; but are willing to go further and plead the propriety and even the absolute necessity of the act itself . . ." Allen reported.[40]

[38] *Herald*, 13 June 1809.
[39] *Herald*, 16 June 1809.
[40] *Herald*, 18, 21 July, 4, 18, 22 August 1809.

The editor of the *Herald* did not let the matter drop there, however. He sensibly reasoned that the coercive power which Non-Intercourse was supposed to have on England was a dead letter, since England had already shown it would not suspend its Orders in Council just because Americans lifted Non-Intercourse. To another commentator Non-Intercourse was clearly unconstitutional, since by it Congress had delegated extravagant powers to the president. A clever columnist carried this argument one step further. Congress had delegated to Madison the power of proclaiming the *end* of Non-Intercourse when in his best judgment he considered Great Britain to have suspended its Orders, "EXAMINER" pointed out. This the president did in his proclamation of April 19. But there his power ceased, the writer insisted, for Congress had never authorized Madison to issue a second proclamation *reviving* Non-Intercourse. Only Congress could do that, "EXAMINER" concluded.[41]

Most observers believed that trade with Britain would continue through roundabout routes and by smuggling, putting the honest trader at a disadvantage. But the merchants had little difficulty finding profitable markets for the West Indian goods which had accumulated during the long months of Embargo. Since late March vessels had been clearing for Baltic and Mediterranean ports, returning with cargoes of hemp, cordage, hardware, and wines. Perhaps the most rewarding voyage of the Non-Intercourse period was that of John Pettingell's ship *Rolla,* which returned from Sumatra in February 1810 with a valuable cargo of pepper, most of which he sent on to Russia along with 100,000 pounds of coffee. In the Caribbean the Swedish island of St. Bartholomew became a popular port of call, along with numerous ports along the South American coast. Although they still complained about Republican restrictions, Newburyport merchants quickly adjusted their commercial activities to the new conditions.[42]

But by the spring of 1810 Newburyport's Federalists once more went on the attack against the national administration. At their March caucus members of the party denounced Madison's dismissal of "Copenhagen" Jackson, the irascible British minister whom

[41] *Herald*, 22, 25, 29 August, 1, 5, 15 September 1809.
[42] *Herald*, 22 August, 5, 19 September 1809; Custom House Records.

Canning had sent to replace Erskine. Not without reason the Federalists suspected that the Republicans' policies would lead eventually to a war with England. Worse than war, however, was the prospect of an alliance with France. Madison's honeymoon with the Federalists was over.[43]

There was little to cheer about in the Federalist camp. Daniel White, just elected a state senator, was disheartened by the political scene. A hopelessness seemed to enshroud the future of his party. Denouncing the folly of the people for returning a democratic state administration, White admitted that of late he had not had much confidence in "our popular sovereigns." "I had hoped for the ascendancy of good principles for a while, though we should be compelled ultimately to succumb," he admitted. Early in the month, while reporting the Republican election riot in New York, editor Allen firmly believed that such conduct could only lead to civil war. Federalists were no fonder of the mob in 1810 than they had been twenty years before.[44]

At the Federalists' Fourth of July banquet in 1810 the young lawyer Samuel Knapp paid his respects to the sacred canons of party dogma in a brilliant speech. Knapp opened by citing the beauty and grandeur of the constitution as first conceived and placed into operation by the great Washington. Opposed to these doings was the Republican party, likened to the serpent "seen lurking in this Paradise, the morning after creation." John Adams was more difficult for the young Federalist historian to deal with, however. "At the name of this man my bosom labors with mingled emotions of reverence, pity and contempt." Had he only followed the great principles of his predecessor "we should on this anniversary be weaving garlands of flowers for his honorable head." Next Knapp briefly examined American relations with France and found them wanting. "[We] have kissed the foot of Bonaparte when it had been lifted to crush our heads in the dust," he concluded. The orator then turned to commerce, "the sacred palladium of our right," whose beneficial effects on civil and political liberties is the country's salvation. Anyone who doubted the value of commerce need only study the history of England, whose strength and influence had

[43] *Herald*, 6 March 1810.
[44] Daniel A. White to James Richardson, 20 May 1810, White Papers (EI); *Herald*, 8 May 1810.

increased with her revenue. "She has increased in spirit and knowledge as she has grown in wealth," for a century past. Federalism
was in short

a combination of intelligence defection [?], and religious belief, a love
of government founded on efficient principles and administered with
firmness and impartiality, a sacred regard to equal rights and a just hatred
of oppression from the many or the few, a union of ability and virtue
against loose principles and violent passions.

The Federalists were now a minority, Knapp grimly recognized,
"but a powerful minority which are yet to save us." [45]

At the Federalist dinner closing the events for the day 400 persons, including Theophilus Parsons, now chief justice of the Massachusetts Supreme Court, were on hand. The political militancy
reflected in Knapp's oration was carried through the banquet proceedings as well. A toast to Timothy Pickering hailed him "the
inflexible patriot, the unwavering politician, and the honorable
man." Two volunteers extolled the virtues of the "Silver Greys."
Their colonel, John Greenleaf, urged that *the band of invincibles*
. . .[be] ever ready to repel the assaults of the infatuated mob,"
while another hoped that its members would never throw away their
muskets "nor flinch at the point of the bayonet when their country's honor or the cause of freedom demands their aid." [46]

The Republicans had their own celebration of Independence Day,
inviting the Reverend Solomon Aiken of Dracut to deliver an
oration. The visiting minister confined himself to recounting the
glories which came with independence, including the absence of
an unnatural aristocracy, freedom from "cruel task-masters and
unfeeling tax-gatherers." But while doing this the clever speaker
raked over the coals of Anglophobia, reminding his audience of
British rule thirty-five years in the past. At the same time Aiken
could not resist slipping in a point for Jefferson, turning to the
latest treasury reports to show how the Republican president had
reduced the national debt despite the Louisiana Purchase.[47]

By the close of 1810 the relations of the political parties had re-

---

[45] Currier, *History of Newburyport*, II, 275–276; *An Oration Delivered at Newburyport on the 4th day of July, 1810, by Samuel L. Knapp* (NPL).

[46] *Herald*, 6 July 1810.

[47] *An Oration Delivered before the Republican Citizens of Newburyport, July 4,
1810, by the Rev. Solomon Aiken* (NPL).

turned to their pre-Embargo norm. On the one hand the extreme vituperation of 1808 and the first few months of 1809 had largely disappeared, but so too had the willingness of some Federalists to meet Madison half way. The dilemma of Newburyport's Republicans remained the same: they were representatives of a national majority party in a town where they were outnumbered by more than two to one.

On May 1, 1810, the laws regulating American commerce underwent their third major change since the ending of Embargo hardly one year before, when Congress replaced the Non-Intercourse Act, due to expire with that session, with Macon's Bill No. 2. The new act completely reversed the principle which the Republicans had previously pursued. Instead of prohibiting American commerce with the belligerents, dangling its restoration as a temptation for either power to end its decrees against neutral shipping, the Macon Act threw open the ports of the world to American shipping. The United States announced its willingness, however, to prohibit trade with one belligerent if the other dropped its restriction against American commerce. The *Herald* announced the demise of Non-Intercourse with characteristically colorful language. "While its offspring here have been idleness, despair, deep-mouth curses, and ghastly poverty—in Europe it has only excited an approved grin from Napoleon and a hearty laugh from John Bull."[48]

For the next nine months Newburyporters enjoyed a freedom of trade, with the important exception of British and French seizures, which they had not known for almost three years. Before the year was out eight of their vessels had returned from Liverpool and many others from British-held possessions in the Caribbean. But important changes in Newburyport's trade patterns had already begun to take place. After the end of Non-Intercourse St. Barts continued to be the most popular call for Newburyporters in the Caribbean. Many of the Spanish possessions, especially Puerto Rico and Cuba, also attracted vessels from the Merrimack. Other ports of call along the South American coast included Orinoco, Cumaná, and Surinam, and even Rio de Janeiro. Another change saw Newburyporters shying away from overconcentration in the sugar trade,

---

[48] Channing, *History*, IV, 410–411; *Herald*, 8 May 1810.

bringing back a more diversified cargo including spirits and cocoa as well as coffee. New routes to Europe quickly became established, and with the backlog of West Indies goods piled up from Embargo days in addition to various American domestic produce, the Newburyporters headed for the Baltic with renewed enthusiasm. Return cargoes included iron, hemp, and a wide variety of cloth goods. Trade with Spain and the Mediterranean also increased, bringing exotic if less valuable commodities such as figs, raisins, and prunes to the Newburyporters.[49]

For awhile the merchants dared to think that a return to the glorious prosperity of pre-Embargo days had actually materialized. Orders were sent up-river for the construction of bigger and better vessels. During the year 1810 seventeen full-rigged ships and fifteen brigs were built for Newburyport owners, and the port's total tonnage climbed to a new high. To the careful observer, however, there were other signs less optimistic than mounting profits. The Baltic trade had to run the gamut of Danish privateers, and French privateers still roamed the seas. In the summer of 1810 four Newburyport vessels were confiscated in Naples, with a loss of nearly $100,000 to their owners.[50]

When the British were invited by Macon's Bill No. 2 to withdraw their Orders in Council in exchange for the suspension of American trade with France, the bargain had little attraction, since virtually no American vessels could slip through the British blockade anyway. In Napoleon, however, the Madison administration found what was thought to be a more amenable customer. The wily emperor saw a chance to trip up the Americans, authorizing his foreign minister to announce the revocation of the Berlin and Milan decrees, effective on November 1, 1810, it being understood that the British should do the same or that the United States would force them to honor its rights. On the same day, however, the emperor consummated his recent seizure of all American shipping in ports under his control by authorizing the sale of confiscated vessels and cargoes, the returns to go to the treasury. Madison's administration, blind to the unprincipled conduct of Bonaparte,

---

[49] Compiled from Newburyport Custom House Records.
[50] *Herald,* 29 October, 10 November 1809, 29 May, 17, 24 August 1810, 1 January 1811; *American State Papers,* VII, 877.

took his offer at face value. The president announced in November that unless the British suspended their Orders in Council within three months, Non-Intercourse would be re-established against her ports, while Americans would remain free to trade with other parts of the world. When the British held fast to their position, Non-Intercourse once again became effective, on February 2, 1811.[51]

Long accustomed to changes in the administration's policy toward commerce, editor Allen of the *Herald* could not resist casting a facetious aspersion when Non-Intercourse was re-established. A large blizzard (elsewhere in his issue called an "Old fashioned Snow-Storm") had prostrated the town on February 2, and Allen entered the fact in the Marine List, commenting that "although the non-intercourse is just revived, the Custom-House could not refuse it entry." Several weeks later, as it became increasingly clear that Napoleon had not in fact repealed his decrees, the editor announced the performance of "THE NEW FRENCH FARCE Entitled DECREES REVOKED, or, NEUTRAL RIGHTS RESPECTED." In his marriage column, Allen heralded the "long-expected Match—the loving NAPOLEON BONAPARTE to the lovely Miss COLUMBIA, in the 35th year of her age, daughter of George Washington. . . . For articles of agreement, see Non-Intercourse Act." [52]

No sooner had the effects of Non-Intercourse begun to grind down the briefly revived prosperity of Newburyport than the town was struck by a devastating fire. Throughout the spring of 1811, small fires, apparently of incendiary origin, destroyed several stables in the crowded business section of town off Market Square. The town watch doubled its vigil, and members of the various fire societies succeeded in confining each blaze to the original building. But on the night of May 31 a fire broke out in an old stable in Mechanic Row, and by the time it was discovered, the flames had already started to spread in all directions, helped by a brisk wind and the fact that no rain had fallen in several weeks. Within minutes the blaze was completely out of control. Firefighters converging on the scene could do nothing at first. Shopkeepers scurried to save their stock and householders their furniture and personal effects.

[51] Channing, *History*, IV, 413–415.
[52] *Herald*, 5 February, 22 March 1811.

By necessity buildings in the path of the conflagration were blown up to help check its spread. Finally, by six in the morning the fire was brought under control, and by noon all that remained in that part of town were smouldering ruins. The business center of Newburyport had been almost completely burned out, the flames covering a crowded area of more than sixteen acres. Altogether nearly 250 buildings were lost, and authorities reckoned the final cost at about $1,000,000.[53]

As extensive as was the devastation wrought by the Great Fire, Newburyporters were only temporarily distracted from the other dangers which had beset them since the laying of the Embargo more than three years before. At a party convention held in Ipswich on March 13, 1811, the Federalists of the county had already protested the admission of the state of Louisiana to the Union as a violation of the spirit of the constitution, contending that each of the original thirteen states should have been consulted. No one doubted the Republicans' intention: it was "to deprive the Northern states of their proportional share of influence in the national government." Newburyporters knew full well the implication of these words, for editor Allen had published Josiah Quincy's famous remarks threatening secession during the House debate on the admission bill.[54]

When the Massachusetts Republicans for the first time gained control of both the legislative and executive branches of the state government in 1812, a political revolution resulted. First the General Court removed Timothy Pickering as United States Senator and then passed the redistricting bill soon to be dubbed the "Gerrymander." This law caused an immediate turmoil in Essex County, where the Federalist towns were grouped together to form a two-senator district; the other towns, including the Republican center of Marblehead, comprised the other district, choosing three senators. In the state election of 1812 the Republicans therefore seated three out

[53] *An Account of the Great Fire . . . in Newburyport on the Night of the 31st of May, 1811* (Newburyport, 1811); Emery, *Reminiscences*, pp. 262, 263.
[54] *Herald*, 25 January, 1, 5 February 1811. The quote printed by Allen on the 25th from Quincy's speech: "If this bill passes, it is my deliberate opinion that it is virtually a dissolution of this union; that it will free the states from their moral obligation, and as it will be the right of all, so it will be the duty of some, definitely to prepare for a separation, amicably if they can, violently if they must."

of five senators from the county, although Federalists registered a 2000-vote plurality.[55]

Political rancor seemed to reach new heights during the electoral season of 1812. Samuel L. Knapp, delivering the main address at the annual dinner of the "Associated Disciples of Washington," reviewed for his listeners the dreadful calamities which had befallen the nation since the retirement of Washington and Adams from office. "You must constantly be on the watch against intrigue and artifice," he warned his audience, "for democracy is perpetually in ambush and springs upon its prey in the dark." Having saddled the opposition with the onus of partisanship, Knapp could blandly assure the assemblage that "no rancour, no malice, no irritation tinges a single thought I have laid before you." [56]

National and state issues were combined as the Federalists of Newburyport took to the friendly pages of the *Herald* to vent their wrath on the hated Republicans. "AMERICANUS" attacked the plan of raising a standing army of 25,000 men, which could be supported only by a swarm of tax-gatherers. The threatened invasion of Canada he saw as a ridiculous undertaking, apparently justified only because it belonged to England and because "we do not have enough territory for the fresh spring Importations from the land of Erin." After the conquest of Canada, "AMERICANUS" asserted, perhaps the Republicans' next objective will be "an expedition to the moon." Of course the release of the Henry Letters by Madison that spring caused a flurry of excitement in Newburyport as elsewhere. Editor Allen dismissed the incident for what it was, a cheap electioneering trick, and displayed his confidence by publishing the letters in the issue of March 20.[57]

It was the possibility of war with England which really brought the shudders to Newburyport's Federalists. The clash between the United States frigate *President* and the British man-of-war *Little Belt* in the spring of 1811 evoked no pride of nationalism in the breast of Newburyporters. Whereas the attack by the American ship had been hailed in other quarters of the country as a settling of the

[55] Channing, *History*, IV, 443–444; *Herald*, 21 February, 3 April, 1, 29 May 1812.

[56] *Herald*, 25 February 1812; *An Oration Delivered before "The Associated Disciples of Washington" on the 22nd of February, 1812 . . . by Samuel L. Knapp, Esq.* (NPL).

[57] *Herald*, 6, 17, 20 March 1812.

old *Chesapeake* score, editor Allen regretted the whole affair. Ship-owner Josiah Bartlett, writing to his wife from New York the following month, concluded that the American commodore, Rogers, had been under orders from the administration to provoke a quarrel with the British, with war the ultimate objective.[58]

The suspense, however, was occasionally worse than the prospect of war itself. Editor Allen showed the strain of waiting for Congress's decision as early as November 1811, when he blurted out: "it indeed is high time that *something* were done. . . . If it be *necessary* in defense of our injured country to take up arms, let us know the worst of it. . . . Even war, horrible as it ever is, is preferable to the listless, stupid, and cowardly procrastination of it, so evident in our Government." In the month following, Allen was somewhat more confident that the cries for war in Congress would ultimately subside and that reason would rule the day.[59]

By the spring of 1812 the situation looked a good deal less optimistic, however. Allen seemed almost resigned to the fact that war was inevitable when on April 14 he had the disagreeable task of publishing the text of the law leveling a ninety-day embargo on foreign voyages. "Heigh ho! here we are again safely landed on another Embargo!!" he wearily reported. "Yes, *embargoed for ninety days;* and what then? Why probably an *enforcing act*—and then a *non-intercourse*—and then a *non-importation*—and then *another War*—So we go." [60]

Numerous citizens gave vent to the frustrations which had built up while they stood helplessly by watching a Republican administration and Congress steer the country still closer to a disastrous war with Britain. "Have we no barrier to thrust against the deluge of misery and disgrace that threaten to engulph us?" cried "AN OLD WHIG." The tension affected Republicans as well. "Such is the dreadful deathlike stillness (in point of business) . . . that the heart sickens at the thought," wrote "A REPUBLICAN." "This state of things cannot be supported for any considerable length of time—it is absolutely impossible. Something must be done to relieve the people," he con-

[58] *Herald,* 28 May 1811; Josiah Bartlett to Sally Bartlett, 26 June 1811, Josiah Bartlett Papers (HSON).
[59] *Herald,* 8 November, 27 December 1811.
[60] *Herald,* 14 April 1812.

cluded, suggesting a petition to the government. Another observer picked up this idea and noted that many towns in the middle and southern states had already petitioned Congress for peace. Allen added to the tempest by printing Pickering's series of open letters denouncing a war with Britain.[61]

For almost three weeks Congress debated the question of war behind closed doors. Finally, on June 18, the decision was made, and Madison signed the declaration the same day. Writing to his brother three days later, Essex North's congressman, Leonard White, painted a gloomy portrait of New England's future. An offensive war declared against a nation "which has it in her power to bring destruction to our defenseless cities and towns on the seaboard" was foolhardy policy, born of malice and revenge. But worse than that was the prospect of an alliance with France.[62]

Since December 1807 the merchants of Newburyport had drifted through more than four years of agonizing uncertainty, their commercial prosperity stifled by an unsympathetic administration. As they watched the Republicans drive the nation along what seemed to them a disastrous course, they could only protest in vain. By the summer of 1812, with the declaration of war against Britain, Newburyporters realized the hopelessness of their position as members of a minority party.

[61] *Herald*, 1, 6 May, 9 June 1812.
[62] Channing, *History*, IV, 453; Leonard White to Daniel A. White, 21 June 1812, White Papers (EI).

Chapter VIII

TO THE BRINK OF SECESSION

At the outbreak of war in June 1812 the merchants of Newburyport in effect suspended their allegiance to the national government and, as hostilities dragged on, acted as though they were totally independent of the Washington authorities. Newburyporters refused to contribute troops or money to the war effort; they cheered the loss of local Republican privateers and ridiculed American military defeats; and they furnished British forces in Canada and in Europe with food supplies. In their opposition to the federal government Newburyporters saw themselves following a path similar to that of their fathers in resisting the tyranny of Great Britain forty years before. When the year 1814 closed with no peace settlement, they were ready to declare more formally the independence which they in fact had assumed for nearly three years, urging their state to sue for a separate peace with England. In January 1815 the merchants of Newburyport stood on the brink of seccession. Only the war's end soon thereafter saved them from utter disgrace. But peace did not bring a restoration of prewar prosperity. Federalist Newburyport was gone forever, and its citizens could only look forward to a generation of stagnation.

When news of the declaration of war against England reached Newburyport, consternation was the immediate reaction. "What are we to do, my friend, now that this overwhelming calamity is at our very door," wrote the merchant-banker William Woart to Daniel A. White on June 24. "I can hardly describe to you the feelings of our best men here." Newburyporters relied as in so many other crises on town meeting to determine what course they should take. Perhaps they still had a choice of action; perhaps Newburyport did not have to go to war with Great Britain even though the Congress declared that hostilities existed.[1]

On June 24 citizens of the town assembled to consider the alarming state of affairs. William Bartlet, as usual, was chosen moderator and also a member of the five-man committee to draft a resolution. The first question was whether the town should address its petition to the national or to the state government. Two merchants, John Pierpont and Thomas M. Clark, suggested that the latter was more appropriate under the circumstances, and the meeting quickly agreed. Edward Little then spoke at some length about the issues of the day—how mismanagement of the nation's affairs by its present rulers had destroyed the earlier prosperity. He called attention to the fact that the northern section of the union did not wish war— that only nineteen out of fifty-seven representatives from New England and New York had voted for the measure. The committee thereupon retired and returned shortly afterward with a lengthy memorial, which was accepted with only three dissensions.[2]

The town made its feelings about the war clear from the start. It was "ruinous and unexpected, a Mad War . . . without object without hope, a war for which the nation is not prepared, but which has been prepared for the nation." Newburyporters believed that this war meant the end of the American republic. Disaster would result not so much from the British as from the French. "The most deadly hostility of Great Britain we regard as a refuge from the storm when compared with an alliance with France." The memorialists staunchly supported Governor Strong's delay in turning over any of the state's militia to the general government, as requested.

By the Constitution of this State our militia are under the Governor as commander-in-chief, whether in war or in peace our governor is the only commander we will recognize. . . . We are ready to march for the purposes expressed in the Constitution of the United States, to suppress insurrections, to repel invasion, and to enforce the laws, but we will march under the command of no other.[3]

Without the immediate command of their "lawful captains" Newburyporters would not stir an inch from their beloved homeland.

[1] William Woart to Daniel A. White, 24 June 1812, White Papers (EI).
[2] *Herald*, 26 June 1812.
[3] Town Records, II, 432.

But that land they would defend unto death. And the threat to their soil was not primarily the British fleet and soldiers; in fact their petition only briefly mentioned these forces. The real source of danger lay elsewhere:

Should a tide from the South and West overwhelm us, that tide, to sweep us away, must rise higher than mountains. Should the tempest of civil commotion destroy us, the tempest must tear us from the bottom of our valleys, for rather than let our blood mingle with the waters of St. Lawrence, or surmount the walls of Quebec, every valley shall be the pass of Thermopolae [*sic*] and every height a Bunkers Hill.[4]

The citizens of Newburyport left no room for doubt concerning their political allegiance. The national constitution was "the proudest monument of legislative wisdom," and if administered in the manner of Washington and his associates (the Federalist party), it would continue to render the people happy. "We are atatched to it [the constitution] as the cement which consolidates our national fabric," the resolution admitted, "but we have a more intimate connexion with the government of our own commonwealth, and we are bound to that if possible by ties still stronger." Newburyporters turned, then, to the state government for guidance. "We look to our Governor as to our political Moses, conducting us through the wilderness of intrigue and terror, like Aaron and Hur." If the governor decided, like Moses before him, to lead his children out of Egypt and into the promised land, the citizens of Newburyport were ready to follow.[5]

In less than a month the towns of Essex County convened at Ipswich to draw up still another series of resolutions expressing their opinion of the state of affairs. With Timothy Pickering in the chair the session denounced the recent Republican policies. Here the emphasis was almost entirely on the iniquitous relation between the administration and France. Nearly all the political evils of the past forty years had come about through the "intrigues and perfidy" of the French, from the original instructions to the American ministers at the treaty of Paris in 1783, jeopardizing the fisheries, to the delay in settling the Florida boundary dispute. The purpose of the

[4] Town Records, II, 433.
[5] Town Records, II, 433.

Canadian expedition, Essex Federalists believed, was to turn that conquered land over to the French "that she may control the Northern States." The resolution condemned the Republican representatives of Massachusetts who had voted for Embargo and war as *"enemies of the Commonwealth."* The session then closed with the appointment of twenty of its members as delegates to a projected statewide convention. Essex County Federalists were united in their determination to stand with their state rather than with their country in the critical days ahead.[6]

Individuals, as well as men joined in convention, went on record against the war declaration, and through their protests ran similar threads. In some the hint of secession occasionally appeared; in all their comments these Newburyporters made it clear that the war with England would get no support from them whatsoever. Editor Allen set the tone in his announcement of the war declaration in the *Herald* for June 26. "The question now is are the PEOPLE of the United States prepared to support this mad career, and become the allies of France, and consequently her vassals; or maintain with spirit their independence as becomes Freemen?" John Lowell, son of the Newburyport lawyer who had become judge of the federal district court, regarded his birthplace as one of the most federal of towns, noting that its inhabitants subscribed to far more copies of his pamphlet "Mr. Madison's War" in proportion to population than in any other town.[7]

Independence is what the Newburyport Federalists called their policy of resistance, but no one knew for sure how the goal was to be achieved. One correspondent suggested that the states opposed to the war meet in a general convention to agree on suitable candidates in the ensuing national election. "A CITIZEN" also adopted the convention idea, but his purposes seemed a little less consistent with the continuation of the union. "We have no time to lose in arresting the progress of our ruin," he wrote in late July. "All those States which wish to be free from slavery" should meet in convention as soon as possible. "SPIRIT OF 1776," showing his devotion to independence,

---

[6] *Declaration of the County of Essex by its Delegates Assembled at Ipswich on Tuesday, the 21st of July, 1812* (NPL); *Herald*, 4 August 1812.

[7] *Herald*, 26 June 1812; John Lowell to D. A. White, 30 July 1812, White Papers (EI).

advocated that New England could manage her affairs "her own way" by dismissing "their traitorous servants" at the next election.[8]

The *Herald* editor was by this time even more precise in what he meant by a spirit of independence. "We have always been led to believe that a separation of the States would be a great evil," he wrote. "We still think it an evil. But rather than prosecute the present war, which will eventuate in the ruin of the Northern and Eastern States . . . , we think it by far the least of the two evils." Allen's statement was as close as any Newburyport observer came to a suggestion of secession in public print during the first two years of the war.[9]

To the Reverend Elijah Parish of neighboring Byfield, however, the course for New England was plain. Since many Newburyporters heard his sermons and others read them as printed by Allen's *Herald* office, his words are relevant here. In his Fast Day address in July Parish declared that the time for petitions had passed. "You have thrown away enough by sending them to the Potomac, to form carpets for her palaces." To Parish the declaration of war was nothing more than "a license given by a Virginia vassal of the French Emperor to the English nation" to destroy the prosperity of New England. "Will you admit southern troops into your borders? Will you permit French soldiers to land on your shores? . . . Protest, did I say, protest? *Forbid this war to proceed in New England*." The Byfield minister then pointed out how the New Englanders should resist the war.

Does *one doubt* perplex your minds concerning the path, which you ought to pursue: What would your fathers have done? What *did* they do? . . . Were your boat fastened to a fireship just ready to explode, would you not cut the painter, and bend to the oar, until the ocean sparkled around you? Then break away from this tremendous war, which is sinking you and your posterity, and your country into the abyss of ruin.[10]

The Republicans were hardpressed to counter this attack on their

---

[8] *Herald*, 10, 28 July, 18 August 1812.

[9] *Herald*, 24 July 1812.

[10] *A Protest Against the War—A Discourse Delivered at Byfield, Fast Day, July 23, 1812, by Elijah Parish, D.D.* (NPL). E. W. Allen published at least two editions of this tract during the summer of 1812.

administration and its war policy. In March a meeting of Madisonians had allegedly declared that "the salvation of this Country depends on War with England," but to justify this statement to fellow Newburyporters was an impossible task. One of the few local Republicans to attempt a public defense of the war against England was the minister John Giles. On August 20, 1812, the day of National Humiliation and Prayer, he delivered two discourses to the congregation of his Second Presbyterian Church. The best Giles could do, however, was to launch a bitter attack against England, his former homeland, for its violations of American rights and its aristocratic government and society. In the afternoon the minister directed his fire against the Federalists. "Men despise our political priveliges [sic] when they use every stratagem to render our government contemptible and to alienate the affections of their fellow citizens from it," he charged. "With all our calamities, we are comparatively a happy people," he found, in reviewing America's current position. "We are not bound as in France or England, to crouch like beasts of burden to those who goad, and add to the weight of their chains." Although Federalists might have been surprised, Giles found France's form of government no more to his taste than the English.[11]

Newburyport's behavior during the war bore out the town's hostility toward the unpopular policy of the Madisonians. No effort was made to support the undertaking unless required by the strict letter of law and backed up by a threat of force. The declaration was scarcely three weeks old when the town took its first step toward throttling the war effort. James Prince and fifteen other local Republicans petitioned the selectmen for a special town meeting to consider providing a bonus to those men drafted into the army. The Federalists controlled the proceedings, however, and voted down the Republican proposal by a ten-to-one margin. Rubbing in their victory, the Federalists then took advantage of the session to vote a resolution favoring the election of a president "who shall be free from foreign influence." [12]

Anything to do with the army, or the war effort on land, was met

[11] Herald, 21 July 1812; Two Discourses Delivered to the Second Presbyterian Society in Newburyport, August 20, 1812 . . . by the Reverend John Giles (NPL).
[12] Town Records, II, 434; Herald, 3 July 1812.

with utmost disdain on the part of Newburyporters. When General William Hull surrendered the North Western army at Detroit in August, Federalists were disgusted. The disgraceful record of the army as the months went by could only be explained by the fact it fought without just cause. "Reasonable men cannot enter heartily into so unrighteous a cause as murdering their neighbors," editor Allen concluded. Newburyporters had little faith that the purpose of that army was solely to conquer Canada. The administration would not hesitate to use their troops, if they could, to perpetuate the Republican regime. As reports of each defeat came in, the Newburyport regiment stayed close to home, entertaining spectators with sham battles and maneuvers. The October proceedings concluded with a grand military ball at Washington Hall. The nation was at war, but Newburyport remained at peace.[13]

The Federalists of Massachusetts made one exception in their blanket disapproval of the war's prosecution. News of victories at sea they welcomed as true measures of protection of commerce. When Captain Isaac Hull of the frigate *Constitution* subdued the British *Guerrière,* Newburyporters rejoiced. As the Washington Benevolent Society expressed it, they felt "a lively sense of those achievements, by which our national character may be raised and vindicated." A licking administered to a ship of the British fleet was too sweet a triumph to be resisted. "All the wrongs we have ever sustained have been of a maritime nature," Allen editorialized; "a maritime force will redress them." Newburyporters were even willing to give direct assistance to the war on the sea. In 1813 Orlando Merrill's yard produced the sloop-of-war *Wasp,* and a call directed to "Men of Patriotism and Promoters of a Navy" was made in the *Herald* for mustering a crew.[14]

Newburyporters took an entirely different attitude toward privateering, however. With a righteousness not in evidence during the Revolution, local Federalists denounced the practice as unprincipled. The merchants understandably feared that attacks on British commerce would provoke retaliation against American vessels. At every opportunity during the first year of the war the *Herald* editor strove to discredit the few privateers which sailed from the Merri-

[13] *Herald,* 4 September, 28 October 1812; 19 January, 19 February 1813.
[14] *Herald,* 1, 4 September 1812, 19 February, 28 September 1813.

mack. When James Prince, Benjamin Merrill, Joseph Williams and other Republicans fitted out the schooner *Manhattan,* Allen disdainfully watched its progress. *Manhattan* returned to port without any prizes in early August, and the editor facetiously congratulated the owners that at least *"she has saved herself."* [15]

On the same day Captain William Nichols cleared the privateer *Decatur,* a fourteen-gun brig with a crew of 160 men. Shortly afterwards Allen announced with evident pride "this town is disgraced with but two privateers (fitted out by democrats) and they are not likely ever to *'set the river on fire.'* " Although *Decatur* could not literally invalidate Allen's prediction, Captain Nichols did the next best to it by capturing in less than two months nine British prizes, including several armed vessels after lively engagements. Even the *Herald* editor was unwilling to deprecate this accomplishment when he announced the triumphant return of *Decatur* to port. The privateer's next cruise began successfully with the capture of three more vessels, but Nichols' luck had run out, and in mid-January he met his match in a thirty-eight gun British frigate aptly named *Surprise.* The Newburyport captain was confined in a cage on the deck of a prison ship for over a month until ultimately exchanged. Although several other privateers cleared the Merrimack and enjoyed brief success, each in turn fell victim to the British fleet. Finally, editor Allen, with little sympathy for the lost crews, could state that "to the credit of this town . . . there is not a privateer owned by its inhabitants. Every one which have sailed from this river have been captured." [16]

The declaration of war at first had little effect on Newburyport's foreign commerce, since the embargo leveled in April 1812 had already severely limited maritime activity. Most of the local vessels still at sea in June continued on their voyages as if nothing had happened, even after learning of the outbreak of hostilities. A number of ships from the Merrimack had for many months violated the Non-Intercourse restrictions on commerce with England. In a six-month period from February through August 1812, for instance,

[15] *Herald,* 14, 21, 24 July, 4 August 1812.
[16] *Herald,* 4, 11, 18 August, 25 September, 25 December 1812, 19 February, 19 March, 5 June, 30 July 1813; Currier, *History of Newburyport,* I, 650–654.

no less than eighteen Newburyport vessels were reported at English ports, many of them sailing with British licenses under the protection of British convoys.[17]

By the end of September 1812 almost all of the Newburyport vessels still at sea had either returned safely back home or had headed for other opportunities. In his *Herald* columns, Allen kept a wry sense of humor when reporting some of the conditions brought about by the stagnation of foreign commerce. When a vessel, apparently under Portuguese flag, unloaded its cargo at one of the wharves, he lamented the "irreparable injury" which had been done the grass growing there. "The pasturing will not be good again for the season, unless the frost should hold off late," he reported. The *Herald*'s Marine List had become the "Horse-Marine List" with entries such as the following:

Thursday arrived the 4 horse ship *Sailors Misery,* Commander Shaw, from Boston, full cargo, dry goods, coffee, etc., came to with every rag of *canvass* set, and half seas over—in *mud.* Spoke, near the *Graves* in *Rowley,* a fleet of 4 sail for Boston, laying to, when they got to the latitude of Salem, intended to *run down the trades!*[18]

The overland route was also popular for smuggling illegally imported goods from one town to another. When Newburyport merchant Luther Waterman learned that a shipment of linen had arrived for him at Kennebunkport, he engaged the services of David Emery and his covered butcher's cart. The goods had been stored in the warehouse of a former West Indies trader, who had plenty of empty rum casks on hand. Certificates for the rum were procured, and the cart set off for Newburyport via back roads. Fortunately the Kennebunkport captain had given Emery a handful of choice Havana cigars, which were effectively distributed to occasional interrogators.[19]

Emery's tavern in Belleville, on the outskirts of Newburyport, was a favorite stopping place for caravans heading south from the Canadian border with smuggled English goods. The mistress of the inn recalled in later life that from the fall of 1812 on as many

[17] *Herald*, Ship Lists, February–August, 1812.
[18] *Herald*, 7 September, 26 November 1813.
[19] Emery, *Reminiscences*, pp. 278–280.

as four or five carts came through every day, and she remembered
once counting as many as a dozen or more drawn up beside the
long barn. The local custom house officers, Ralph Cross and Jacob
Whitmore, paid an occasional visit to the establishment, which
required the lady of the house to entertain them in the parlor while
her husband drove off to West Newbury with whatever illegal
goods happened to be on hand. Although Mrs. Emery did not recall
what these carts transported on the trip north to the border, it is
probable that a considerable quantity of flour and other provisions
passed through Newburyport to Canada in payment for the cloth
goods brought back. Emery grew rich on the two-way traffic past
his tavern. The fact that the northbound goods fed the British
forces in Canada probably did not bother his conscience, for he
was as patriotic in his way as most of his neighbors, serving as a
major in the local cavalry regiment.[20]

At first Massachusetts Federalists had hopes that the outbreak of
war would bring about a victory for their party in the national
elections of 1812, and to this end they supported the nomination of
New York's De Witt Clinton. Newburyporters voted for the
"Peace Ticket" by the overwhelming margin of 695 to 135. Perhaps
most surprising was that over one hundred voters still supported the
Republican administration, but they represented only 20 percent
of the electorate. With each year of the war Federalists gained
further strength, and in the fall of 1814 the Republican candidate
for congressman received no votes at all in Newburyport.[21]
Federalists kept up a steady clamor against the continuation of
hostilities in the *Herald*'s friendly columns. Occasionally, when
interest seemed to be flagging a bit, a group of citizens called a
meeting. Thus in March 1813 the Federalists published a notice
requesting all those unwilling to pay high taxes or to die in the
snows of Canada to assemble in protest. "ONE AND ALL—let the
enemies of New England find us watching over our constitution
and rights," the declaration closed. The Reverend Elijah Parish
did not slacken his campaigns against the sinful war from his pulpit

[20] Emery, *Reminiscences*, p. 275.
[21] *Herald*, 5 April, 20, 23 October, 3, 6, 8 November 1812, 9 April 1813; Town
Records, II, 464–465, 481.

in Byfield. April Fast Day in 1813 was an occasion for yet another onslaught. "Do not, I beseech you, do not move a finger to promote this wicked war," he urged his listeners.[22]

When peace had not come by the autumn of 1813, the patience of some was nearly exhausted. "ARISTIDES" went so far as to protest the pride with which most New Englanders greeted American triumphs at sea. Newburyporters had not matched Boston, where a town meeting unanimously voted to honor Commodore Perry's recent victory on Lake Erie; but throughout the war, the inhabitants had shown undisguised joy in the few moments of glory which the American fleet had achieved. To "ARISTIDES" it was a matter of principle. "If the war is immoral and unjust—and this, federalists have generally professed to believe—it is immoral to rejoice at any success which may attend its progress." The correspondent feared most that such victories would sufficiently annoy the British to tempt them into more vigorous prosecution of the war, a matter of common concern along the exposed New England seaboard. "ARISTIDES" hoped above all that bloodshed could be avoided; he was not advocating that Americans should rejoice at British victories. But within nine months Newburyporters and Federalists throughout the country would be doing just that.[23]

When the Republican administration had exhausted all of its meager resources for combatting illicit coastwise trade, Congress passed an embargo law in December 1812, designed to put an absolute ban on American waterborne commerce. Again the Custom House Collector enjoyed sweeping powers of enforcement, and again partisan politics quickly became entangled in the debate. "AN OLD WHIG" was one of many to protest the new measure, but as usual he exercised extreme caution. Urging that the town petition the General Court to furnish protection "from the scourges of an unjust, wanton, and cruel government," he hastened to add that such measures should be limited to those "consonant with the national compact." Others were probably talking about stronger steps to prompt this specific reservation.[24]

[22] *Herald*, 30 March 1813; *A Discourse Delivered at Byfield on . . . April 8, 1813*, by *Elijah Parish* (NPL).
[23] *Herald*, 12 October 1813.
[24] *Herald*, 23 December 1813, 4 February 1814; Robert G. Albion and Jennie B. Pope, *Sea Lanes in Wartime* (New York, 1942), p. 117.

When the town did meet on February 7, 1814, at the behest of eighty-seven prominent citizens, the resolution which it finally submitted to the General Court also stopped short of suggesting secession. Basing their complaint on the recent Embargo Act as well as on the usual grievances stemming directly from the war, the petitioners sought relief. "In this unhappy and almost desperate condition of our beloved country we rejoice that we have in our state government a constitutional barrier against acts of violence and oppression." Once more the Newburyporters turned to the Commonwealth to interpose its authority between the national government and themselves. Allen was optimistic that the General Court would take the necessary action. "We believe the morn of liberation dawns. . . . The legislature is now acquainted with the sentiments of the great body of the people—let them act," the editor demanded, "and while they proceed with prudence and discretion, let them act with FIRMNESS and ENERGY." But the General Court failed to act, and the old wounds continued to fester.[25]

As the year 1814 went by, the grievances of Newburyport's oppressed citizens grew more numerous and more serious. When Congress made provision for military and naval enforcement of the recent Embargo Act, one local observer declared it to be yet another attempt on the part of Virginia to depress Massachusetts and the other maritime states. The presence of a troop of cavalry enlisting men in Newburyport nearly caused a riot in March, as its recruiter enticed a thirteen-year-old lad to sign up and then gave him twenty lashes for desertion when the boy changed his mind a few days later.[26]

Not until June 1814 did the progress of the war give Newburyport's Federalists anything to cheer about, and then it was for the victory of the British and their allies over Napoleon. Word of the capture of Paris and the fall of the French emperor filled the pages of the *Herald*'s June 7th issue. On the 14th the selectmen authorized a public demonstration, and on the next day the town rejoiced in the French defeat. A bust labeled "ALEXANDER THE DELIVERER" graced

[25] Town Records, II, 456–458; *Herald*, 11 February 1814.
[26] *Herald*, 4 March 1812; Miss Mary Harrod to Capt. Benjamin Harrod, 7 March 1814, Harrod Papers (EI).

Town Hall, while a sign beneath announced "NAPOLEON DE-THRONED—EUROPE FREE." [27]

So united was the town on the matter of praising the English victory that the Reverend Daniel Dana, normally a more restrained minister, challenged his audience at a July Fourth celebration: "Do any object, that to rejoice in the recent triumphs of the allied powers, is to rejoice at the success of our enemies?" The *Herald* proclaimed that this was the first Fourth of July that the town could celebrate in many years. Federalist toasts on that occasion praised "Alexander the Deliverer," "Field Marshal Wellington," and "Louis XVIIIth, a new master of the Old School. As he rides over the ruin of despotism, many his car be guided by justice and his course be sacred to freedom." [28]

The Federalists' hatred of Mr. Madison's War took strange forms as 1814 drew to a close. That summer a writer to the Republican Boston *Patriot* had claimed that "a Tory mob" in Newburyport had surrounded some British prisoners being conducted through town with an eye toward releasing them. A correspondent to the *Herald* heatedly denied the charge, as did the editor, both insisting that the Newburyporters simply wanted to offer the captives food since they had not been fed all day. When the British captured and burned Washington, editor Allen showed little sympathy. "We know the subject has become too serious for levity," he admitted, but who will say that they [the Madison administration] do not richly deserve their calamity?" Perhaps a new standard of defiance was reached by an anonymous correspondent when he reproved the administration for its recent efforts to unite the country behind the war. Since the Republicans asked for the war and pledged their lives and fortunes to support it, "how pitiful and degrading then to call on the federalists in the humble tone they now use to assist them!" [29]

At the same time that the Newburyport Federalists welcomed the victories of the allies on the Continent, they realized that the Eng-

[27] Town Records, II, 476; *Herald*, 17 June 1814.
[28] *Discourse Delivered in Newburyport, July 4 1814, in Commemoration of American Independence and of the Deliverance of Europe,* by Daniel Dana (NPL); *Herald*, 8 July 1814.
[29] *Herald*, 12 July, 2, 20 September 1814.

lish would soon be able to turn their full military attention toward
the United States. The town had long pondered the prospect of
attack from the sea, especially after the Plum Island fort, built by
the Jeffersonians in 1808, had fallen in ruins. Newburyport's best
defense was the bar at the mouth of the Merrimack, which prohibited vessels drawing over eighteen feet from coming closer than
three miles from the town. Although out of range of the larger
units of the British fleet, inhabitants still feared the possibility of
a British landing party. A committee therefore was assigned the
task of investigating the town's defenses when it became clear by
the spring of 1814 that the national administration would not or
could not defend the New England coast.[30]

Several groups of armed men had already been formed. The
Sea-Fencibles, a band of shipmasters and mates stranded ashore
because of the war, met for the first time in late September 1813
to organize a company. By the following spring there were about
thirty members and in August the company made its first public
appearance. In the fall of 1813 Newburyport and neighboring Newbury assembled a force of 2000 men for a sham battle on the Plains
of Newbury. Infantry, artillery, and cavalry were all present, an
impressive sight to the large spectator group. Any of the army
commanders on the frontiers would have welcomed their help, but
the editor thought too highly of the Newburyport troops for that:
"The ragamuffins who have foolishly marched to the frontiers
would suffer, in every point of view, by a comparison with such
militia as we have been speaking of." [31]

As the summer of 1814 progressed, other units were formed to
strengthen local defenses. Since few of the young men of the
community volunteered for national service, there was a considerable pool available for duty. The elderly "Silver Greys" stood along-
side a company organized from the Leonidas Fire Society. An
advisory group, the Merrimack Military Society, brought together
experts of the region into a sort of academy for the dissemination
of military knowledge. Fort Phillips, named for the lieutenant
governor, rose from the sands of Plum Island that summer and
was manned by successive companies of local soldiers to ward off

[30] *Herald*, 18 June, 13 November 1813, 1 July 1814; Town Records, II, 445.
[31] *Herald*, 28 September, 15 October 1813, 28 June, 30 August 1814.

any attack from the sea. These defenses gave immediate comfort when units of the British fleet began to appear offshore almost daily.[32]

Occasionally the Newburyporters could reassure themselves that the British would not harm them. When Richard Coffin, off on a short fishing trip in the bay, was captured by a barge from the British brig *Leander,* he returned with an encouraging report. The British lieutenant, after inquiring about the force stationed at Plum Island, explained that they did not intend to molest the coast of Massachusetts unless provoked. Reported Coffin: "The burden of the war was to be carried on in the Southern States, as they knew very well what section of the Union made the war." This of course simply encouraged the Federalists in their policy of refusing to support the national administration. But the British fleet was a clearly visible danger, no matter what the stated intentions of its officers. Its blockade of the New England coast had tightened so firmly that hardly a coaster or boat escaped inquiry. Barges from the larger vessels poked into nooks and crannies of the coastline, raiding island communities for provisions, and bringing the war to New England's front door. Salem was in a panic in September; families fled to the countryside, with Republicans, it was said, leading the way.[33]

By September 1814 Newburyport too had become increasingly worried about its safety. A special ten-man committee, including at least two Republican members, was authorized to strengthen the town's defenses wherever possible. Correspondents to the *Herald* submitted suggestions for the construction of breastworks in the river, partly to obstruct hostile navigation as was done during the Revolution, partly also to provide public works for the unemployed. An impressive military review held in late September brought Newburyport's entire force onto the field, infantry "much reduced in numbers," artillery and cavalry, Washington Light Infantry ("with this corps there cannot be much more room for improvement"), Sea-Fencibles, and other companies. Miss Judith Stickney presented

[32] Town Records, II, 448; *Herald,* 5 August, 13 September 1814; Currier, *History of Newburyport,* II, 515–528.
[33] *Herald,* 26 July 1814; Mrs. —— to Mrs. Daniel A. White, September 1814, White Papers (EI).

the troops with an elegant standard, perhaps the five-starred New
England flag later reported flying at Fort Phillips. "While you have
been advocates for PEACE and contemners of this WAR," the pretty
young miss asserted, "you have associated for our defence; and if
a hostile foot ever profane our shores, we are sure you will among
the first to repel them." With this encouragement the Sea-Fencibles
took up their lonely watch on Plum Island, planting their standard
and firing a *"New England* salute of 5 guns and 5 cheers." [34]

The danger of assault from the sea was but one of the conditions
of war which profoundly disturbed the inhabitants of Newburyport. The federal government's direct tax was a heavy burden
which many property holders refused to pay. And conditions on
the home front worsened with each month. Although food was not
generally scarce, prices of such commodities as sugar, coffee, and
tea, as well as clothing and other articles long since regarded as
essential, had risen sharply. According to the complaint of one shopkeeper in town, these goods were not actually in short supply.
Rather, merchants with sufficient capital simply hoarded their stocks
until demand drove prices steadily higher. Quantities of food and
clothing were also stored away in country barns, awaiting a further
rise in the market price. Firewood became increasingly expensive,
until proposals were made to bring in supplies from the eastward
in coastal schooners, manned by unemployed seamen, for distribution to the poor. By the spring of 1814 the town was appropriating
over $5000 annually for the support of the poor, including seventy-
one inhabitants of the almshouse. Fear of invasion, the mounting
cost of living, taxation, and grinding poverty all contributed to the
rising tide of discontent. Newburyport, along with other New
England towns, was ready for revolution by the end of 1814, and
plans for such action had already begun to take form. [35]

Secession had been discussed in Newburyport from the days of
Embargo, but only by individuals and in theoretical terms rather
than as an actual possibility. Earlier plans, such as those of Pickering
and his Junto, received little support in town. By 1814, however, talk

[34] Town Records, II, 480; *Herald,* 6, 30 September, 14 October 1814.
[35] *Herald,* 14 January, 19 July, 1 December 1814; Town Records, II, 471; Emery,
Reminiscences, pp. 275–276.

of a separate northern confederacy had gained considerable head-way. Its most outspoken local advocate was the Reverend Elijah Parish, who kept up a continual assault on the national government from his Byfield pulpit. In a pamphlet widely circulated at the Port, the radical minister made his proposal more concrete than ever in his Fast Day sermon in April. Likening New Englanders to the children of Israel, he noted that the latter had separated themselves from their oppressors. New Englanders, however, could not physically leave their homeland—"Will the sons of New-England give up their traffic and their homes to dwell with the ferocious hordes of Kentucky and the West? No!" was his vehement reply. The implication was clear. Parish then listed the advantages which accrued to the Israelites when they dissolved their union with Egypt, placing particular emphasis on how they escaped the judgments of a God made angry by the sins of Egypt. Pointing out that New England would be hard-pressed to defend herself in case of invasion by British forces, Parish concluded: "Do you not owe it to yourselves, owe it to your children, and owe it to your God, *to make peace for yourselves?*" [36]

By November talk of secession had become more common. Allen of the *Herald* picked up an inflammatory article from the Baltimore *Federal Republican,* which looked to the forthcoming Hartford convention for action. Since information concerning this convention was not widespread in Newburyport at the time, inhabitants may have relied on this account for an impression of what to expect from the session. The *Federal Republican* predicted that the convention would frame a new constitution to be submitted to the legislatures of the states. The new government was to take effect "as soon as two, three, or more of the states *named* [New England] shall have adopted it." The editor of the *Federal Republican* flatly predicted that "On or before the 4th of July [1815] if James Madison is not out of office, a new form of government will be in operation in the eastern section of the union." [37]

By December Newburyporters had become impatient for action. When the Custom House officials did their duty by seizing seven

[36] *A Discourse Delivered at Byfield on the Public Fast, April 7, 1814 by Elijah Parish* (NPL).
[37] *Herald,* 8 November 1814.

wagons admittedly loaded with English goods, Allen snapped, "Thank God the time is coming, and we trust speedily, when it will not be in the power of a few men . . . to trample on the rights of their fellow-citizens with impunity." Through the long weeks of December and early January, Newburyporters waited, with the rest of New England, for the result of the convention at Hartford.[38]

When the convention report reached Newburyport in the second week of January, residents were disappointed by its moderate language. The formation of a new confederacy was specifically ruled out and no suggestion was made of a separate peace with England. In fact none of its recommendations would have alleviated the immediate distress of New England. Sixty-one citizens immediately petioned the selectmen to call a special town meeting "to express to the Legislature . . . their sufferings, their feelings, and their opinions of the doings of the late Hartford Convention." [39]

Newburyport's meeting of January 16 appointed a committee of three to draw up a memorial. For some reason no copy of the resulting petition was ever entered in the Town Records, but fortunately editor Allen published it in the *Herald*. The citizens of Newburyport were happy enough with the Hartford convention report as far as it went. "It is for the purpose of expressing our assent to all its doctrines and our willingness to support to the last hazard and extremeity the measures which it proposed, that we now approach you," the petitioners stated. Despite their interest in long-range correction of the evils of a national government dominated by the southern and western Republicans, however, the Newburyporters wanted direct action which would safeguard their homes and bring about the cessation of hostilities. They therefore suggested that a desperate step be taken, far beyond the cautious recommendations of the convention. If spring still found the nation "bending under domestic tyranny and exposed to foreign invasion," the citizens of Newburyport proposed to "consider our State Legislature as the sole, rightful and bounded judge of the course

[38] *Herald,* 6 December 1814.

[39] "Petition of sixty-one inhabitants of Newburyport, January 11, 1815," O. B. Merrill Papers (HSON); Town Records, II, 482; Theodore Dwight, *History of the Hartford Convention* . . . (Boston, 1833).

which our safety may require, without any regard to the persons still assuming to be the National Government." [40]

With full allegiance transferred to the Commonwealth, the Newburyport petititioners would then be prepared to go further. They were convinced that the citizens of the Northern states

ardently as they are attached to the Union, would in that event, under the guidance of their enlightened sages, standing in the spirit and upon the extreme boundary of their constitutional privileges,—Would declare that our resources shall be appropriated to our defence, that the laws of the United States shall be temporarily suspended in their operation in our territory, and that hostilities shall cease towards Great Britain on the part of the free, sovereign and independent States of New England.[41]

Thus to the brink of secession the Federalists of Newburyport would go. Just how to justify such action as being within the "extreme boundary" of the constitution was not discussed, although of course that document expressly prohibited any state from entering into an agreement or compact with any other state or with a foreign power, without congressional approval. One thing was certain: there was no doubt in the minds of the Newburyporters that a state could interpose its authority between the national government and its own citizens, that the union was dissoluble, and that secession was a theoretical possibility. But the Newburyporters were no longer concerned with the niceties of constitutional law. The war must be ended, and immediately, or the New England states should sue for separate peace.

Fortunately for New England and perhaps for the union as well, news of the war's end reached America in early February. Newburyport hailed the event as if its town meeting of January 16 had never been held. Such a display of patriotism had not been seen in the town since the *Chesapeake-Leopard* affair nearly eight years before. With the roaring of cannon and ringing of bells the inhabitants launched themselves on a two-day celebration of the joyful news, with all business suspended. A hastily called meeting authorized the firing of a federal salute on the 14th, and a subscription

[40] *Herald*, 27 January 1815.
[41] *Herald*, 27 January 1815.

was circulated to raise money for the illumination of the town hall and other prominent buildings. The Sea-Fencibles fired a deafening volley from their eighteen-pounders as the Union Jack and Old Glory again flew side by side from shipping and buildings throughout the port.[42]

The celebrations at last over with the anniversary of Washington's birthday, the men of Newburyport confidently looked to the future for a return of the prosperity of which they had so long been deprived. "We trust the time is not far distant when American canvas is to whiten every sea," predicted the *Herald* editor. Although Newburyporters could not then know it, perhaps some suspected that for them there would never be a return to the glories of the past.[43]

When Newburyporters complained that the War of 1812 was ruining their fortunes, the charge was not exaggerated. In the three years between 1812 and 1815 the town's total valuation dropped from $6,074,600 to $3,853,200, to less than two thirds of the prewar figure. Valuation had already fallen by over $600,000 in the five years of Embargo, Non-Intercourse, and the Great Fire, so that the over-all loss reduced the Newburyporters' worth to nearly half of 1807's high-water mark. Few citizens escaped the paralyzing effects of Embargo and war. Average wealth per poll dropped from 1807's $5089 to $2716 at war's end. But the median fell even more sharply, from $1600 to $500. Hardest hit were the maritime artisans, mariners, and laborers, whose skills and services were no longer needed on the grass-covered wharves. Poverty meant in political terms an end to the phenomenon of a broadening electorate which prosperity had brought. In 1807 all but 109 of the town's adult males had met the requirements for voting in state elections. But by 1815, despite a small rise in population, three times as many men owned no assessable property at all, nearly a quarter of the town's adult males. Many of these men were among the 237 families at least partially dependent on the town for support, a service costing local taxpayers $10,000 a year by 1815. Wealthy members of the community suffered also. The number of men worth $25,000 or more dropped from

[42] *Herald*, 14, 17 February 1815.
[43] *Herald*, 24 February 1815.

thirty-six in 1807 to twelve eight years later. The broader class of affluent men, those with holdings of at least $10,000, fell by nearly half to 62.[44]

With few exceptions those who had great wealth in 1807 still led the town eight years later, though with reduced fortunes in most cases. William Bartlet and Moses Brown occupied their customary positions at the head of the assessors' list, Bartlet losing not a penny of his $500,000 estate. Nineteen of 1807's top twenty-five property-holders were still living in Newburyport at the end of the war. Thirteen of these men retained top standing, and three others, while suffering losses, still held at least $10,000 worth of property. Only three of 1807's top twenty-five were reduced to straitened circumstances in the eight chaotic years which followed.[45]

One of the men who had lost most heavily by the end of the war was the mastmaker and importer Zebedee Cook. Having amassed an estate worth $30,000 by 1807, Cook watched his fortune melt away to $2700 by 1815. Another man who had done well during the neutral-trade period, blacksmith Nathaniel Noyes, suffered heavy losses too. His estate, worth $5000 in 1807, fell to $1700 by war's end. John Libby, laborer, nearly held his own, losing only $100 of his $500 property valuation. Ropemaker John Akerman's wealth, which had been a modest $165 in 1793 and had then grown to $4000 in 1807, dropped back to $800 by 1815. Oddly enough, the man whose gains had equaled the median rise during neutral trade, wheelwright Jesse Dorman, lost enough in the eight ensuing years nearly to match the median drop. Dorman's holdings decreased from $1500 in 1807 to $600 in 1815.[46]

At first many Newburyporters thought they could pick up where they had left off before the war and that with enterprise and hard work the prosperous days which had been theirs would soon return. When peace came, shipowners scurried to get their vessels to sea. Editor Allen likened the activity to the "good old times." In the first nine months after the war thirty-eight vessels were dispatched to the familiar West Indies, returning with the usual cargoes of

[44] Valuation Lists for the Years 1807 and 1815 (Assessors' Office, Newburyport City Hall); Town Records, II, 496. As late as 1835 population and valuation figures remained virtually unchanged.

[45] Valuation Lists for the Years 1807 and 1815.

[46] Valuation Lists for the Years 1793, 1807, and 1815.

sugar, coffee, and molasses. But there the chain of commerce stopped, for the nations of Europe were at peace and no longer depended upon the American neutral trader to transport their colonial produce. Local merchants soon sensed this, for only two vessels cleared Newburyport for European ports in 1815, both for Marseilles.[47]

Already a new pattern of commerce had begun to replace the old. The end of neutral trade sharply curtailed exchange with the West Indies to the "normal" level of imports which could be sold locally. Direct runs from Newburyport to Europe held little promise of gain, as always, because the Continent remained a poor market for New England goods. Recalling the European demand for southern agricultural products in the years before the war, Newburyport merchants sent altogether thirty-seven vessels south in 1815 for the exports necessary to pay for importation of European manufactured goods. Picking up a freight of tobacco, cotton, or flour, the ships carried the cargoes to their European destinations. The master or supercargo then loaded a return cargo, purchased by the freight charges, and returned home. Sometimes the supercargo bought the tobacco or flour outright and looked for the best possible market for his venture in Europe. The risks were greater, but so too were the profits.

The consequence of this new pattern soon revolutionized Newburyport's commerce. The town itself gradually lost importance as a base of operations. Since New England produce was in little demand in the south, the only reason for a vessel to return home at all was to discharge its cargo of European goods. But Boston and New York were better markets for such goods, especially when transportation systems became centralized. As a result of the freighting business, fewer Newburyport vessels returned to their home port; their crews increasingly came from other areas; the profits from maintenance work went to artisans in other ports. The West Indies trade fell off from the heyday of 1807, and the demand for New England products gradually decreased, depriving fishermen and lumbermen of their markets. These and other inhabitants of the Merrimack valley were therefore less able to buy the goods which Newburyport importers brought from Europe, which further

[47] *Herald,* 7 March 1815, Marine Lists 1815; Newburyport Custom House Records (EI).

encouraged the merchants to drop Newburyport as a port of call altogether. The final step, not taken for many years by some merchants, saw the shipowners themselves leaving Newburyport for Boston, or New York, or entering new lines of business elsewhere. The process was slow, but inevitable. By 1820 most Newburyporters realized that their town would not soon again see the prosperity of Federalist days. Total tonnage registered and enrolled in Newburyport continued to fall, until 1820's figure barely exceeded 20,000 tons. Population declined too, in a period when the rest of the country rapidly expanded. Only 6852 inhabitants remained in town by 1820, and valuation dropped even more rapidly. Five years after the end of the war the average adult male held $2491 worth of property, although the median holding remained at $500. The number of men in the $10,000 bracket dropped by a third. The lower classes fared no better, 335 inhabitants remaining with no property at all. Altogether, nearly 30 percent of the male adults failed to qualify as electors, an increase of 6 percent from 1815. When the Constitutional Convention of 1820 removed property qualifications, therefore, 350 Newburyporters gained the right to vote which many of them had lost in the years since 1807.[48]

In the half-century 1764–1815 two generations of Newburyport merchants saw the birth and early development of American nationalism. Its first manifestation came in the decade 1764–1775 as Newburyporters abandoned the assumption that they were merely "British inhabitants of America," realizing that their New World experience had made them different from Englishmen. Inhabitants of other colonies underwent a similar change in outlook, and to the colonial merchants of Newburyport it seemed both logical and desirable to unite with them in an assertion of their right as Americans to be free. Even before the independence of each colony was achieved, Newburyporters recognized that Americans had much in common, although in the years following the war political allegiance was directed more toward the General Court of Massachusetts than toward the Congress of the United States. A spirit of unity generated by wartime cooperation remained, however, and out of this grew a new nationalism. Once convinced of

---

[48] Valuation Lists for the Years 1807, 1815, and 1820.

the need for a more centralized government, the Newburyport merchants laid aside their suspicions of southerners to join them in the new federal union.

As the merchants of the second generation took over in Newburyport, they adopted the nationalism of their predecessors, for allegiance to the administrations of Washington and Adams meant supporting a national government which advanced the interests of New England commerce. When Jefferson gained control of the central government in 1800, however, the Federalist merchants saw the new president not just as a Republican but as a southerner threatening their own sectional interests. The price of nationalism was thereby increased beyond the level these men were willing to pany, and they began to consider themselves primarily as citizens of Massachusetts or at best of New England.

During the crisis of 1807–1815 the Federalist merchants often thought of their struggle against the central government as similar to their predecessors' fight for independence from Great Britain. But the two situations were quite different. While the earlier generation had ceased to be Englishmen and had become Americans by 1775, there was nothing else the Federalists could become. For no single cause joined the northerners of 1812 as the defense of slavery would unite southerners a half-century later. Moreover, the fact that they tried to justify their actions in terms of 1776 showed how deeply they were committed after all to their American heritage. It was to this past that Newburyporters turned after the War of 1812 to find once again the nationalism they had lost in the years since 1800.

When President James Monroe visited Newburyport in the summer of 1817, Federalists William Bartlet and Moses Brown joined Republicans Joseph Marquand and Josiah Smith on the fifteen-man bipartisan committee to welcome the one man perhaps most responsible for the declaration of war against England five years before. Monroe was met at the town line and escorted by troops which had stood ready three years before to resist the federal government. As he proceeded through the streets of town, the Virginia-born president received the loud hurrahs of the crowd. In front of the Court House waved a flag which had flown during the Revolution. When the procession halted at the steps of the Eastern Stage House on

State Street, Monroe was greeted by the largest throng ever before assembled in Newburyport. Speaker of the day was staunch Federalist Ebenezer Moseley, chairman of the board of selectmen, who as moderator of town meeting on January 16, 1815, had signed the resolution suggesting a temporary disruption of the union and a separate peace with England. But now Moseley turned to Monroe and, overlooking all the differences which had once separated them, praised the president for his contributions forty years before to the establishment of America's independence, the strongest article of faith which the two men had in common.

In their past Newburyporters found strength to face the future, a future which promised for most of them little more than a small share in national greatness. Newburyport merchants had been, after all, patriots as well as partisans.

BIOGRAPHICAL SKETCHES

Among the several hundred merchants and professional men who resided in Newburyport during the half-century 1764–1815 were a number of inhabitants whose public services and private careers gave them particular distinction. Following are brief biographical sketches of twenty-five prominent Newburyporters of the period.

WILLIAM BARTLET

William Bartlet was born in 1747, the son of a successful cordwainer, Edmund Bartlet, through whom he was descended from one of the original settlers of Newbury. William began to accumulate property in his own right before the end of the Revolution and through careful management was able to purchase wharves, warehouses, and vessels from merchants of the older generation who were faced with financial difficulties. From his wharf at the foot of Federal Street, his fleet of vessels sailed mainly to the West Indies and to northern Europe. In 1807 Bartlet's ship *Pomona* was the first Newburyport vessel to complete a voyage to India. In the fourteen years of neutral trade between 1793 and 1807, his wealth increased fivefold to over $500,000, maintaining him as Newburyport's richest inhabitant. Bartlet invested in many other enterprises, including the Newburyport Woolen Manufactory, the Merrimack Bank, the Newburyport Marine Insurance Company, and the Newburyport Turnpike. He was instrumental in raising money for construction of the sloop-of-war *Merrimack*, built in 1798 to cruise against the French. Bartlet donated his time and money to many local charitable organizations, notably the Newburyport Academy, the Athenaeum, and the Bible Society, but the principal recipient of his largess was the Andover Theological Seminary, to which he gave altogether over $150,000. In politics Bartlet was a staunch Federalist, serving three terms as a representative to the General Court, moderating many important town meetings, and sitting on numerous special committees. He died in 1841 at the age of ninety-four, having lived the last forty-two years of his life in the fine brick house he had built at 13 Federal Street, not far from the foot of his own busy wharf.

MOSES BROWN

Moses Brown was born in 1742 and was at first a chaisemaker by trade. In the years just before the Revolution he invested some of his earnings in molasses and sugar cargoes, which he sold at a good profit. Following the war he turned full time to mercantile activities and by 1790 he ranked second in wealth to William Bartlet. During the period of neutral trade Brown's holdings increased fourfold to $272,500 in 1807, but after 1812, like most of his colleagues, he suffered heavy losses. Brown carried on an extensive trade between the West Indies and northern Europe, transferring the cargoes at his wharf at the foot of Green Street. In 1810 his ship *Nancy* cleared for Sumatra, returning with pepper the following year. Brown invested his profits in local real estate and in such undertakings as the Newburyport Woolen Manufactory, the Merrimack Bank, the Newburyport Marine Insurance Company, and the Plum Island Turnpike. In 1791 Brown bought Tristram Dalton's mansion at 94 State Street, which he occupied until his death in 1827 at the age of eighty-four. He was a loyal Federalist, although he took little part in political activities.

NATHANIEL CARTER

Nathaniel Carter was born in 1716 and established himself as a merchant at the "waterside" part of Newbury long before the incorporation of Newburyport. He took an active role in the separation movement and served as the new town's first treasurer. Carter joined other Newburyporters, most of whom were younger than himself, in supporting the patriot cause in the years before the Revolution, sitting on several important town committees. At this time he ranked second in wealth among Newburyport inhabitants, behind the Tracy family. Carter invested his profits carefully, in local real estate for the most part, and scrupulously avoided privateering and other financial risks. As a result he was one of the few older merchants who retained his wealth through the postwar depressions. At his death in 1798 he ranked third behind William Bartlet and Moses Brown. Carter passed a fortune worth well over $60,000 to his widow and to his three sons, Nathaniel, Jr., Joshua, and Thomas, who continued to operate the family mercantile house.

DAVID COFFIN

David Coffin began his mercantile career with modest ventures in coastal trade, first as a shipmaster, then as a shopkeeper, offering Virginia coal among other commodities for sale at his store in Market Square. He had acquired enough profits to invest in the carrying trade when the European war broke out in 1793 and by 1807 his fortunes had increased elevenfold to over $90,000, making him Newburyport's sixth wealthiest inhabitant. Coffin also invested in the Newburyport Woolen Manufactory, the Plum Island Turnpike, the Merrimack Bank, and the Marine Insurance Company. Unlike several of his relatives, notably Samuel Coffin, David was a staunch Federalist, although he took little active part in public affairs. He died in 1815, apparently by drowning.

WILLIAM COOMBS

William Coombs was born in 1736, the son of shipbuilder Philip Coombs, whom he accompanied to Lake Ontario in 1756 to build vessels for the British-American forces during the Seven Years' War. He was captured and sent to France, but returned to Newburyport, where he became a shipmaster. Coombs took an active role in the deliberations which preceded the Revolution, and during that war he served as a captain of artillery and invested in several privateers. After the war Coombs went into general mercantile work. In 1790 he ranked fourth among the wealthiest inhabitants, but his financial affairs did not markedly improve and his relative position declined during the next two decades. Coombs remained a highly respected member of the community. He served for twenty-two years as the president of the Newburyport Marine Society, resigning in 1804, and was a representative to the General Court during the four-year period 1799–1802. He regarded himself a loyal Federalist. Coombs invested in a wide variety of local business enterprises, commencing in 1792 with the "Proprietors of Locks and Canals on Merrimack River," a corporation which after many alterations became the nucleus for the mill operations at Lowell. He also held shares in the Newburyport Woolen Manufactory, the Merrimack Bank, the Essex-Merrimack Bridge Company, the Newburyport Marine Insurance Company, and the Newburyport Turnpike. He lived for many years in the house he had built in 1783 on Water Street, near the corner of Lime, and he died there in 1814, at the age of seventy-eight.

STEPHEN CROSS

Stephen Cross was born in 1731, one of two sons of the prominent shipbuilder Ralph Cross. He accompanied his father on the expedition to Lake Ontario in 1756 to build vessels for the British-American forces there. During the Revolution he and his brother Ralph, Jr., constructed several warships for the Massachusetts navy, but by that time the family had already branched out into other activities, investing in West Indies ventures and operating a distillery. Although moderately successful at first, neither brother prospered after the war and at his death in 1809 Stephen's estate was worth a modest $6000. Stephen took an active role in politics beginning with the struggles with England preceding the Revolution. He was a member of the convention which drew up *The Essex Result* in 1778 and was a delegate to the state Constitutional Convention the following year. Although he did not overtly oppose ratification of the federal constitution, Cross was nevertheless known later as an antifederalist, and with the development of two-party politics at the turn of the century, he became a leading Jeffersonian. His last public office was as postmaster of Newburyport, which he held until his death at the age of seventy-eight. He had lived for many years in a house on Merrimack Street, directly across from the family shipyard.

TRISTRAM DALTON

Tristram Dalton was born in 1738, the son of Michael Dalton, a prominent merchant residing along the "waterside" in Newbury. After graduating from Harvard in 1755, Tristram joined his father's business and three years later married Ruth Hooper, the daughter of Marblehead's wealthy merchant, Robert "King" Hooper. But this alliance, and his own aristocratic upbringing, did not prevent

Dalton from giving his wholehearted support to the patriot cause preceding and during the Revolution. He was on most of the important local committees and after the war took an active part in state politics, serving as Speaker of the House and sitting as a delegate to the convention ratifying the federal constitution. Dalton was chosen in 1788 as one of the first two United States senators from Massachusetts, but he drew the short two-year term and was not reappointed. He had already moved to his elegant country seat at Pipe-Stave Hill, in Newbury, and in 1791 he sold his mansion on State Street to Moses Brown, leaving Essex County for his new residence in Georgetown, D.C. Dalton's financial affairs had suffered severely during the postrevolutionary depression, and hard luck continued to dog him until his death in Boston in 1817, at the age of seventy-nine.

ANTHONY DAVENPORT

Anthony Davenport was born in 1752, one of two sons of William Davenport, who owned Newburyport's popular inn, the General Wolfe Tavern. After his father's death in 1773, Anthony operated the inn with his brother Moses for several years. During the Revolution he invested in several privateering ventures and following the war left the inn in his brother's hands to become a merchant. By 1793 he was one of the ten richest inhabitants of Newburyport, owning a large wharf at the foot of which he lived. During the period of neutral trade Davenport's wealth did not expand so rapidly as that of others, and by 1807 he ranked only twenty-fifth, with property worth about $30,000. He was able, however, to build a fine house at 78 High Street, which he occupied until his death. Davenport was a Federalist but took little part in political matters, serving only briefly as a selectman in the 1790's. He died in 1836 at the age of eighty-four.

TIMOTHY DEXTER

Timothy Dexter was born in 1748, coming to Newburyport at the age of twenty-one, where he established himself as a leatherdresser. He acquired a considerable estate during the 1780's, and, by the end of that decade he ranked sixteenth in wealth among the town's inhabitants. Having invested heavily in depreciated government notes during this period, Dexter realized a fivefold increase in his holdings by 1793, at which time he ranked fourth behind William Bartlet, Moses Brown, and Nathaniel Carter, with property worth about $45,000. Although he continued his importing business and invested in such ventures as the Essex-Merrimack Bridge, Dexter's estates dwindled slowly through his remaining years until, at his death in 1806, he was worth about $35,000. Despite his personal eccentricities, Dexter remains an important historical figure. The fact that a nearly illiterate glover could purchase in succession the mansions of Nathaniel Tracy (1791) and Jonathan Jackson (1798) and become one of the wealthiest inhabitants of Newburyport points up the instabilities and opportunities of the postrevolutionary period.

WILLIAM FARRIS

William Farris, born in Ireland in 1753, came to Newburyport at the age of twelve. By the outbreak of the Revolution he had become an experienced shipmaster, and during the war he commanded several letters-of-marque as well as taking part in Arnold's Quebec expedition. With the restoration of peace Farris formed a prosperous partnership with Ebenezer Stocker, engaging in banking and importing. In 1800 Farris was worth $44,000, and ranked eighth in wealth, but financial difficulties stemming in part from losses suffered during the naval war with France drove the firm out of business. By 1807 Farris's holdings had declined in value to $7000, although he continued to be an active member of the community. He was a determined Federalist, serving on numerous local committees protesting national policies during the period 1807–1815. Farris died in 1837, at the age of eighty-four, dependent in his last years on a government pension awarded him for his services during the Revolution.

BENJAMIN GREENLEAF

Benjamin Greenleaf, born in Newbury in 1732, graduated from Harvard with the class of 1751. After a brief period in Kittery, Maine, Greenleaf returned to Newbury in 1761, where he became active in public affairs. He served several terms as representative to the General Court and was a member of many local committees in the years just before the outbreak of the Revolution. In 1775 Greenleaf was appointed chief justice of the Court of Common Pleas and in 1779 he became judge of probate for Essex County. Until this time he maintained a wharf and store in Newburyport and throughout his life invested in local real estate. In 1793 Greenleaf ranked twentieth in wealth, although at his death in 1799, at the age of sixty-six, his relative position had declined considerably.

JONATHAN GREENLEAF

Jonathan Greenleaf, a cousin of Judge Benjamin Greenleaf, was born in 1723. After the death of his father, Jonathan was apprenticed to the shipbuilder, Edward Presbury, from whom he learned the business and whose daughter he married in 1744. Greenleaf soon established his own yard at the foot of Federal Street, constructing vessels for sale abroad as well as for local customers. He built several armed warships during the Revolution, but after the war his business languished, although he was never in straitened financial circumstances. At his death in 1807, at the age of eighty-four, he was worth slightly over $10,000. Jonathan Greenleaf had a long and active role in public affairs. He served on most of the important local committees during the quarrel with Great Britain and was a representative to the General Court or a state senator almost continuously from 1769 to 1791.

STEPHEN HOOPER

Stephen Hooper was born in 1741, the son of Marblehead's wealthy merchant, Robert "King" Hooper. After graduating from Harvard in 1761, he moved to Newburyport, where his sister had come after marrying Tristram Dalton and where his classmate, Jonathan Jackson, had established himself as a merchant. Hooper also entered into business, owning several vessels in the West Indies trade. He took an active part in public affairs, serving on the local committees protesting British policies before the Revolution. During the war Hooper joined in outfitting a number of privateers and ultimately suffered severe financial losses along with his colleagues. In 1786 he was still worth over $27,000 and ranked second in wealth among the inhabitants of Newburyport, but four years later, after the settlement of his debts, Hooper's holdings were reduced in value to $8000. He remained active in town affairs until about 1800 when he retired to his country seat at Pipe-Stave Hill, where he died two years later at the age of sixty.

JONATHAN JACKSON

Jonathan Jackson, born in 1743, was the son of a prosperous Boston merchant. After his graduation from Harvard in 1761 he came to Newburyport, where he worked for a short time as a clerk for the prominent merchant, Patrick Tracy. In 1765 he formed a partnership with another Boston-born Harvard graduate, John Bromfield, specializing in the importation of English goods. Jackson married Hannah Tracy, Patrick's daughter, in 1771, and three years later joined his brothers-in-law, John and Nathaniel, to establish a major mercantile house. Jackson had already become a leading figure in the public life of Newburyport, serving on numerous committees and taking a firm stand against British policies. Jackson, Tracy & Tracy fared very well in the months before the outbreak of the Revolution, but during the war the firm outfitted a large number of privateers, eventually suffering heavy losses. With the restoration of peace the firm broke up, and after several years of struggle Jackson abandoned the attempt to re-establish himself in trade. He relied on appointments to various public offices, and in 1795 he sold his mansion at 201 High Street and moved to Boston the following year. There he made a remarkable comeback, becoming president of the Boston Bank in 1806 and treasurer of Harvard the year following. At his death in 1810 at the age of sixty-six Jackson's estate was worth about $25,000.

WILLIAM P. JOHNSON

William P. Johnson, born in 1745, was one of several sons of the shipbuilder, Eleazer Johnson, and he married the daughter of another prominent shipyard owner, Jonathan Greenleaf. William began his career at sea, sailing for a number of years as the master of several West Indiamen. After the war he became a merchant and shipowner in his own right, specializing in the West Indies trade, and by 1790 he ranked tenth among Newburyport's wealthy citizens. During the next decade he profited greatly from neutral trade, increasing his estate tenfold to over $72,000, and ranking

BIOGRAPHICAL SKETCHES   215

third behind William Bartlet and Moses Brown in 1800. Although a dependable Federalist, Johnson did not take much interest in politics, leaving that role to his younger brother, Nicholas. William died in 1802, at the age of fifty-seven.

JOSEPH MARQUAND

Joseph Marquand was born in 1748, the son of merchant Daniel Marquand. He became a prominent shipowner during the Revolution, when he invested in a large number of privateering ventures, suffering considerable losses. As late as 1786 Marquand ranked fifth among the town's wealthiest citizens, but for the next decade his fortunes dwindled steadily. Although recouping somewhat during the later years of neutral trade, Marquand never regained his former financial stature. With the emergence of a two-party political system in the late 1790's, Marquand became a prominent Jeffersonian. Although this stand made him quite unpopular among his fellow townsmen, his loyalty was rewarded in 1811 when he was appointed Collector of Customs for Newburyport, a post he held until his death in 1820 at the age of seventy-one. Marquand lived for most of his life in the house his father had built on Water Street at the foot of Mill Street.

THEOPHILUS PARSONS

Theophilus Parsons was born in Newbury in 1750, the son of Byfield's minister, Moses Parsons. He graduated from Harvard in 1769 and then studied law with Theophilus Bradbury in Portland. Upon opening a law office in Newburyport in 1777, Parsons took an immediate interest in public affairs. He dominated the county convention held at Ipswich in 1778 and wrote its report, *The Essex Result*, criticizing the proposed state constitution. In the following year Parsons was a member of the convention which drew up the Constitution of 1780, and in 1788 he was instrumental in persuading John Hancock to support the proposed federal constitution at the state ratifying convention. He trained a number of young lawyers in his Newburyport office, the most famous of whom were John Quincy Adams and Rufus King. Parsons was a conservative Federalist during the latter part of his life, often identified with that elusive company, the "Essex Junto." He lived at the corner of Green and

Washington Streets in the house he built in 1789. Moving to Boston in 1800, Parsons became chief justice of the state Supreme Court six years later. He died in Boston in 1813, at the age of sixty-three.

JOHN PETTINGELL

John Pettingell was born in 1745. He received his first training as a cordwainer, but just before the Revolution he opened a shop in Market Square where he sold West India goods. During the war he owned shares in at least two privateers and afterward gradually expanded his mercantile interests, although he did not begin to grow prosperous until the outbreak of the European war in 1793. For a while he was associated with Josiah Smith, but that partnership dissolved around 1800. During the fourteen years of neutral trade his holdings increased nearly tenfold in value, so that by 1807 he ranked fourth in wealth among Newburyporters with an estate worth $108,000. Pettingell sent several of his vessels to North European ports and in 1809–1810 his ship *Rolla* made Newburyport's first voyage to Sumatra for pepper. His investments included shares in the Newburyport Marine Insurance Company, the Merrimack Bank, and the Newburyport Turnpike. He owned houses at 164 High Street (until recently the home of the Historical Society of Old Newbury), at 41–43 Green Street, and at Pipe-Stave Hill. Although not active in politics, Pettingell served several terms as selectman in the 1790's and was a staunch Federalist in later years. He died in 1828 at the age of eighty-three.

JAMES PRINCE

James Prince was born in 1755, the son of the Reverend Moses Prince. Records of his early years are missing, but by 1790 he had become active in business, keeping a store in Market Square where he sold a variety of imported goods. In 1800 Prince ranked twelfth among the wealthy citizens of Newburyport, with holdings worth over $31,000. In that year he bought the Nathaniel Tracy mansion at 94 State Street, now the public library, but financial difficulties forced him to rent it in 1807 as an inn. Prince took a leading role in the incorporation of the Newburyport Turnpike Company in 1803 and was a founder of the Phoenix Marine and Fire Insurance Company in 1809. The latter business was wiped out in the Great Fire of

1811, adding further to his financial embarrassment. In politics Prince was a confirmed Jeffersonian and was the last of his party to be elected to public office for many years, serving as selectman in 1799. Prince was appointed Collector of Customs in 1821, on the death of another Jeffersonian, Joseph Marquand, and he remained in that post until his own death in 1830, at the age of seventy-five.

DR. MICAJAH SAWYER

Micajah Sawyer was born in 1737, graduated from Harvard in 1756, and returned to Newburyport shortly thereafter to establish a medical practice. He served on the Committee of Safety and Correspondence during the Revolution and maintained a strong interest in public affairs after the war. Sawyer was an incorporator of the Newburyport Turnpike Comany and the Newburyport Bank in 1803 and became the first president of the Merrimack Humane Society in 1804. His medical practice prospered, and with careful investments he became one of the town's wealthiest inhabitants, ranking seventh in 1807 with property worth $73,000. He lived in the house he had built in 1766 at the corner of State and Pleasant Streets until his death in 1815 at the age of seventy-eight.

LEONARD SMITH

Leonard Smith began his career as a sailmaker but after the Revolution became a merchant. He joined with John Pettingell in the importing business for a few years, but that partnership was dissolved around 1800, and the two carried on separately thereafter. By 1807 Smith had acquired an estate worth over $50,000 and was ranked ninth among the wealthy citizens of Newburyport. He owned several vessels engaged in neutral trade and invested profits in the Newburyport bank and in the Marine Insurance Company. Although not prominent in public affairs, he gave firm support to the Federalist cause. Embargo hurt Smith badly, for he was soon forced to sell the houses he had built in 1805 at 37 Green Street and 5 Harris Street to satisfy his creditors. He apparently left Newburyport around 1812.

EBENEZER STOCKER

Ebenezer Stocker began his career as a mariner, serving as master of several vessels prior to the Revolution. He was a shopkeeper for several years after the war, but in the 1790's he went into partnership with William Farris, owning a number of vessels engaged in the West Indies trade. In 1798 Stocker built and occupied a house at 75 High Street. He was an organizer of the Merrimack Bank in 1795 and of the Newburyport Marine Insurance Company four years later. By 1800 Stocker had acquired an estate worth $68,500, making him the fifth wealthiest inhabitant of Newburyport. But the firm of Farris and Stocker suffered severe losses as the result of the naval war with France, and the partnership dissolved soon after. Stocker apparently moved away from Newburyport around 1808.

JONATHAN TITCOMB

Jonathan Titcomb was born in 1727. During the Revolution he played a leading role in guiding Newburyport through the crisis. He served on many of the important town committees before the outbreak of hostilities and then became a colonel and later a brigadier of the Second Militia Regiment, which included Newburyport's companies. Titcomb also held seats both on the Board of Selectmen and in the General Court during most of the war years and invested in several privateering ventures as well. Originally a blacksmith, he soon turned to mercantile interests but never became wealthy. In fact, after the war's end he was largely dependent on appointive office, notably as naval officer at the customs house during much of the 1780's. He took little part in public affairs after serving as a delegate to the state convention ratifying the federal constitution in 1788. Titcomb lived most of his life in a house on Merrimack Street at the foot of Green Street, which he had built in 1761. He died at the age of eighty-nine in 1817.

NATHANIEL TRACY

Nathaniel Tracy was born in 1751, one of two sons of the prominent merchant, Patrick Tracy. Nathaniel graduated from Harvard with the class of 1769 and after an additional year at Yale returned to Newburyport to enter his father's mercantile house. In 1774, along with his brother John, Nathaniel formed a partnership with Jonathan Jackson, who had married their sister Hannah three years before. The firm of Jackson, Tracy & Tracy enjoyed considerable success in the short time remaining before the outbreak of hostilities, and during the war fitted out a large number of privateers, only a few of which showed any long-run profit. Tracy briefly enjoyed prodigious wealth, entertaining lavishly in his mansion at 94 State Street, now the public library. By 1786, however, his fortunes along with those of his former partners had almost completely disappeared, and he was forced to liquidate most of his assets to satisfy his many creditors. Tracy lived the last decade of his life in retirement at his country estate at Pipe-Stave Hill, dying at the early age of forty-five in 1796.

ABNER WOOD

Abner Wood established himself as a merchant in Newburyport during the first years of the 1790's. At the beginning of the period of neutral trade his property was worth a little over $2000; by 1807 his holdings had increased nearly fiftyfold to just under $100,000, which placed him fifth among the town's wealthy inhabitants. Wood owned several vessels during this period which he employed in voyages to North European ports, and he also owned stock in the Newburyport Bank. In politics he was a determined Federalist, serving as selectman and representative to the General Court for several terms during the period 1800–1810. In 1792 he built a house at 166 High Street which he occupied until 1819.

BIBLIOGRAPHICAL NOTE

I. PRIMARY SOURCES

A. Personal Papers of Merchants and Professional Men

Most of the merchants and professional leaders of Newburyport during the period 1764–1815 were of course broadly speaking relatively minor historical figures. Few of them corresponded with great men of the period, and fewer still apparently had their own letters and personal papers preserved for posterity. As a consequence there are virtually no extensive collections of personal manuscript materials to aid the historian of Newburyport, with the important exception of the papers of the Jackson and the Tracy families. The personal papers upon which I have relied for this study are arranged below alphabetically by author.

ADAMS, JOHN QUINCY. One letter to John Phillips, 1788, in Phillips Papers (MHS); *Life in a New England Town, 1787-1788—Diary of John Quincy Adams while a Student in the Office of Theophilus Parsons at Newburyport,* Boston, 1903; Worthington C. Ford, ed., *The Writings of John Quincy Adams,* 2 vols.

BARTLET, WILLIAM. Several letters to the Assessors of Newburyport in Bartlet Papers (HSON).

BARTLETT, JOSIAH. One letter to his wife, 1811, in Bartlett Papers (HSON).

CARTER, NATHANIEL. Two letters, 1762, 1766, to Samuel Savage in Savage Papers (MHS).

DALTON, TRISTRAM. One letter, 1788, in Ballard Papers (MHS); a miscellaneous group of letters in Dalton Correspondence (EI); a few letters in Dalton-Deblois Correspondence (HSON); one letter, 1779, in Davis Papers (MHS); one letter, 1789, in French Papers (MHS); several letters in Eben F. Stone, "The Letters of Tristram Dalton," Essex Institute *Historical Collections,* LXXI (January 1935), 7–15; in Eben F. Stone, "A Sketch of Tristram Dalton," Essex Institute *Historical Collections,* XXIV (January 1888), 7ff.; and in Eben F. Stone, "Parsons and the Constitutional Convention of 1788," Essex Institute *Historical Collections,* XXXV (April 1899), 81–102.

HARROD, MARY. One letter, 1814, in Harrod Papers (EI).

HASKELL, CALEB. L. Washington, ed., *Caleb Haskell's Diary, May 5, 1775–May 30, 1776,* Newburyport, 1881.

HODGE, CHARLES. Journal, 1809, of a voyage to Cork, Ireland, and return (EI).

HUDSON, HENRY. A large number of letters, accounts, and journals in Hudson Family Papers (EI); several letters to his father-in-law, John Rogers, and business records in Hudson-Rogers Correspondence (NYPL).

INGERSOLL, JONATHAN. Auction Record Book, 1779–1781, and Insurance Receipt Book, 1779–1780 (EI).

JACKSON, JONATHAN. A large number of letters to his brother-in-law, Oliver Wendell, in Austin H. Clark Collection (Washington, D.C.); business papers of the firm of Jackson & Bromfield, 1766–1771, in Patrick Tracy Jackson, Jr., Collection (Boothbay Harbor, Maine); business papers of the firm of Jackson, Tracy & Tracy, 1774–1776, in Patrick Tracy Jackson, Jr., Collection (Boothbay Harbor, Maine); record book as United States Marshal, 1789–1792, Jackson Papers (MHS); one letter from Henry & Thomas Bromfield to Jackson & Bromfield, 1769, in Lee-Cabot Papers (MHS); several letters, 1777–1785, in Putnam Papers (MHS); two letters, 1790–1791, in Sedgwick Papers (MHS); Jackson & Bromfield Invoice Book, 1764–1771, "Letterbook 1765" of Jackson & Bromfield, 1765–1773, "Letterbook 1774," of Jackson, Tracy & Tracy, 1774–1777, and several letters all in Henry L. Shattuck Collection (MHS); letters while Congressman in 1782 in Edmund C. Burnett, ed., *Letters of Members of the Continental Congress,* 10 vols., Washington, D.C., 1933; letter to Oliver Wendell, 1774, in Massachusetts Historical Society *Miscellany No. 2,* July 1955; letter to Richard Price, 1785, in Massachusetts Historical Society *Proceedings,* 2d ser., XVII (1903), 327; many of the business letters and papers and personal correspondence noted above have been printed in Kenneth W. Porter, *The Jacksons and the Lees,* 2 vols., Cambridge, 1937.

KING, RUFUS. Letters written while a Congressman in Edmund C. Burnett, ed., *Letters of Members of the Continental Congress,* 10 vols., Washington, D.C., 1933; many letters in Charles R. King, *The Life and Correspondence of Rufus King,* 6 vols., New York, 1894–1900; one letter to Jonathan Jackson, 1786, in Massachusetts Historical Society *Proceedings,* XLIX (1915–1916), 85–86.

O'BRIEN, JEREMIAH. One letter, 1776, in Edes Papers (MHS).

PARSONS, THEOPHILUS. Several letters, 1779–1780, in Dane Papers (MHS); two letters, 1781, in Paine Papers (MHS); miscellaneous materials, including a manuscript record of the Ipswich Convention of 1778, in Parsons Papers (BPL); correspondence with Timothy Pickering, 1786–1790, in Pickering Papers (MHS); several letters in Samuel E. Morison, *The Life and Letters of Harrison Gray Otis,* 2 vols., Boston, 1913; some correspondence in Theophilus Parsons, *Memoir of Theophilus Parsons,* Boston, 1859; several letters in Eben F. Stone, "Parsons and the Constitutional Convention of 1788," Essex Institute *Historical Collections,* XXXV (April 1899), 81–102.

PIKE, NICHOLAS. One letter, 1785, in Belknap Papers (MHS); one letter, 1787, in Bowdoin-Temple Papers (MHS).

PIKE, WILLIAM. Two letters, 1789, in Knox Papers (MHS).

TITCOMB, JONATHAN. One letter, 1787, in Keith Papers (MHS).

TRACY, JOHN. In addition to business papers of Jackson, Tracy & Tracy, listed under Jonathan Jackson, above, there are additional business papers, 1781–1785, in Patrick Tracy Jackson, Jr., Collection (Boothbay Harbor, Maine); several letters, 1788–1791, in Knox Papers (MHS); two letters, 1788–1790, in Sargent Papers (MHS); correspondence with Jonathan Williams in "Jonathan Williams' Letterbooks" (YUL); and miscellaneous items in Kenneth W. Porter, *The Jacksons and the Lees,* 2 vols., Cambridge, 1937.

TRACY, MARGARET. One letter in Knox Papers (MHS).

TRACY, NATHANIEL. In addition to business papers of Jackson, Tracy & Tracy, listed above under Jonathan Jackson and John Tracy, there are several letters, 1785, 1790, in Knox Papers (MHS); one letter, 1785, in the Tucker Papers (HUL); and miscellaneous items in Kenneth W. Porter, *The Jacksons and the Lees,* 2 vols., Cambridge, 1937.

WHITE, DANIEL A. Several letters in White Papers (EI).

B. *Published Writings of Merchants and Professional Men*

Aiken, Solomon. *An Oration Delivered before the Republican Citizens of Newburyport,* July 4, 1810 . . . (NPL).

Bannister, William. *An Oration Delivered at Newburyport on the 34th Anniversary of American Independence.* Newburyport, 1809 (NPL).

Boddily, John. *A Sermon Delivered at Newburyport on the 22nd of February, 1800.* Newburyport, 1800 (NPL).

Cogswell, Nathaniel, Esq. *An Oration Delivered before the Republican*

224   BIBLIOGRAPHICAL NOTE

Citizens of Newburyport on the 4th of July, 1808. Newburyport, 1808 (NPL).

[Dalton, Tristram]. Reports of his speeches in the Senate of the United States in William Maclay, *Sketches of Debates in the First Senate of the United States,* Harrisburg, Penna., 1880.

Dana, Daniel. *A Discourse Delivered in Newburyport, July 4, 1814, in Commemoration of American Independence and of the Deliverance of Europe.* Newburyport, 1814 (NPL).

Giles, John. *Two Discourses Delivered to the Second Presbyterian Society in Newburyport, August 20, 1812, on the Day [of] National Humiliation and Prayer.* Haverhill, Mass., 1812 (NPL).

[Jackson, Jonathan]. *Thoughts upon the Political Situation of the United States of America . . . with some Observations on the Constitution for a Federal Government.* Worcester, Mass., 1788.

Knapp, Samuel L. *An Oration Delivered at Newburyport on the 4th Day of July, 1810.* Newburyport, 1810 (NPL); *An Oration Delivered before "The Associated Disciples of Washington" on the 22nd of February, 1812.* Newburyport, 1812 (NPL).

Miltimore, James. *An Address in Commemoration of the Independence of the United States of America, July 4, 1808.* Newburyport, 1808 (NPL).

Parish, Elijah. *A Discourse Delivered at Byfield on the Annual Fast, April 8, 1813.* Newburyport, 1813 (NPL); *A Discourse Delivered at Byfield on the Public Fast, April 7, 1814.* Newburyport, 1814 (NPL); *A Protest Against the War—A Discourse Delivered at Byfield, Fast Day, July 23, 1812.* Newburyport, 1812 (NPL).

Pierpont, John. *"The Portrait:" A Poem Delivered before the Washington Benevolent Society on the Evening of October 27, 1812.* Newburyport, 1812 (NPL).

Spring, Samuel. *A Discourse in Consequence of the Late Duel* [Hamilton-Burr] . . . Newburyport, 1804 (NPL); *Two Sermons Addressed to the Second Congregational Society in Newburyport, April 6, 1809.* Newburyport, 1809 (NPL).

C. Manuscript Materials Pertaining to Newburyport

"Abstracts of English Shipping Records Relating to Massachusetts Ports —Salem Custom District 1714–1717 and 1754–1765 [photostatic copy] (EI).

"Account of Sundries expended for the Publick Service of the Town of Newburyport 1775 [–1781]" (HSON).

Assessors' Account Book, 1784–1797 (Newburyport City Clerk's Office).

Entrances into the Newburyport Custom District, 1790–1792 (EI).
Essex County Deeds, Books 120 through 210 (Essex County Court House, Salem).
Essex-Merrimack Bridge Papers (HSON).
Home Militia List [no date] (EI). Apparently a list of those subscribing as members of the "Silver Greys," 1808.
"Innholders and Retailers Licenses" [1764–1820] in Ichabod Tucker Papers (EI).
"List of Persons that refuse to sign against . ˙. . Tea . . ." in Eben F. Stone Papers (EI).
Marine Society of Newburyport Papers (HSON).
Newburyport Committee of Correspondence Papers in Bancroft Collection (NYPL), Heath Papers (MHS), and Stone Collection (EI).
Newburyport Custom House Records (EI) as follows:
Abstracts of Drawbacks Payable. 3 vols. 1802–1815.
Abstracts of Exports. 3 vols. 1796–1815.
Abstracts of Imports. 3 vols. 1792–1815.
Impost Books of Imports. 2 vols. 1792–1795; 1809–1815.
Marine Hospital Records. 4 vols. 1798–1815.
Registry of Seamen. 2 vols. 1805–1812.
Ship Registers. 3 vols. 1792–1815.
Newburyport Merchants' Non-Importation Agreement, April 16, 1768, in Savage Papers (MHS).
Petition to General Court from Merchants and Traders of Newburyport, [no date: 1785?] (Mass. Archives).
"Records of all Vessels arriving in [and departing from] Newburyport in 1780," Hudson Papers (EI).
Records of the First Parish Church, Newburyport, 1788 and 1789 (HSON).
Records of the Town of Newburyport, Massachusetts (Newburyport City Clerk's Office). Volume I, 1764–1789; Volume II, 1790–1820.
Selectmen's Minute Books, 1764–1793 (Newburyport City Clerk's Office).
Tax Collector's Book for the Year 1771 [South End of town only] (NPL).
Tax List for the Town of Newburyport, 1767 [incomplete], (EI).
Valuations of the Town of Newburyport for the Years 1768, 1771, and 1784 [list for 1771 is imperfect] (Mass. Archives).
Valuation Lists for the Years 1780, 1786, 1790, 1793, 1800, 1807, 1815, and 1820 (lists for 1780, 1786, and 1790 in NPL; the others are in the Assessors' Office, Newburyport City Hall).

Valuation for 1781 and Share of State Tax for Newburyport, 1786, in Dane Papers (MHS).

Voters' Lists for the Years 1769, 1773, and 1774 (HSON).

Miscellaneous materials as follows:

one letter from Samuel Adams to James Warren, 14 May 1774 in Adams-Warren Papers (MHS).

one letter from Nathaniel Cogswell to Thomas Jefferson, July 1808, in Jefferson Papers (LC).

D. Printed Materials Pertaining to Newburyport

An Account of the Great Fire . . . in Newburyport on the Night of the 31st of May, 1811. Newburyport, 1811.

Acts and Resolves of Massachusetts, 1780–1797. 9 vols. Boston, 1890–1896.

Acts and Resolves of the Province of Massachusetts Bay . . . 21 vols. Boston, 1869–

Bentley, Rev. William, *The Diary of William Bentley.* 4 vols. Salem, 1905–1914.

Brissot de Warville, in George F. Dow, *Two Centuries of Travel in Essex County . . .* Topsfield, Mass., 1921.

Constitution and Form of Government for the State of Massachusetts-Bay . . . 1778. The rejected constitution of 1778, published in the appendix of the *Journal of the [1780] Convention* (see below).

Debates and Proceedings in the Convention of the Commonwealth of Massachusetts Held in the Year 1788 . . . and which Finally Ratified the Constitution of the United States. Boston, 1856.

Declaration of the County of Essex . . . by its Delegates Assembled at Ipswich on Tuesday the 21st of July, 1812. Salem, 1812 (NPL).

Department of Commerce and Labor, Bureau of the Census, *Heads of Families at the First Census of the United States Taken in the Year 1790: Massachusetts.* Washington, 1908.

Dwight, Timothy, *Travels in New England . . .* London, 1823.

Emery, Sarah A., *Reminiscences of a Nonagenarian.* Newburyport, 1879.

Force, Peter, ed., *American Archives.* 9 vols. Washington, D.C., 1837–1853. Contains a number of letters from the Newburyport Committee of Correspondence.

Journal of the Convention for Framing a Constitution of Government for the State of Massachusetts-Bay, 1779–1780.

Journals of Each Provincial Congress of Massachusetts in 1774 and 1775. Boston, 1838.

Resolves of the General Court of the Commonwealth of Massachusetts 1806–. Boston, 1806.

BIBLIOGRAPHICAL NOTE   227

Result of the Convention of Delegates Holden at Ipswich in the County of Essex who were Deputed to Take into Consideration the Constitution and Form of Government Proposed by the Convention of the State of Massachusetts-Bay. Newburyport, 1778. A copy of *The Essex Result* is printed in Theophilus Parsons, *Memoirs of Theophilus Parsons.* Boston, 1859, pp. 359–402.

Tonnage Registered and Enrolled at Newburyport, in *American State Papers,* vol. VII. 38 vols., Washington, 1832–1861.

Value of Exports in *American State Papers,* vol. VII.

E. Newspapers

Essex Journal [Whig], December 4, 1773–February 13, 1777; [Hancockian] July 9, 1784–April 2, 1794.

Impartial Herald [Federalist], May 18, 1793–October 27, 1797.

Morning Star [Federalist], April 8, 1794–December 3, 1794.

Political Gazette [Federalist], April 30, 1795–October 27, 1797.

Newburyport Herald [Federalist], October 31, 1797–1815–.

Merrimack Gazette [Republican], March 21, 1803–February 18, 1804.

New England Repertory [Federalist], July 6, 1803–January 21, 1804.

Political Calendar [Republican], March 26, 1804–June 17, 1805.

Newburyport Gazette [Republican], April 7, 1807–September 18, 1807.

Statesman [Federalist], August 15, 1808–March 9, 1809.

Independent Whig [Republican], March 22, 1810–May 2, 1811.

II. SECONDARY SOURCES

A. Newburyport History

By far the most useful works on Newburyport are the several volumes of history by John J. Currier: *"Ould Newbury": Historical and Biographical Sketches* (Boston, 1896); *History of Newbury, Mass., 1635–1902* (Boston, 1902); and *History of Newburyport, Mass., 1764–1905* (2 vols., Newburyport, 1906). Into these four volumes Currier crammed an extraordinary amount of factual material without, unfortunately, any regard for organization or interpretation. Currier also wrote a short study of the local shipbuilding industry, *Shipbuilding along the Merrimack* (Newburyport, 1889), a business in which his family was active for many years. Other local histories, better written but less thorough are: (Mrs.) E. Vale Smith, *History of Newburyport* (Newburyport, 1854), in which the author undertakes to interpret, with considerable success, Newburyport's place in the nation's history; Joshua Coffin, *A History of Newbury, Newburyport, and West Newbury* (Boston,

1845), a standard, mid-nineteenth-century chronological study; and William T. Davis, "Newburyport," in D. Hamilton Hurd, ed., *The History of Essex County, Massachusetts,* vol. II (Philadelphia, 1888). More specialized studies include William H. Bayley and Oliver O. Jones, *History of the Marine Society of Newburyport* . . . ([Newburyport], 1906), a poorly organized but rich collection of data concerning shipmasters and their activities; James M. Barriskill, "The Newburyport Theatre in the Eighteenth Century," Essex Institute *Historical Collections,* XCI (July–October 1955), and "The Newburyport Theatre in the Federalist Period," Essex Institute *Historical Collections,* XCIII (January 1957); and H. Follansbee Long, "The Newburyport and Boston Turnpike," Essex Institute *Historical Collections,* XLII (April 1906).

B.   Colonial and Revolutionary Periods

Carl Bridenbaugh, *Cities in Revolt: Urban Life in America, 1743–1776* (New York, 1955), provides an excellent examination of social and cultural development in five important urban centers of colonial America. For the role of the merchants in the revolutionary crisis, Arthur M. Schlesinger, *The Colonial Merchants and the Coming of the American Revolution, 1763–1776* (New York, 1918), remains an indispensable study. The pattern in which most of the merchants in major American ports behaved, however, does not hold for many merchants in the outports. For general background I have found John C. Miller, *Origins of the American Revolution* (Boston, 1943), the most useful of several recent studies of the coming of the war. More specialized works for this period include Oliver M. Dickerson, *The Navigation Acts and the American Revolution* (Philadelphia, 1951), in which he explodes the idea that the colonial merchants felt oppressed by the Navigation Acts; Lawrence A. Harper, *The English Navigation Laws* (New York, 1939), which provides an excellent evaluation of the laws and their operation; Edmund S. and Helen M. Morgan, *The Stamp Act Crisis: Prologue to Revolution* (Chapel Hill, N.C., 1953), a model study of the Stamp Act and its effects; and Robert E. Brown, *Middle-Class Democracy and the Revolution in Massachusetts, 1691–1780* (Ithaca, N.Y., 1955), a masterful examination of political democracy in colonial Massachusetts and its significance during the revolutionary period. Although we differ as to the extent of real democracy present in the urban centers where the Revolution began, I have found Brown's work of great value to the present study. Among the many articles devoted to more particular aspects of the revolutionary movement in Massachusetts I have found the following most useful: Charles M. Andrews, "The Boston Merchants and the Non-Importation Movement," Colonial Society of Massachusetts *Publications,* XIX (1918); Robert S. Longley, "Mob Activities in Revolutionary Massachusetts," *New England Quarterly,* VI (March 1933); Edmund S. Morgan, "Colonial Ideas of Parliamentary Power," *William and Mary Quarterly,* 3d ser., V (July 1948); and Arthur M. Schlesinger, "Political Mobs and the American Revolution," American Philosophical Society *Proceedings,* XCI (August 1955). For a listing of privateers and their owners, see Gardner W. Allen, *Massachusetts Privateers of the Revolution* (Boston, 1927).

C. Confederation and Constitution

Essential for an understanding of the struggle for a state constitution in Massachusetts during the period 1776–1780 are three studies by Samuel E. Morison: *The History of the Constitution of Massachusetts* (Boston, 1917); "Vote of Massachusetts on Summoning a Constitutional Convention, 1776–1917," Massachusetts Historical Society *Proceedings,* L (April 1917); and "Struggle over the Adoption of the Constitution of Massachusetts, 1780," Massachusetts Historical Society *Proceedings,* L (May 1917). General works for the Confederation period include two by Merrill Jensen: *The Articles of Confederation: An Interpretation of the Social-Constitutional History of the American Revolution, 1774–1781* (2d ed., Madison, Wisc., 1947), and *The New Nation: A History of the United States during the Confederation, 1781–1789* (New York, 1950), both of which advance the thesis that distinctions between "radicals" and "conservatives" remained clear from 1774 on. In the latter work Jensen also maintains that prosperity returned long before the end of the 1780's and that therefore economic depression was not a cause of the movement for a stronger central government.

The difficulty of comparing "radicals" and "conservatives" of the prewar and Confederation periods is brilliantly presented by Oscar and Mary F. Handlin, "Radicals and Conservatives in Massachusetts after Independence," *New England Quarterly,* XVII (September 1944). Other studies of the Confederation period give ample evidence, at least as far as Massachusetts is concerned, of continued economic depression until the late 1780's. Allan Nevins, *The American States During and After the Revolution, 1775–1789* (New York, 1927); Oscar and Mary F. Handlin, *Commonwealth: A Study of the Role of Government in the American Economy: Massachusetts, 1774–1861* (New York, 1947), and their "Revolutionary Economic Policy in Massachusetts," *William and Mary Quarterly,* 3d ser., IV (January 1947); Ralph V. Harlow, "Economic Conditions in Massachusetts during the American Revolution,"

Colonial Society of Massachusetts *Publications*, XX (May 1919); Charles
J. Bullock, "Historical Sketch of the Finances and Financial Policy of
Massachusetts from 1780 to 1905," American Economic Association
Publications, 3d ser., VIII (May 1907); William B. Norton, "Paper
Currency in Massachusetts during the Revolution," *New England
Quarterly*, VII (March 1934); Samuel E. Morison, *The Maritime History of Massachusetts, 1783–1860* (Boston, 1921); Benjamin W. Labaree,
"Nantes to Newburyport: Letters of Jonathan Williams," Essex Institute *Historical Collections*, XCII (January 1956); and Robert A. East,
"The Massachusetts Conservatives in the Critical Period," in Richard B.
Morris, ed., *The Era of the American Revolution* (New York, 1939).
For Massachusetts politics during the Confederation period see also
John C. Miller, *Sam Adams, Pioneer in Propaganda* (Boston, 1936), and
Herbert S. Allan, *John Hancock, Patriot in Purple* (New York, 1948).
The composition of the Massachusetts convention ratifying the federal
constitution in January 1788 is skillfuly analyzed in Forrest McDonald,
We the People: The Economic Origins of the Constitution (Chicago,
1958), a successful refutation of Beard's classic *Economic Interpretation
of the Constitution*. The standard work on the convention itself is Samuel B. Harding, *The Contest over the Ratification of the Federal Constitution in the State of Massachusetts* (New York, 1896), while Anson
E. Morse, *The Federalist Party in Massachusetts to the Year 1800*
(Princeton, 1909), presents a less satisfactory account. For the "bargain"
between the Federalists and Hancock George H. Haynes, "Conciliatory
Propositions in the Massachusetts Convention of 1788," American Antiquarian Society *Proceedings*, new series, XXIX (October 1919), is
necessary but disappointing. A far better picture is given by studies of
the participants themselves, including Charles R. King, *The Life and
Correspondence of Rufus King* (6 vols., New York, 1894–1900); Richard E. Welch, Jr., "Rufus King of Newburyport: The Formative Years
(1767–1788)," Essex Institute *Historical Collections*, XCVI (October
1960); Theophilus Parsons, *Memoir of Theophilus Parsons* (Cambridge,
1859); William V. Wells, *The Life and Public Services of Samuel
Adams* (3 vols., Boston, 1888); Eben F. Stone, "Parsons and the Constitutional Convention of 1788," Essex Institute *Historical Collections*,
XXXV (April 1899); and his "Sketch of Tristram Dalton," Essex Institute *Historical Collections*, XXIV (January 1888).

D. *Federalist and Jeffersonian Party Politics*

There have recently been published a number of excellent works
concerning the party politics of the 1790's and 1800's. For a general
survey of the period see John C. Miller, *The Federalist Era* (New York,

1960), and the older but still valuable work by Edward Channing, *A History of the United States,* vol. IV, 1789–1815 (New York, 1927). Joseph Charles, *Origins of the American Party System* (Williamsburg, 1956), presents a valuable interpretation of the beginnings of the two-party system during the 1790's. Manning G. Dauer, *The Adams Federalists* (Baltimore, 1953), and Stephen G. Kurtz, *Presidency of John Adams* (Philadelphia, 1957), are two excellent studies of the Federalist party in office, while Samuel E. Morison, *The Life and Letters of Harrison Gray Otis* (2 vols., Boston, 1913), provides a wealth of material concerning the party in Massachusetts. The significance of foreign policy is seen in Samuel F. Bemis, *Jay's Treaty* (New York, 1923); Alexander DeConde, *Entangling Alliance: Politics and Diplomacy under Washington* (Durham, N.C., 1958); and the older study by Charles M. Thomas, *American Neutrality in 1793* (New York, 1931). The war with France is well covered by Gardner W. Allen, *Our Naval War with France* (Boston, 1909), while the impact of the Federalist Alien and Sedition Acts is examined by John C. Miller, *Crisis in Freedom: The Alien and Sedition Acts* (Boston, 1951), and by James M. Smith, *Freedom's Fetters* (Ithaca, N.Y., 1956). The rise of the Jeffersonians is traced by Eugene P. Link, *Democratic Republican Societies* (New York, 1942); Noble E. Cunningham, Jr., *The Jeffersonian Republicans: The Formation of Party Organization, 1789–1801* (Chapel Hill, N.C., 1957); William A. Robinson, *Jeffersonian Democracy in New England* (New Haven, 1916); and Claude G. Bowers, *Jefferson in Power* (Boston, 1936).

E. Embargo and the War of 1812

For the Embargo Act and its enforcement Louis M. Sears, *Jefferson and the Embargo* (Durham, N.C., 1927), and Walter W. Jennings, *The American Embargo, 1807–1809* (Iowa City, 1921), are still useful. For the attitude of one embittered Federalist see Hervey P. Prentiss, "Pickering and Embargo," Essex Institute *Historical Collections,* LXIX (April 1933). Alfred T. Mahan, *Sea Power in its Relations with the War of 1812* (2 vols., Boston, 1905), analyzes the commercial policy of the Jeffersonians, while Robert G. Albion and Jennie B. Pope, *Sea Lanes in War Time* (New York, 1942), give a good account of the problems of neutral trade in the years preceding the outbreak of the war. Federalist reaction to the War of 1812 is seen in Charles R. Brown, *The Northern Confederacy According to the Plans of the Essex Junto, 1796–1814* (Princeton, 1913); Henry Adams, ed., *Documents Relating to New England Federalism* (Boston, 1877), John Q. Adams's collection of materials concerning the radical Federalists; and Theodore Dwight, *History of the Hartford Convention . . .* (Boston, 1833).

INDEX

Bowditch, Nathaniel, *New Practical Navigator,* 138
Bowdoin, James, 56, 68, 69, 70, 76, 90
Bowdoinites, 79, 86, 105
Bradbury, Theophilus, 52, 105, 106, 112, 215
Brazil, 110
Brewery, 65–66
"Broken voyages," 151–152
Bromfield, Henry and Thomas, 22
Bromfield, John, 20, 36n, 84, 214
Brown, Moses, 95, 99, 100, 117, 133, 136, 137, 139, 159, 201, 204, 209, 211, 212, 215; family, 141; biographical sketch, 208
Brown, Robert E., 15n
Bulfinch, Charles, 134
Burr, Aaron, 124–125, 130, 146

Cabot, George, 79, 86, 113, 163
Cambridge, 51
"CAMILLUS." *See* Hamilton
Canada, 160, 162, 178, 181, 184, 187, 190
Canning, George, 170, 172
Caribbean island trade, 59, 97, 98, 106, 132, 174
Carleton, William, 144
Carter, Nathaniel, 12, 21, 38, 84, 99, 212; biographical sketch, 208–209
Cato, 60, 61
Cavalry, 192, 194, 195
Cayetano and Co., Messrs., 139
Charleston, S.C., 7, 111
Charlestown, 39
Chase, Capt., 148
Chastellux, Marquis de, 89
Chatham, Earl of, William Pitt, 23
Chesapeake affair, 148–149, 179, 199
Clark, Thomas M., 182
Clergy, and politics, 144–145
Clinton, De Witt, 190
Cloths, 5–6, 7, 27, 61
Clubs, 10, 102
Coal, 24
Cobbett, William, 143
Cocoa, 98
Coercive Acts, 30–32
Coffee, 98, 132, 153, 202
Coffin, David, biographical sketch, 209
Coffin, Richard, 195

Cogswell, Nathaniel, 156
College, merchants attended, 96–97, 141
Columbian Centinel, 124
Commerce: colonial, 2, 3, 6, 7, 93, 95, nonimportation, 20–27, ban on, 36–40; *1780's,* 42–43, 58–66, 68–71, 73, 204; early *1790's,* 96, 97–100, 204; neutral trade during European war period, 106, 108–111, 113–114, 131–133, 174, 202, problem with British, 147–150, 151–152; under Embargo, 152–161 *passim,* 166; under Non-Intercourse, 168–171; under Macon Bill, 174; change in patterns, *1810,* 174–175; during War of *1812,* 187, 188–189, 191; postwar, 201–203
Committee of Correspondence, 28, 29; on Embargo, 159
Committee of Inspection, pledge against tea, 25–26
Committee of Safety and Correspondence, 36–37, 38, 42, 96, 217; in *1809,* 167
Committee of Seven, *1768,* 20–21
Concerts, 101, 117
Confederacy, northern, 162, 197. *See also* Secession
Confederation, Newburyport attitude toward, 70–71, 75
Congregationalists: and tea, 25; in Mass. constitution, 52; clergy and politics, 144
Congress, U.S., 75, 76, 105, 127, 128, 161, 164, 179, 191, 203; elections of 1800, 122–123
Constitution, Mass.: formulation and adoption, *1778–1780,* 42, 43–56, 66; Declaration of Rights, 51, 52. See also *Essex Result*
Constitution, U.S.: ratification of, 67, 68, 71–78, 92, 211, 215; political factions resulting from, 78–84, 106; and attitude toward Embargo, 162, 164, 166–167; Newburyport allegiance to, 182–183. *See also* Government
Constitution, 187
Constitutional convention, Mass.: *1779–1780,* 49, 50–52, 54–55, 210, 215; *1820,* 203
Constitutional convention, U.S., 57, 69, 70, 71, 74

passim, 169, 173; Message to Congress, *1805,* 148–149
Jeffersonians. *See* Republicans
Johnson, Daniel, 133
Johnson, Eleazer, 37, 96, 214
Johnson, Capt. Nicholas, 99, 114, 215
Johnson, William P., 113; biographical sketch, 214–215
Judiciary: appointment to, in *Essex Result,* 48, 50; in Constitution of *1780,* 52; in recommended amendments to U.S. constitution, 76
Judiciary Act, 128
July 4 festivities, political significance, 116–117, 143, 145, 193
Juno, 148

Kennebunkport, 189
Kilham, Daniel, 73–74, 81–84, 141n
King, Rufus, 57, 68–69, 70, 71, 74, 75, 76, 78, 79, 80, 83, 86, 215
Kittredge, Dr. John, 122, 123, 131
Kittredge, Thomas, 163
Knapp, Samuel, 172–173, 178
Knox, General Henry, 76, 78, 79, 87, 89, 90, 91

Laborers, 5, 13, 14, 15, 93, 132, 154, 200
"Labradore Tea," 25
Lane Son & Fraser, 39, 61, 88
Lawyers, 8, 11, 13, 14, 57, 93, 97, 137, 140
Leander, 195
Lear, Tobias, 86
Legislature: in *Essex Result,* 46–47, 48, 49; in Constitution of *1780,* 52, 53, 54
Leonidas Fire Society, 194
Leopard, 148–149, 199
Levant trade, 157
Libbey, John, 132, 133, 201
Liberty: and political freedom, 18; and attitude toward Napoleonic wars, 110
Library, 101
Lincoln, Benjamin, 79, 80, 82, 83
Liquor, 98
Lisbon, 39
Little, Ebenezer, 84
Little, Edward, 182
Little, Capt. Josiah, 122
Little Belt, 178–179
Little-Dick, 155

Livermore, Edward St. Loe, 140, 163, 164, 168
Locke, John, 45, 46
Locks, construction of, 100, 135
Locks and canals company, 100, 204
London, 39, 132, 138
Louisiana: purchase, 128–130, 143, 173; admission as state, 177
Lowell, Francis Cabot, 100
Lowell, Hannah Jackson, 11
Lowell, John, 7, 8, 11
Lowell, John (younger), 11, 38, 51, 57, 80, 83, 87, 184
Lowell, John Cabot, 11
Lowell (city), 100
Loyalists, 16, 42
Lumber, 2, 7, 59, 61, 98, 132, 153
Lunt, Ezra, 9

Macon's Bill No. 2, 174–176
Madison, James, 169–170, 171–174, 178, 186, 193, 197; declaration of war, 180
Maine, 25, 96
Malaga, 7
Manhattan, 188
Manufactures, 64, 65, 66, 132; imports, *1790's,* 98. *See also* Shipbuilding
Manuscripts, bibliography of, 224–226
Marblehead, 16, 21, 28, 33, 130, 177
March, Angier, 101, 113–114, 115, 118, 119, 121, 122, 125
Marine insurance company, 99, 138
Marine List, 9, 176, 189
Marquand, Daniel, 215
Marquand, Joseph, 12, 141, 204, 217; family, 140; biographical sketch, 215
Marsh, Rev. Mr., 25
Martinico, 108, 148
Massachusetts: and colonial congress, 35; establishment of state government, 42, 43–56; postrevolutionary economic problems, 57–59, 63; ratification of federal constitution, 67, 68, 71–75; Newburyport attitude toward, 198–199; politics in, *see* Politics
Massachusetts Bay, 1
Massachusetts Bay Colony, 2; "Act for the better Regulating . . .", 35
Merchants: and growth of nationalism, 203–205; biographical sketches, 207–219

Harvard Historical Studies

(Out of print titles are omitted.)

59. *Richard Humphrey.* Georges Sorel, Prophet without Honor: A Study in Anti-Intellectualism. 1951.
60. *Robert G. L. Waite.* Vanguard of Nazism: The Free Corps Movement in Postwar Germany, 1918–1923. 1952.
62. *John King Fairbank.* Trade and Diplomacy on the China Coast: The Opening of the Treaty Ports, 1842–1854. Vol. I. Text. 1953.
63. *John King Fairbank.* Trade and Diplomacy on the China Coast . . . 1842–1854. Vol. II. Reference Notes, Appendices, Bibliography, Glossary. 1953.
64. *Franklin L. Ford.* Robe and Sword: The Regrouping of the French Aristocracy after Louis XIV. 1953.
65. *Carl E. Schorske.* German Social Democracy, 1905–1917. The Development of the Great Schism. 1955.
66. *Wallace Evan Davies.* Patriotism on Parade: The Story of Veterans' and Hereditary Organizations in America, 1783–1900. 1955.
67. *Harold Schwartz.* Samuel Gridley Howe: Social Reformer, 1801–1876. 1956.
68. *Bryce D. Lyon.* From Fief to Indenture: The Transition from Feudal to Non-Feudal Contract in Western Europe. 1957.
69. *Stanley J. Stein.* Vassouras: A Brazilian Coffee County, 1850–1900. 1957.
70. *Thomas F. McGann.* Argentina, the United States, and the Inter-American System, 1880–1914. 1957.
71. *Ernest R. May.* The World War and American Isolation, 1914–1917. 1958.
72. *John B. Blake.* Public Health in the Town of Boston, 1630–1822. 1959.
73. *Benjamin W. Labaree.* Patriots and Partisans: The Merchants of Newburyport, 1764–1815. 1962.